COMMUNALISM IN
POSTCOLONIAL INDIA

This book reconceptualises the idea of communalism in independent India. It locates the changing contours of politics and religion in the country from the colonial times to the present day and makes an important intervention in understanding the relationship between communalism and communal violence. It evaluates the roles of state, media, civil societies, political parties and other actors in the process as well as ideas such as secularism, nationalism, minority rights and democracy. Using new conceptual tools and an interdisciplinary approach, the work challenges the conventional understanding of communalism as time and context independent.

This topical volume will be useful to scholars and researchers in South Asian politics, political science, history, sociology and social anthropology, as well as the interested general reader.

Mujibur Rehman is member of faculty at the Dr K.R. Narayanan Centre for Dalit and Minorities Studies, Jamia Millia Islamia, New Delhi, India.

'This rich collection of essays . . . brings together several theoretical and empirical approaches to the problem of communalism and secularism; at times disturbing the analytic and political slumber. . . . This timely collection ought to invite serious social debate and political action.'

Upendra Baxi, *University of Warwick, UK*

'Communalism, and associated violence, has been a feature of India since the colonial period. This important collection of essays examines the phenomenon especially towards the end of the twentieth century.'

Francis Robinson, *Royal Holloway, University of London, UK*

'Through new theoretical approaches and case studies, these . . . essays pursue the restless and mercurial spectre of communal conflict that continues to haunt Indian society.'

Nile Green, *University of California, Los Angeles, USA*

COMMUNALISM IN POSTCOLONIAL INDIA

Changing contours

Edited by Mujibur Rehman

Routledge
Taylor & Francis Group

NEW DELHI LONDON NEW YORK

First South Asia edition 2016

First published 2016
by Routledge
2 Park Square, Milton Park, Abingdon, Oxon OX14 4RN

and by Routledge
711 Third Avenue, New York, NY 10017

*Routledge is an imprint of the Taylor & Francis Group, an informa
business*

British Library Cataloguing-in-Publication Data
A catalogue record for this book is available from the
British Library

Library of Congress Cataloging-in-Publication Data
A catalog record has been requested for this book.

ISBN: 978-1-138-63983-6

Typeset in Goudy
by Apex CoVantage, LLC

Digitally Printed at Replika Press Pvt. Ltd.

For sale in India, Pakistan, Nepal, Bhutan, Bangladesh and Sri Lanka only.

CONTENTS

CONTENTS

vi

CONTRIBUTORS

Savio Abreu is director of Xavier Centre of Historical Research (XCHR), Goa. He received his Ph.D. from the Indian Institute of Technology, Mumbai, on a sociological study on New Christian movements in contemporary Goa. He has published articles in various journals, including *Indian Church History Review, Seminar, Social Action*, and so on. Among his recent publications include, 'Contribution of Jesuits to Higher Education in Goa' in a Universidad de Navarra publication, Pamplona (2012).

Shibani Kinkar Chaube is retired professor of Political Science at the University of Delhi, India. He is an expert on North-East, and also on Constituent Assembly Debates, and has authored several books on the subject.

Sanjoy Hazarika is professor and founding director of the Centre for North-East Studies and Policy Research at Jamia Millia Islamia, New Delhi. He also holds the Dr Saifuddin Kitchlew chair and is widely acknowledged as a specialist on issues related to the region and its neighbourhood. He is the author and co-author of several books on North-East. The widely acclaimed *Strangers of the Mist* (1994) is the most well-received of his books.

Ramin Jahanbegloo is an Iranian–Canadian political philosopher. He was a fellow at the Center for Middle Eastern Studies at Harvard University and is presently an associate professor of political science at York University and a professor at the Barcelona Institute for International Studies (IBEI). Among his 24 books in English, French and Persian are *Conversations with Isaiah Berlin* (1992), *Gandhi: Aux*

Sources de la Nonviolence (1999), *India Revisited: Conversations on Contemporary India* (2007), *The Clash of Intolerances* (2007), *The Spirit of India* (2008), *Beyond Violence* (2008), *Talking Politics* (2010), *Civil Society and Democracy in Iran* (2011), *The Gandhian Moment* (2013) and *Democracy in Iran* (2013).

Heewon Kim has recently completed her doctorate on 'United Progressive Alliance (2004–14), equality of opportunity and Muslims: a paradigm shift or political pragmatism?' at the School of Oriental and African Studies (SOAS), University of London. She is currently a post-doctoral research associate in the Department of the Study of Religions, SOAS.

M. Ashok Kumar is assistant professor of sociology in the School of Humanities and Social Sciences, Indian Institute of Technology, Mandi. He obtained his Ph.D. from the Indian Institute of Technology, Bombay. His research areas of interest include sociology of religion, caste, Christianity and religious minorities in India.

Prateep K. Lahiri had a distinguished career as an Indian Administrative Service officer. In the 1960s, serving as district magistrate in several regions, he had first-hand experience in dealing with communal conflicts and riots. Based on his experiences and study of the subject he authored the book *Decoding Intolerance: Riots and Emergence of Terrorism in India*, an authoritative work on communal disturbances in the country. During 1991–95 he served as India's executive director on the resident board of directors of the Asian Development Bank (ADB), Manila.

Harsh Mander is a social worker and writer and works with survivors of mass violence, hunger, homeless persons and street children. He is associated with social causes and movements, such for communal harmony and justice, tribal, Dalit, child and disability rights, homeless people and bonded labour. His books include *Unheard Voices: Stories of Forgotten Lives*, *The Ripped Chest: Public Policy and the Poor in India*, *Fear and Forgiveness: The Aftermath of Massacre*, *Fractured Freedom: Chronicles from India's Margins*, *Untouchability in Rural India* (co-authored) and his latest *Ash in the Belly: India's Unfinished Battle against Hunger*. He regularly writes columns for *The Hindu* and *Hindustan Times*. He teaches courses on poverty and governance in the Indian Institute of Management, Ahmedabad and St Stephen's College, Delhi.

Martha Nussbaum is Ernest Freund Distinguished Service Professor of Law and Ethics at the University of Chicago, United States. Her books include *The Clash Within* (2007) and *The New Religious Intolerance* (2012).

Hitendra K. Patel is associate professor of history at Rabindra Bharti University, Kolkata. He is the author of *Communalism and the Intelligentsia in Bihar 1870–1930: Shaping Caste, Community and Nationhood* (2011).

Mujibur Rehman (Mujibur Raheman, Shaikh) is member of faculty at Dr K.R. Narayanan Centre for Dalit and Minorities Studies. He has received graduate research training at the University of Texas, United States; the University of Heidelberg, Germany; and Indian Institute of Technology (IIT), Delhi. His recent publications include 'Muslim Politics in India and 15th General Election', in A.K. Mehra (ed.), *Emerging Trends in Indian Politics* (Routledge, 2010); 'L' enjeu des Mussalmans indiens', in *Outre-Terre 24*, *Revue européenne de politique*, *Académie européenne de Geo Politique* (French). He is currently working on electoral politics in India. (smujib2000@yahoo.com)

Rowena Robinson is a professor at the Department of Humanities and Social Sciences, Indian Institute of Technology, Bombay. She has also taught at Delhi University and Jawaharlal Nehru University. Among other publications, she is author of *Tremors of Violence: Muslim Survivors of Ethnic Strife in Western India* (2005) and *Christians of India* (2003), editor of *Minority Studies* (2012), and co-editor of *Religious Conversion in India: Modes, Motivations and Meanings* (2003) and *Margins of Faith: Dalit and Tribal Christianity in India* (2010).

Dilip Simeon taught history at Ramjas College, Delhi University (1974–94). From 1984 onwards, he participated in a citizen's campaign against communal violence, known as the Sampradayikta Virodhi Andolan. He has been a visiting scholar at institutions such as in Surat, Sussex, Chicago, Leiden and Princeton. From 1998 till 2003 he worked on a conflict-mitigation project with Oxfam and is now chairperson of the Aman Trust, which works to reduce violent conflict. His publications include an academic monograph on labour history published in 1995 and a political novel, *Revolution Highway* (2010).

Pritam Singh teaches economics at Oxford Brookes University, Oxford. His books include: *Economy, Culture and Human Rights: Turbulence in Punjab, India and Beyond* (2010); *Federalism, Nationalism and Development: India and the Punjab Economy* (2008); *Punjabi Identity in a Global Context* (co-edited with Shinder Thandi) (1999) and *Equal Opportunities in the Curriculum* (co-edited with Martin Pearl) (1999). He is on the editorial board of several journals including *World Review of Political Economy*, *South Asian History and Culture* and *Journal of Punjab Studies*, and on the executive committee of several organisations including World Association of Political Economy and Association of Heterodox Economics (UK). He has been a visiting professor at Jawaharlal Nehru University, Delhi and Moscow State University, Moscow.

PREFACE

On 6 December 1992, Babri Masjid was demolished, triggering cycles of riots and ethnic violence in different parts of India. This changed the politics and democracy of India. It also contributed to the change of discourse on minority rights and secularism. On 6 December 2013, I went over headlines after headlines, pages and pages, news items after news items of various newspapers such as the *Times of India, Indian Express, Hindustan Times, The Hindu* and many others, and did not find any mention about the Babri Masjid demolition or the violence that followed. This negligence by the Indian media has been happening for a few years now. This gives some hint about how key moments of India's difficult struggle for multi-culturalism and secularism are reported and articulated in public debate.

The subject of communalism, riots and ethnic violence have been topics of conversation around which I grew up. As I child, I used to run my fingers over a deep cut mark on the bald head of a victim of the Rourkela riot that took place in the early 1960s. He was a distant relative of my mother. During my college days, I wrote a story on this victim. It won the Mansingh Memorial award.[1] In the aftermath of the demolition of Babri Masjid, I travelled by a train as the university closed down, through the heart land of Uttar Pradesh by changing my name on the advice of many secular Hindu friends at the Delhi University. Some of them apologised for the circumstances. Only few days before my travel, there was a disturbing report about how some Kashmiri students of Aligarh Muslim University, who were returning home, were thrown out of a running train. Overall, the Indian political climate in northern India was so frightening that I found it wise to helplessly endorse the suggestion to change my name. A few days before the Babri Masjid demolition, an activist of a Hindutva organisation knocked at my door in order to identify the Muslim person living in the upstairs apartment of the University of Delhi's North campus. At the time I did not know he was a Hindutva activist; it came to my notice when I saw his photograph in a major Indian weekly. Communalism was in the air all the time. When Gujarat 2002 happened, I was a graduate student at the University of Texas, in the United States. Some of my close secular friends, born as Hindus and working in different parts of India, e-mailed me their apologies for the violence and expressed deep remorse for the erosion of humanity. I had the pleasure of working on a project on the Gujarat violence with noted activist and writer Harsh Mander a few years later and visited Ahmedabad. This gave me the opportunity to meet with a few victims. The most enlightening part of my few visits to Ahmedabad was to spend time with Mallika Sarabai, who was at the receiving end of the Hindutva forces. Her courage to stand up to such forces is very inspiring for all those who believe in secularism and multi-culturalism. When I joined the Geneva-based Women's International League for Peace and Freedom (WILPF) to investigate women's condition during the anti-Christian violence in Kandhamal, Odisha, I had close interaction with recent victims of Kandhamal in various relief camps. Over the years, I had the pleasure to interact, and collaborate, with many activists working on the issue of communalism and secularism. Intellectually, these associations and experiences have shaped my understanding of the subject.

This book is partly an outcome of a national conference, which I put together at Jamia Millia Central University in March 2012 at the behest of Dr K.R. Narayanan Centre for Dalit and Minorities of the university. Among the participants included Dilip Padgaonkar, former editor of the *Times of India*, and also former member of the National Commission of Minorities (NCM), Government of India, New Delhi; late Asghar Ali Engineer, noted Islamic scholar and activist; Prof. Faizan Mustafa, former vice-chancellor of National Law University, Cuttack, Odisha; Harsh Mander, author and former member of National Advisory Council (NAC) headed by Sonia Gandhi, chairperson of the United Progressive Government (UPA I and II); Prof. Monirul Hasan, professor of political science, University of Assam, Guwahati; Prof. Rowena Robinson, professor of sociology at the Indian Institute of Technology (IIT), Mumbai; Prof. Mukul Kesavan, Department of History, Jamia Millia Islamia, New Delhi; Prof. Hitendra K. Patel, Associate Professor of History at Rabindra

PREFACE

Bharati University, Kolkata, West Bengal; Dr Nonica Datta, Department of History, Miranda House, Delhi University; Dr D.R. Santosh, faculty at the Indian Institute of Technology (IIT), Chennai; Dr Ashraf Azeez, Department of Islamic Studies, University of Kerala, Trivandrum; Madhu Trehan, noted journalist; Shazia Ilmi, former journalist; and Mujibur Rehman. Wajahat Habibullah, chairperson of the National Commission of Minorities (NCM), New Delhi, gave the valedictory address.

Some of the contributors in the volume were invited later to speak at Martha Nussbaum, University of Chicago, United States; Dr Pritam Singh, Oxford Brookes University; Ramin Jahanbegloo, York University, Canada; Heewon Kim, a doctoral student at the School of Oriental and African Studies (SOAS), London; Sibani K. Chaube, retired professor of political science at Delhi University, India; Prof Rowena Robinson, faculty at IIT, Mumbai; Savio Abreau; M. Ashok Kumar; and Sanjoy Hazarika, director of North-Eastern Studies, Jamia Millia Islamia, New Delhi.

Some people who have contributed to my intellectual understanding of the problem and the politics associated with it over the years, are as follows: Harsh Mander, Dieter Rothermund, Robert Hardgrave, Rob Moser, Water Dean Burnham, Romila Thapar, Mushirul Hasan, Ravinder Barn, Gurharpal Singh, Uma Chakravarty, Eleanor Newbeign, Margrit Pernau, Feryal Ali Gauhar, Late Asghar Ali Engineer, Vidhu Verma, Nirja Jayal Gopal, Sudha Pai, Manoranjan Mohanty, Neera Chandoke, M.P. Singh, S.K. Chaube, Andre Beteille, Badal Mukherjee, Kaushik Basu, Ujjawal Singh, Yogendra Yadav, Madhulika Banerjee, late Dharma Kumar, Lolita Chakravarty, Partho Ghosh, Abu Saleh Shariff, V. Upadhyaya, Kamal Narayan Kabra, Dwaipayan Bhatacharya, Swagato Ganguly, Rajeev Bhargava, Robert Toscano, Giancarlo Bosseti, Nina Zu Furstenberg, Ramin Jahanbegloo, Sunila Kale, John Harriss, E. Shidharan, Ramu Manivannan, Daron Shaw, Harris Gazdar, Jean Dreze, Javed Alam, Jyotirmaya Sharma, Siddharth Varadharajan, Tarun Saint, Deewa Zafir, Padmanabh Samarendra, Prashant Negi, Narender Kumar, James Galbraith, Thom Wolf, Linda Wolf and many others.

Note

1 This award was named after Mayadhar Mansingh, a noted poet of modern Oriya and also the father of diplomat Lalit Mansingh.

INTRODUCTION

Mujibur Rehman

This book makes two-fold claims: first, owing to changed roles of political parties, state, media and civil societies in postcolonial India, the forms of communalism have undergone a change compared to what it used to be during the 1930s and 1940s. Second, new conceptual tools and resources emanating from inter-disciplinary traditions are needed to advance our understanding of this puzzle. There is some evidence about this trend, though scant in nature, available in recent research. In an influential essay, 'Secularist, Subalterns, and the Stigma of Communalism', Ayesha Jalal calls for rethinking the notion of communalism. She writes:

> If secularists still acknowledge the significance of historical context and contingent events albeit by re-affirming the stigma of communalism, the recent subaltern interventions deem pain and violence – the attended lives of ordinary people – to be far more important fact than the political fact of partition. The apparently irreconcilable, yet partially in imbricated, secularist, and subaltern positions with their loud claims and equally deafening silences afford an opportunity *to rethink the notion of communalism* (italics mine) and reappraise the debate over the history and meaning of Partition.
>
> (Jalal 1996: 681–737)

Interestingly, it is not just the idea of communalism, but even secularism is context dependent or in the words of philosopher Akeel Bilgrami, 'relevance of secularism is contextual in very specific ways' (Bilgrami 2014:

1

3). He further adds, 'If secularism has its relevance only in context, then it is natural and right to think that it will appear in different forms and guises in different contexts' (Bilgrami 2014: 4). Given the relationship between the idea of secularism and communalism in India's political domain, it will be only appropriate to argue that serious reflections on communalism could be extended focussing on the context – almost in the manner that philosopher Bilgrami has advanced the analysis with regard to secularism. Of course, there are specificities that demand a particular form of articulation for a sophisticated understanding of the idea of communalism. Furthermore, more comprehensive scholarship on the subject of communalism will add value to our knowledge of democracy and minority rights. The chapters in this volume promise to shed substantive insights on this question and help grasp various dimensions of its menacing forms. In a nutshell, it does claim to have pushed for new possibilities for further scientific exploration.

Scholars have long pointed out to a unique meaning of communalism – mainly pejorative and negative – in the context of South Asian history and polity (Pandey 2006; Singh 2014). The dominant formulations have employed communalism as a monolithic notion. Put simply, whatever *communalism* meant in the 1930s and 1940s in India remains largely the same in subsequent periods, during the 1980s and 1990s and continues to have a similar connotation in contemporary times. Conceptually, it is treated as both time- and context-independent. This formulation is challenged by our research. It urges the scholarly community to respond imaginatively to the new era of communalism with its changing forms with the help of new concepts and methodologies.

Communalism as an idea, I argue, is a typical attitudinal disease with infinite capacity to generate suspicion, fear, hate, violence and discriminatory tendencies among members of communities of real or perceived differences. Further, it could often find collective expression or take the form of an ideology with its own assumptions and counter-assumptions. In so doing, it stands in conflict with normal, rational human relationships based on trust, solidarity and other larger human values. It also unsettles and even destroys human experiences inspired by sympathy, compassion, care, mutual respect, forgiveness and human dignity as a legitimate mode of human conduct. In a nutshell, it contributes to the pernicious processes of de-humanisation and unleashes various forms of beastly brutalities on society.

What is indeed heartening is the availability of abundant high-quality scholarship not just on the subject of communalism, but also on its outcomes or consequences such as discrimination, ethnic violence, riots, pogroms, genocides and so on. Each chapter has engaged and built its narrative on this rich scholarship, giving rise to fresh ideas and new arguments.

Until the late 1980s, the scholarship on the subject was dominated by professional historians. Moreover, a very productive internal debate inspired by methodological disputes, among nationalists, neo-colonialists, Marxists/Leftists, subalternists, and so on has taken place. The dominant arguments on this subject during the immediate years of post-independent India lent the impression that Partition and the politics that preceded it or resulted thereof is the key factor behind communalism. Indeed, owing to the debate over communalism as a political ideology and its impact on the division of this sub-continent into three nation states – India, Pakistan and Bangladesh – historians found it necessary to pay enormous attention to address numerous puzzles, contested and unresolved, of South Asian history. As scholars from other disciplines such as political science, sociology, psychology and even economics began to join the investigation on communalism, there has been further deepening of our understanding on this question. At the level of methodology, a multi-disciplinary and inter-disciplinary tradition has found firm and irreversible footing. For instance, Sudhir Kakar's *Colors of Violence* (1996) has employed tools of psychology to address the issue of ethnic conflict. Amartya Sen's *Identity and Violence* (1998) and Amiya Bagchi's essay, 'The Predatory Commercialisation and Communalism in India' (1991) brought insights of economics to its analysis. Likewise, Steve Wilkinson's *Votes and Violence: Electoral Competition and Ethnic Riots In India* (2004), Paul Brass's *The Production of Hindu-Muslim Violence* (2003) and Ashutosh Varshney's *Ethnic Conflict and Civic Life* (2002) have used methodologies of political science. Additionally, the volume edited by Veena Das, *Mirrors of Violence* (1990), has brought insights from sociology. The works of Siddharth Varadarajan, *Gujarat: The Making of a Tragedy* (2002), and M.J. Akbar, *Riot after Riot* (2003) have brought out rich journalistic narratives on the subject. Also, there are scholars such as Ornit Sahani, whose book, *Communalism, Caste and Hindu Nationalism: The Violence in Gujarat* (2007), has sought to show

3

the connection between caste and communalism. Scholars such as Aijaz Ahmed's *On Communalism and Globalization: Offensives of the Far Right* (2004) and Jan Breman's *The Making and Unmaking of an Industrial Class* (2004) have attempted to show the connection between globalisation and communalism. Such a growing body of scholarship has also opened new frontiers of research.[1] Among major contributions, Ashis Nandy's essay titled, 'Anti-Secular Manifesto' (1995), has been the most provocative.

Theoretically, the interrogation of the notion of communalism is conducted more effectively in conjunction with other ideas such as secularism, nationalism, minority rights, democracy and so on. Often how these relationships are defined and interpreted has determined the nature, quality and impact of scholarship. For instance, Amartya Sen seeks to explain the idea of communalism by unravelling various criticisms of the idea of secularism (Sen 1998). Louis Dumont has sought to achieve the same by analysing the idea of nationalism (Dumont 1970). Neera Chandoke explained communalism by reflecting on the idea of minority rights and democracy (Chandoke 1999). Martha Nussbaum used the dimensions such as democracy and tolerance to describe communalism (Nussbaum 2007).

It is also crucial to reflect on how the idea of communalism and secularism should be debated in the context of democracy. To further illustrate this point, the bulk of the classic text *Capitalism, Socialism and Democracy* (1942) by Joseph Schumpeter is devoted to the analysis of political parties. The methodological insight that can be drawn from this work is that analysis on democracy demands serious understanding of political parties. However, often scholars have made profound statements on democracy without alluding to the role of political parties. An important example of this genre of analysis is the writings of Amartya Sen on democracy. Interestingly, on the subject of communalism and secularism as well, scholars of various disciplines have recognised the role and position of political parties as vital to make sense of Indian democracy. Furthermore, the understanding of the relationship between secularism and minority rights is indispensable for explaining the enigma of democracy. In the Indian case, this could be most effectively explored by asking a question such as: What has the democratic practice done to this relationship between communalism, secularism and minority rights during the last six decades or more? What has made minorities vulnerable are the

4

imperfections in secular practices, making it less desirable for its citizens and the major blame for this has to go to political parties.

Since the late 1980s, particularly the rise of the Bharathiya Janata Party (BJP) and the Ayodhya movement have inspired Western scholarship on the subject of communalism, minority rights and secularism. The writings of Christopher Jaffrelot, Thomas H. Hansen, Steve Wilkinson, Paul Brass and several others represent that tradition. Several volumes by Indian scholars based in India and also in Western universities have contributed to this burgeoning body of scholarship. Furthermore, the rise of BJP has introduced new concepts and brought new dimensions to the discussions on the subject of communalism and secularism. For instance, notions such as 'positive secularism' and 'negative secularism' were evoked repeatedly by the BJP and other like-minded organisations and also by scholars and commentators sympathetic to Hindutva politics during the 1980s and 1990s in an attempt to highlight the shortcomings in the practice of secularism. After remaining for little more than a decade in Indian public debate during the period from the late 1980s to 1990s, these notions have now literally disappeared. Also interestingly, noted historian Perry Anderson has observed that 'Indian secularism is Hindu confessionalism by another name' (Anderson 2012: 142).

Another front for an attack on secularism was launched by branding Indian state policy towards minorities, particularly Muslims, as case of appeasement. Apparently, this appeasement allegation against Indian Muslims has been rather old and could be easily traced to anti-colonial days. One of its early evidence could be noted in a letter by Prime Minister Nehru. In his Letter to Chief Ministers on 15 October 1947, Nehru wrote, 'I know there is certain amount of feeling in the country. . . . That the Central Government has somehow or other been weak and following a policy of *appeasement* (italics mine) towards Muslims.'[2] This accusation continues to exist in Indian public debate. Its presence, and continuation as a part of the active language of discourse on secularism and minority rights, has weakened the foundations of Indian secularism and contributes to the promotion of hostile attitude towards Muslims and other minorities. Interestingly, the Gopal Singh panel report (1983) contains enormous evidence of extremely abysmal socio-economic conditions of Indian Muslims. The failure of

India's supposedly secular political elites, intellectuals and activists to use data presented by the Gopal Singh panel report to counter the onslaught on Indian secularism gave legitimacy to the appeasement accusation by the BJP and its sister organisations during the late 1980s and early 1990s. This was a period when the appeasement allegation gathered momentum. The data presented by the Sachar Report (2006) has given further resources to substantiate the findings to the Gopal Singh panel report.

In recent years, there are prominent incidents of communal violence in different parts of India, such as Muzaffarnagar (2013), Kokrajhar (2012), Kandhamal (2008) and Gujarat (2002). Among these cases, Gujarat 2002 is widely discussed and researched, and seen as an example of Indian style of ethnic cleansing or fascism (Vardharajan 2002; Shani 2007; Mander 2008). Given that political ideology of secularism plays a key role in Indian electoral politics, political elites are sensitive to their secular image. Consequently, some political elites are reluctant to endorse inter-religious conflict as a communal violence and feel more comfortable to describe it as ethnic conflict as if the latter is a conflict of lesser kind and normal. Hoping that such attempts by lending a new label to communal violence would not tarnish their secular image, these political elites view such descriptions of less consequential electorally. There was prominent use of this conceptual manoeuvring by political elites during the Kandhamal violence in 2008. The leaders of the Biju Janata Dal (BJD), including the chief minister of Orissa, Naveen Patnaik, chose to explain it as an ethnic conflict quite frequently. Similar attempt by the political elites of the Samajwadi Party, the ruling party in Uttar Pradesh, was made to explain the Muzzafarnagar violence in 2013.

For Indian polity, what is crucial is how the relationship between communalism and violence is perceived and how the future discourse on secularism is going to unravel around this relationship. At the time of the Babri Masjid demolition in 1992, the BJP which led the Ayodhya movement was running a few state governments. These states had remained riot free under the BJP rule. When the Narasimha Rao government at the Centre decided to dismiss these governments owing to the BJP's connivance in the demolition of the Babri Masjid, a debate erupted around the question: What is the good evidence of secularism for a political party: a political party claiming to be secular but fails to contain violence against minorities and Muslims during its reign or a political party that does not claim to be secular but its regime is violence free? Similar arguments questioning the meaning of secularism in Uttar Pradesh are now raised with regard to the Samajwadi Party. My sense is, that this will be a dominant question in the Indian public debate in the coming years. What is good for minorities and Muslims: a secular regime with frequent eruptions of violence and riots or a regime that claims to be non-secular but its rule free of violence or riots?

What is the relationship between communalism and violence? Communalism, I believe, could exist without violence, though riot is its violent manifestation in extreme sense. There could be non-violent communalism in a society showing signs of normalcy at the surface, but discrimination and prejudices are practiced covertly or overtly. Absence of violence or riot does not offer concrete evidence of absence of communalism from a society. Since such prejudicial attitudes have tendencies to accumulate, it could explode at a critical time, leading to some of the worst forms of ethnic violence or riot as evident in Gujarat (2002) or Muzzafarnagar (2013).

This collection also reflects on different dimensions of communalism using their vantage points. Contributions by Pritam Singh, Dilip Simeon and Prateep Lahiri reflect more on the theoretical debate on communalism and engage with changing terms of discourse. Pritam Singh's chapter, 'Institutional Communalism in India', develops the notion of institutionalised communalism on the lines of institutionalised racism in Britain. He discusses how the idea is debated in the context of South Asia as well as Western societies. A bulk of his analysis is devoted to India. In his attempt to demonstrate the limitations of current usage of communalism, he discusses various institutions such as the judiciary, and the media among others. In his chapter, he discusses in detail various cases and incidents associated with Muslim and Sikh minorities in elaborating the relevance of majority communalism and highlights the pernicious aspect of institutionalised communalism. Prateep Lahiri's chapter, 'Tracing the Trajectory of Communalism and Communal Violence in India', discusses various dimensions of communalism and shares his insights with the arguments of other prominent scholars such as Bipan Chandra, Paul Brass, Amartya Sen, and Ashutosh Varshney. He devotes substantial space to the analysis of Hindutva and how organisations such as the Rashtriya Swayamsevak Sangh (RSS) and Vishwa Hindu Parishad (VHP) contribute to the polarisation of society. In conclusion, he shows optimism and argues that economic expansion creating further opportunities would contribute to the decline of communal violence.

Dilip Simeon's chapter, 'The Philosophy of Number', analyses the predicament of the conceptual analysis of the idea of communalism. It seeks to accomplish this objective by understanding how the idea of majority, minority, nation and state evolved. The chapter also invests considerable space in the analysis of how some prominent communists looked at the issue of communalism and Partition. It touches upon some thoughts of Ambedkar's analysis of Partition. Simeon sheds light on the shortcomings of the dominant interpretations of communalism. On the other hand, Ramin Jahanbegloo's chapter, 'Gandhi's Critique of Religious Fanaticism', not only explores Gandhi's position on communalism and religious fanaticism, but it also makes an attempt to demonstrate how Gandhi's ideas developed during the extremely challenging phase of his political career.

In 'Reflections on Secularism and Communalism in Constituent Assembly Debates and Beyond', Shibani K. Chaube approaches the question by analysing various interpretations in the process of evolution of the Indian Constitution. The chapter devotes considerable space to the discussion of the idea of secularism in the Constituent Assembly debates and how the modern Indian state dealt with it. It exposes the ambiguities associated in the way the Indian state employed the notion of secularism. Though he makes a strong case for secularism in a pluralist society, it is perhaps the failure to grasp the real meaning that seems very paradoxical for Indian society.

Martha Nussbaum's chapter, 'The Diaspora Community', offers detailed analysis of how the Indian diaspora contributes to the rise of Hindu fundamentalism in India, large through donations. It provides a comprehensive understanding about these organisational channels and their networks. However, it appears that the contributors to these donations are perhaps unaware of the intent of these organisations and the end towards which the fund was generated. Savio Abreu, Ashok Kumar and Rowena Robinson's chapter, 'Indian Christians: History and Contemporary Challenges', share insights about the changing circumstances of Indian Christians in modern India. Despite the fact that there are constitutional provisions and legal standing of their rights in India, there is a growing threat to their existence in various parts of India. A sizeable number of Indian Christians, owing to the fact that they have emerged out of the womb of various tribal identities, confront peculiar challenges, particularly with regard to affirmative action policies and its politicisation in the context of majoritarian politics. Heewon Kim's chapter, 'United Progressive Alliance (I) and India's Muslims: Redefining Equality of Opportunity?', situates the analysis of the UPA(I) regime that lasted from 2004 to 2009 in the larger context of the global political development in the post-9/11 world, in which securitisation of Muslim community became a prominent trend all over the world. It then focuses on the approach of the regime under study in the context of the rival BJP-led National Democratic Alliance (NDA) regime. It argues for the need for further assessment of the UPA (I)'s regime policy interventions towards Muslims in the hope of deepening the value of equality of opportunity. It almost asserts that equality of opportunity approach is the most effective way to deal with Muslim backwardness and discrimination.

There are contributions based on more specific case studies, for instance, the chapters by Harsh Mander, Sanjoy Hazarika, Hitendra Patel and Mujibur Rehman. Harsh Mander's 'Communal Violence in India: Ending Impunity' explores the challenges in the formulation of an effective, anti-communal violence bill for this country. As a member of the National Advisory Council in the UPA (II) government, Mander had the opportunity to contribute to this debate and also in the formulation of this bill. He discusses the various incidents of violence, especially Gujarat in detail, and analyses the possibilities of prevention, secrets of statecraft and the role of civil society. Sanjoy Hazarika's chapter, 'Conflict and Attrition in the North-East: Identity, Impunity and Inequality', reflects on the enduring nature of violence with a special focus on Kokrajhar violence in 2012. He situates this conflict in the larger historical sense and seeks to locate with narratives about various other tribal conflicts that have erupted in the region. He states that this multi-ethnic region of India has more than 22 large ethnic groups, and its Muslim population is the second largest in terms of ratio to the overall population next to Jammu and Kashmir. According to him, the Indian state has committed the blunder of granting enormous power to security forces without accountability, as embodied in the notorious Armed

---

Forces Special Powers Act (AFSPA). Ethnic conflict in this region, he recognises, erupts owing to multiple reasons, such as state indifference, lack of intent by political elites to deal with unresolved issues, adverse implications of draconian laws such as AFSPA and substantive ignorance about the region, its history and people.

Hitendra Patel's chapter 'Aspects of Hindu–Muslim Divide in Literature and the Role of Intelligentsia', explores the evidences available in various literary traditions in the late nineteenth and twentieth centuries. The mystery of how communalism existed in several parts of India with no communal organisations could be unravelled by reading about communal thoughts in various literary works. Given that Hindu–Muslim history is deep and complex, it evidently gives enough material for a variety of imaginative interpretations. But there are also evidences to the contrary, about Hindu–Muslim amity and brotherhood. Using various sources such as Bhartendu, Rangalal Bandyopadhyaya, Dinabandhu Mitra and Pratap Narayanan Mishra, the author addresses one of the key enigmas of Indian society. Mujibur Rehman's chapter, 'Politics of the 2008 Anti-Christian Violence in Kandhamal, Odisha', explores the circumstance in which the anti-Christian violence took place in Kandhamal and the future challenges that Indian Christians are facing. It claims that state negligence and the rise of far-right Hindutva ideology with its organisational machinery, such as the RSS and the VHP, have contributed to the increase in violence not just in Odisha but also in other parts of India. It analyses the role of political elites as well. It forcefully argues that it was an anti-Christian violence and expresses deep concerns about the pernicious trends owing to the violent Hindutva politics.

Notes

1 In addition to this, a good sample on the existing literature of various disciplines addressing different dimensions of communalism and its relationship with other key ideas such as secularism, minority rights, democracy and so on could be as follows: Achin Vinayak (1998); Rajeev Bhargava (1998); Tapan Basu et al. (1993); Sarvapali Gopal (1991); Thomas B. Hansen (1999); Romila Thapar, Harbans Mukhia, and Bipan Chandra (1969); Gyanendra Pandey (1996); Ayesha Jalal and Sugata Bose (1997); Mushirul Hasan and Amrita Basu.
2 See Parthasarathi (1985–89), 24.

1

REFLECTIONS ON SECULARISM AND COMMUNALISM IN CONSTITUENT ASSEMBLY DEBATES AND BEYOND

Shibani Kinkar Chaube

Confusion on secularism in India

Because of the nature of Indian politics surrounding the 1947 Partition, much debate has grown on the questions of communalism and secularism in India. First, secularism and communalism are pitted against each other, putting religion at its centre. It is assumed that communalism is embedded in religious conviction and secularism is the opposite of religiousness, which means that a secular person cannot be communal and vice versa – a communal person cannot be secular – forgetting that Mohammad Ali Jinnah, the communalist par excellence, had not much interest in religion and Gandhi, a great adherent to religion, and his illustrious follower, Abul Kalam Azad, an equally devout man, could by no means be considered communal.

The second mistake is to regard secularism as a social phenomenon identifying it simultaneously with atheism and Protestantism. The argument goes on that Indian society, particularly the Hindu society, is steeped in religion and secularism – a Western vice in India. It also identifies Protestantism with atheism, ignoring the historical fact that right from the early colonization of America, religion, particularly Protestant Christianity, has played a major part in the formation of the US society. And, yet, the United States, by separating the state from the church, through the first amendment to its Constitution, became the mother of modern secularism.

The exactly opposite argument is: 'The Indian/Hindu society is essentially secular', its *reductio ad absurdum* being 'The Hindu religion is essentially a secular religion'. Those who use such clichés really mean that the Hindus are a tolerant people – indeed a questionable assertion. The fact is that no person can be secular without being an atheist. Neither can a society be secular. There is in almost every human being a place for religion as there is a large secular area. There is in every society a large role of religion as there is a large secular area too. Secularism does not mean denial of religion. It seeks to confine religion in its proper place. On the other hand, institutions engaged in secular affairs can be secular – like a football club, or a bank or a state.

A tendentious variant of the allegation that secularism is a Western product is a division between 'Western secularism' and 'Indian secularism'. Secularism is assumed to be a lifestyle – comprising the food habit of the common man, the dress code of the politician and the like. It is neither. It is not even an ideology. It is a scientific concept like gravitation or relativity; the West is its author. If a concept means something according to the authors, we have to accept that meaning provided that it is clearly stated. Notwithstanding the fact that one has the right to reject it, no one has the right to change its meaning. There cannot be an 'Indian' theory of secularism as there cannot be an Indian theory of gravitation or relativity. Secularism is a strategy or theory of administration – an administration by a government that wants different religious communities under its span of control to live in peace and amity. Secularism is about state policy and not about social relations where communalism works.

These two mistakes have led to two kinds of demands: (1) Alleging that the Indian Constitution is 'pseudo-secular' a political group demands that the present Constitution of India be scrapped and replaced by a 'genuinely secular' constitution based on the doctrine of Hindutva laid down by V.D. Savarkar in 1923.[1] (2) During the emergency in 1975 Prime Minister Indira Gandhi reinvented the hoary doctrine of *sarva dharma samabhāva* (equal respect for all religions). This private ethic had been developed into a political principle by India's philosopher president, S. Radhakrishnan, in 1961: 'I want to say authoritatively that secularism does not mean irreligion. It means we respect all faiths and religions. Our state does not identify itself with any *particular* religion' (*The Statesman*, 21 August 1961.

Italics added). This definition was different from the one given by B.R. Ambedkar, India's first law minister who had led the Drafting Committee of the Constituent Assembly:

> All that a secular state means is that this Parliament shall not be competent to impose any particular religion upon the rest of the people. This is the only limitation that the Constitution recognises. We are not here to flout the sentiments of the people. (*Parliamentary Debates, Part II*, Vol. VII: 1959)

At the height of obfuscation of secularism during the period of emergency (1975–77), while moving the Forty-Second Amendment bill, Law Minister H.R. Bharadwaj said: 'Let anyone say that "socialism" or "secularism" is incapable of definition. Well, if that argument was to be accepted, even "democracy" in that sense is incapable of definition because, is it not understood in different ways in different countries? But we understand what kind of democracy we stand for' (*Lok Sabha Debates*, 25 October 1976, c 58).

Definition of secularism

The above discussion raises the question of definition of secularism. Literally, the word 'secular' originated from the Latin word *secularis* (*Seculum* in Latin means generation, age, time). Max Weber translated the secular as this-worldly. In other words, it means temporal, mundane, in contrast with the word 'sacred', which concerns the other-worldly affairs of life. Secularism is the practice or a norm of attachment to this-worldly affairs. It is pointless to distinguish between the 'public' and the 'private' spheres of religious life. All religious congregations, Hindu, Muslim, Christian, Sikh, Buddhist, have a public character, while all religious practices have a private, meditative aspect. By the same token, when we speak of a 'secular person' in common parlance what we mean is a rational person – one who can distinguish between the sacred and the secular domains of life and choose to act appropriately in different situations: one who does not start praying in the midst of a cricket game or gamble on the premises of a temple.

Now, as Max Weber said that there is no society without religion (Parsons 1966: xxxvii), there cannot be a secular society. While society, as a whole, encompasses both the secular and the sacred aspects of life, very few, if any, social institutions can encompass them together. The modern state is one institution concerned with the secular and material affairs of the society. In fact, Machiavelli, the world's first modern political philosopher, firmly pronounced the materialistic end of state.

Of the various cultural criteria that define a community, religion has proved to be most sensitive. Religious differences have produced some of the bloodiest and longest conflicts all over the world. Any state with the desire to avoid such conflicts will adopt secularism. 'Secularism in the realm of philosophy is a system of utilitarian ethics, seeking to promote greatest human happiness or welfare, quite independent of what may be called either religious or the occult,' pronounced the Supreme Court of India in the *Ziauddin Burhanuddin Bukhari v. Brijmohan Ramdass Mehra* case (AIR 1975 SC 1788, p. 1800). Secularism prevents the state from discriminating against any particular religion as also interfering with any. It is a cultural laissez-faire that infuses confidence in the governments of the modern state, invariably made up of several religious communities. But it has its problems. It cannot effectively undertake social reform as many of the customs and practices of a traditional society are tied up with religious faiths and practices. It may also not be able to effectively protect minorities from the pressures and attacks of majorities on religious ground (e.g. cow slaughter, religious processions).

Secularism in history

Secularism's antithesis is theocracy, more a myth than a reality today. *The Concise Oxford English Dictionary* (1486) defines theocracy as 'a system of government in which priests rule in the name of God or a god,' and cites the Commonwealth of Israel from the time of Moses until Saul became the king.

In the primitive societies it was not the priest but the magician, often the rainmaker and the medicine man, who became a secular ruler (Frazer 1957: 111). In a more advanced, ancient period the Mesopotamian priests were the masters of secular authority and the Egyptian kings thought themselves to be gods (Wells 1922: 61). Historical data, however, are not clear about the secular–sacred divide of power in those societies. In Mahayana Buddhist Tibet, the Dalai Lama was given both secular and spiritual powers by the Mongol overlord. But it came to be exercised by the Panchen Lama. In Bhutan the dualism of the *Dharma-raja* and the *Devaraja* prevailed up to 1907, when a divine-right kingship was established. A divine-right kingship is an appropriation of divine right by an ordinary mortal either at the connivance of the priests or after their subordination.

In spite of the notoriety of the Asians' attachment to religion and other worldliness, it should be noted that none of the rulers of ancient Mesopotamia, China and India claimed to be God or a god incarnate,[2] whereas Alexander, probably inspired by the Pharaos of Egypt, and the Roman Cæsers, inspired by Alexander, conceived themselves as gods. In the confessional religions the prophets did not claim to be God or a god; they led their followers in the name of God. When, in the third century A.D., Constantine adopted Christianity, he surrendered his divinity to the Christian God. When he moved his capital from Rome to Constantinople, he lost his grip over the western part of the Roman Empire. It fell upon the Pope in Rome to strive to keep Christian unity under his leadership in the western part of the former empire.

The dichotomisation of the sacred and the secular is as old as the period before the papacy undertook wide reform in the church. In England of the seventh century, for instance, the parish church was organised on territorial basis around Bishoprics, independent of the control of the roving missionary type of Celtic church belonging to the monasteries. The king supported the Bishopric and, in turn, got the support of the Bishops to their 'divine right' to rule. The clergy was divided between the 'regular'– celibate ones in the monastic tradition – and the 'secular' parish priests who could marry. The distinction between the clergy and the lay was not clear in the Anglo-Saxon period though some of them were imputed divinity (Trevelyan 1959: 66–68). All the rulers, however, carved out their own secular domain of authority. It was William the Conqueror who separated the spiritual from the secular courts (ibid.: 114–15). King Henry II's effort to control the top of the Bishopric produced the tragedy of Thomas Becket. The spiritual courts claimed and exercised autonomy over the administration of justice; but they transferred severe criminal cases to 'the secular arm' of justice. While the parish courts had the support of the kings who allowed limited judicial and civil administrative functions by the secular parish priests occasionally along with the sheriff, the reform that the papacy introduced in the eleventh century gradually replaced them by regular priests and sought to impose its control over the parish church. The kings, in return, gradually divested the parish churches of judicial and administrative functions and transferred them to secular courts and administrative bodies. Secularism, thus, meant this worldliness (and not profanity) as against 'regulated' other-worldly life of celibacy and abstinence.

Incomplete grasp of Western history has led to the accusation that secularism is a Protestant faith. Protestantism is older than the separation of the church and the state. Indeed, religion as an organised system of faith cannot be traced older than the Roman Empire adopting Christianity in the fourth century A.D. After the collapse of the Roman Empire the Roman Church claimed to be the legitimate medium of handing over divine sanction to Christian kings. But Charlemagne did not like taking the crown from the Pope and did not intend to follow his diktat. Medieval unity of the Christian church could not stop wars among European rulers. Between Nicole Machiavelli (Italy) and Martin Luther (Germany), who followed him shortly, the essence of Protestantism grew and demanded the freedom of the state from the church's control. In England this movement led to the establishment of the Church of England under the British Crown subordinating the church to the jurisdictionalist state.[3] It was the Puritans who felt unhappy with the Church of England and wanted complete separation of the state and the church. This happened in the United States. The very foundation of the United States owes itself to the settlement of the separatist Pilgrim Fathers, an intensely religious group, followed by the Presbyterians. The subsequent migration of Irish Catholics and East European Jews only added colour and complexity of this picture. A further development in the growth of secularism was the campaign by the Quakers, that religious faith is a private affair, a belief inconsistent with the congregational prayer of all Christian denominations. Not until 1940, however, could the US Supreme Court impose the church–state separation in the states of the federation that had taken shelter under their separate constitutions (See Sandel 1998: 75–79). Secularism, thus, became a vital component of the freedom of thought and, therefore, democracy – a gift neither of Reformation, nor of Renaissance, but of Enlightenment. Its justification was based on individual freedom and multi-culturalism as the governing principle of states.

However, religion and politics may not be completely separated either because politics is a social and an individual matter concerning the state. It is not possible to ban religion from them. But social and political institutions may surely be separated from religion. Such separation did take place after the American and the French revolutions in the late eighteenth century. It took place in 1905 in France, in 1917 in Russia and, later, in the Union of Soviet Socialist Republics (USSR). It took place in Turkey in 1924 when the Islamic Caliphate was altogether abolished.[4] Yet, rulers often use religion for the pursuit of secular interests. The British rulers of India made subtle use of religion in fomenting communal differences among their subjects.

Secularism in the Constituent Assembly of India

The Indian Independence Act, 1947, which partitioned British India, never spoke of a 'Hindu-majority' or a 'Muslim-majority' dominion. It created two 'independent dominions' (which happened to be, respectively, Hindu-majority and Muslim-majority). None of the Indian political parties, during the freedom movement, including the Hindu Mahasabha, had asked for a Hindu state. No one moved a resolution in the Constituent Assembly of India proposing a Hindu state even though there were demands for abolition of cow slaughter[5] and the like. What all the parties, other than the Muslim League, wanted was a united India (*Akhand Bharat*). (Even the demand for Sikh 'homeland' did not envisage a separate state.) At the time of Partition, there were more Muslims in India than in Pakistan. Yet the Partition strengthened political Hinduism in India and political Islam in Pakistan. *Hindutva* is the epitome of political Hinduism based on the argument of 'cultural nationalism', first propounded by the philosophers of Nazism in Europe.

Transfer of power was a political revolution without the accompaniment of a social revolution in India. A great deal of continuity with her past remained alive. One element of this continuity was the influence of religion aggravated by Partition and the communal riots. They continued to haunt the builders of the new nation. They had to remain satisfied after abolishing communal electorate but granting cultural and educational rights to the minorities under the rubric of equal rights. A number of social reforms involving rights of women and Scheduled

Castes required separation of religion and politics, which could not be achieved at one stroke. Such a situation exposed the political leadership to two kinds of danger. First, given the inter-communal tensions in the country, the policy-makers are frequently viewed by the minorities to be committed to the majority ethos and seeking to impose them on the minorities. In contrast, the majority community looks at them as unduly placating the minority communities as vote banks. This eventually leads the state to be branded as sectarian by all sides. Hindus blame the government of tolerating polygyny of the Muslims; Muslims and Sikhs blame it for trying to curb their social practices and cultural distinction and Christians blame them of obstructing proselytization.

A study of the proceedings of the Constituent Assembly of India will show that there was not much debate on the first principles of the Constitution (Gadgil 1948: Preface; Chaube 2000: 235). In a way they had been settled during the freedom struggle. Whatever major decisions were taken beyond them was in the committees of the Constituent Assembly comprising leaders and lawyers. At the early stage of its work, the Fundamental Rights Sub-Committee received a note from K.M. Munshi and a memorandum from B.R. Ambedkar (before he had become chairman of the Drafting Committee). Ambedkar proposed that the state shall not recognise any religion as state religion (paragraph 18. Shiva Rao 1968: 87) and that

> Religious associations shall be entitled to levy contribution on their members who are willing to pay them if their law of incorporation permits them to do so. No person may be compelled to pay taxes the proceeds of which are specifically appropriated for the use of any religious community of which he is not a member. (Para 20, ibid.)

On 26 March 1947 the Fundamental Rights Sub-Committee of the Advisory Committee adopted the first proposal of Ambedkar with verbal modification. The second sentence of his second proposal, that agreed with Art VI, Clause (4) of Munshi's draft (Shiva Rao 1967a), was also adopted (ibid.: 123). By the time the Fundamental Rights sub-committee met again on 14 April 1947 there was a new member in the sub-committee, Sardar K.M. Panikkar. In the absence of reports of proceedings of the committees, it is difficult to know what exactly happened in this session. But the minutes of April 16 say that Munshi and Panikkar promised to bring a fresh draft the next day so as to provide for those cases where religion was already accepted as a state religion (Shiva Rao 1967a: 165). The minutes of April 17 on the clause have 'No Comments' (ibid.: 202). In the final report of the sub-committee the prohibition part is missing. It did not come back in the Constitution.

The net effect of the proceedings was that the draft constitution desisted from proclaiming secularism though it substantially ensured it by and large. That substantial right was given in a circuitous way in the draft constitution prepared by the constitutional adviser in October 1947, following Munshi's draft, in this form: 'No person may be compelled to pay any taxes the proceeds of which are specifically appropriated in payment of expenses for the promotion or maintenance of any particular religion or particular denomination'(Clause19, Shiva Rao 1967b: 10). There was no prohibition on the state recognising any religion as state religion or spending a part of the general revenue for the benefit of any particular religion or religious denomination, however. It remained so in spite of an amendment proposed by B. Pattabhi Sitaramayya and others, in 1948, on the lines of Ambedkar's original proposal to the Fundamental Rights Sub-committee of the Advisory Committee: 'No religion shall be recognised as a state religion nor shall any tax be levied for the promotion or the maintenance of any religion' (Shiva Rao 1968: 42). (The word 'specifically' was missing in Sitaramayya's amendment. 'Specifically' was later replaced by 'exclusively'.) The Drafting Committee's comment was: 'This amendment seeks to substitute a new article. The existing article 21 is based on the last paragraph of article 49 of the Swiss Constitution. The proposed amendment involves a question of policy'(Shiva Rao 1968: 42).

On the floor of the Constituent Assembly one amendment each from a Hindu congressman, Professor K.T. Shah, and a Muslim League member Moulana Hasrat Mohani demanding the declaration of India as a 'secular, socialist, federated republic' (Shiva Rao 1968: 141–42; Chaube 2000: 182), however, were rejected. The weakness of the demand was its composite character. The assembly, naturally, put its attention on the points of 'federative' and socialism about which there were strong objections. Ambedkar, chairman of the Drafting Committee, argued that a constitution is a political document and should

19

not lay down social and economic policies; they should be left to the future legislatures (CAD, VII, 392 403; Shiva Rao 1968: 141; Chaube 2000: 176). The point of state religion was lost in the maze of ideological debate. How could this be explained?

There is a circumstantial evidence suggesting an explanation. During the debate on the permissibility of religious instruction in schools, Renuka Roy's amendment that, 'No denominational religious instruction shall be provided in schools maintained by the State. No person attending any school or educational institution recognised or aided by the State shall be compelled to attend any such religious instruction' got powerful support from S. Radhakrishnan and H.N. Kunzru but was opposed by Vallabh Bhai Patel and K.M. Munshi on ground of some practical difficulty. India would be a secular state. The provinces would also be secular states. But the princely states were not all secular and democratic. Unless the princes agreed, it would not be advisable to establish such a fundamental right throughout the country. Ultimately the Constituent Assembly overcame that fear (CAD V 1968: 380–81; Shiva Rao V 1968: 263–64). The impact of at least one of the princely states on Indian secularism was permanently stamped. This was the state of Travancore. Since 1811, when the British resident assumed the position of dewan, the properties of the temples were taken over by the state, which took up the maintenance of the temples. The cost of appropriation of their wealth by the state, however, was so big that it would be impossible to settle the liability of the government at a time. The government, therefore, decided to pay an annual maintenance out of the state's exchequer (Menon 1956/1961: 269–71). It was later agreed to incorporate that agreement in the Constitution.

Now, both K.M. Munshi and K.M. Panikkar had deep knowledge of the states' politics. Panikkar had been dewan of the state of Baroda, besides personally hailing from the state of Travancore, and K.M. Munshi was a leader in the States' Peoples' Movement. Sardar Patel was the kingpin of the process of integration of princely states with independent India, Pattabhi Sitaramayya, on the other hand, had not only been a close associate of Gandhi and Nehru but also president of the Indian National Congress at the time. It is impossible to believe that the Drafting Committee, chaired by Ambedkar himself, would reject his amendment without the support of Vallabh Bhai Patel. There is reason to believe that the Congress leaders were cautious in respect of integration of states and willingly desisted from proclaiming secularism though they substantially did it.

Secularism and the Indian state

Although the Constitution could not declare India a secular state there are enough provisions in the Constitution that 'substantially' grant India a secular state but allow the state to go beyond the limits of secularism. There are grey areas in the Constitution of India, including Article 25. But they were so left not out of any malice or prejudice on the part of the Constitution makers. Pressures of circumstances forced the Constituent Assembly to leave them like that. Some of the subsequent state legislations and executive actions have come in for uninformed and unkind criticism. Partha Chatterjee, for instance, takes exception to two legislations that violate the liberal democratic principles of secularism: (1) passage of the Madras Hindu Religious and Charitable Endowments Act, 1951(Chatterjee 1998: 354) and (2) extension of Shari'at Act 1937 to the former princely state of Cooch Behar (ibid.: 363). Both these aberrations were mandated by the integration of states and the need to apply the rule of law. The first was required following the constitutional provision on *Devaswom* Trust (per Art. 290A as on today). The second followed the requirement to apply civil laws uniformly, the only exception being the Scheduled Tribal areas. The first had a commitment of the state of India to the ruler of Travancore as its justification, but the second was not accompanied by such commitment except to the principle of rule of law. It should be noted that the impact of the Hindu Marriage Act and the Hindu Women's Succession Act was to abolish the traditional rights to property of the Hindu Nayar women of Kerala.

Article 25 is reinforced by other articles in the Constitution. Article 27 provides that no person shall be compelled to pay taxes, the proceeds of which are specifically appropriated for the purpose of any religion or denomination. This is a prohibition of a *ziziya*-like tax, but it does not stop state funding of religion. According to Article 28 no religious instruction would be imparted in wholly state-funded educational institution. This prohibition does not apply to a state-aided endowment or trust institution, which is required to impart religious instruction, although they may not compel any student to take religious instruction. No citizen may be denied admission in a state-aided school on ground of race, religion, caste, language or any of them [Article 29(2)]. All minorities, religious or linguistic, have the right to establish and administer educational institutions of their choice. The state shall not discriminate against any such minority institution (Article 30). Of course, some cultural and educational rights may encourage and facilitate the exploitation of minority communities by their own trusts and religious bodies. It was the poor pay structure of the teachers of the trust colleges of Kerala that moved the communist government of the state to take over the management of such colleges in 1957, provoking a huge protest that ultimately led to the dismissal of the state government in 1959. The government is unable to take ameliorative steps on the plight of Muslim women on the same ground.

Did India turn away from secularism?

Donald Eugene Smith called India a secular state, despite the existence of problems.

> India is a secular state in the same sense in which one can say
> that India is a democracy. Despite various undemocratic features
> of Indian politics and government, parliamentary democracy is
> functioning, and with considerable vigour. Similarly, the secular
> state; the ideal is clearly embodied in the Constitution, and it is
> being implemented in substantial measure. (Smith 1998: 193)

According to Smith, the rejection of the proposal to declare a secular state in the Constituent Assembly by the law minister (Ambedkar) was correct because '[t]he inclusion of such an article in the Constitution, however laudable the intention behind it, would certainly have produced a conflict with Art. 25, which . . . permits extensive state intervention with religion in the interest of social reform' (ibid.: 103).

'The debates in the Constituent Assembly leave little doubt', says M.C. Setalvad, one of the finest legal brains that India has ever produced, in his Patel Memorial Lectures, 1965, adding, 'what was intended by the Constitution was not the secularization of the State in the sense of its complete dissociation from religion, but rather an attitude of religious neutrality, with equal treatment to all religions and religious minorities'(Setalvad 1990: 482). Setalvad's justification of this phenomenon was that the Indian, particularly the Hindu society, needed social reform involving religion too:

> A secular state in the strict sense may, indeed, by reason of its
> policy of total non-interference in religious matters, feel itself

powerless to promote a secular attitude in the citizen in social and political matters, and fail to induce him to confine religion and religious practices to a narrower sphere. (ibid.: 484)

What Setalvad really meant by a secular attitude is a rational attitude. He cited the problem of framing a uniform civil code as a critical issue in the area (ibid.: 490). But a careful reading of Article 25 that grants the Indians the right to freedom of religion clearly would distinguish between religion and social reform. Clause (2) of this Article enables the state to make any law (a) regulating or restricting any economic, financial, political or other secular activity which may be associated with religious practice and (b) providing for social welfare and reform or the throwing open of Hindu religious institutions of a public character to all classes and sections of Hindus. Sub-clause (a) thus makes a clear distinction between secular activity associated with religious practice and purely religious activity. The first includes, but does not exhaust itself with, economic, financial, political activities and is under the domain of the state. Sub-clause (b) enables the state to undertake social welfare and reform of all sections of the population. Read together, under the principle of harmonious construction, social welfare and reform would be considered to be belonging to the secular domain of society.

There is some misunderstanding about the second part of sub-clause (b) that enables the state to throw open the Hindu religious institutions of a public character to all sections of Hindus. This has been criticised as the state's intervention in religious affairs of the Hindus. Further, Explanation II furnished under the same sub-clause provides that the reference to the Hindus is to be construed as including a reference to persons professing the Sikh, Jaina and Buddhist religions. Some Akali politicians in the past have taken strong exception to being clubbed with the Hindus.

It will be more logical to connect this provision with Article 17, which abolishes untouchability and sees it in the light of the long temple-entry movement since the 1920s. In a broader sense, the matter is a part of the caste system that has condemned the untouchable castes. The Sikh society practised untouchability. Most of the Buddhists in India had belonged to the untouchable castes, B.R. Ambedkar being the iconic figure among them. The possibility of presence of untouchability among the Buddhists cannot be ruled out. Though untouchability among the Jains is not apparent on the surface, they have virtually converted themselves into a caste equivalent to the Hindu trading castes and have free intermarriage with them. In any case, caste discrimination has been definitely prohibited by the Constitution of India as far as the public affairs are concerned. Islam and Christianity abhor untouchability at least in theory, though among the Catholics of South India it is discerned in respect of their burial grounds. So they are untouched by this regulation (Chaube 2012: 214).

There is some misconception about the provision of social reform. It is assumed that social reform is constitutionally permitted only for the Hindus, the Sikhs, the Jains and the Buddhists and not the Muslims. Orthodox Muslim opinion insists Muslim personal law (i.e. laws on marriage and succession). The *Hindutavadis* take the same argument to allege that the Indian Constitution discriminates against the Hindus and allows polygyny among Muslims. Extremist Sikhs have resented state intervention in their marital affairs too. Rajmata Vijay Raje Scindia openly criticised the police action against burning of widows, a Hindu religious practice, in Rajasthan. One has only to note that an overwhelmingly Hindu Union government failed to pass the Hindu Code Bill in 1949. The substance of the bill had to be passed part by part over the entire next decade.

There is no exception for the Muslims under the Indian Constitution. Social reform is not restricted to any particular community. In fact Article 44 of the Directive Principles of State Policy recommends a uniform civil code on this ground. It is a different matter that no government has found it possible to frame such a law. With regard to Muslim personal laws the governments in the past 60 years have argued that the initiative for reform must come from a leader of the Muslim community. Interestingly, Pakistan and Bangladesh have abolished Muslim polygyny, but not Hindu polygyny.[6] Of course, in Bangladesh and Pakistan, polygyny is occasionally practised by the Muslims in violation of law. In India Muslims are allowed by Muslim Personal Law to marry up to four wives, the Quranic condition being that one treats all wives equally. Influential Hindus also can and do violate the rule of monogamy. One legal escape route is conversion to Islam in order to get a marriage dissolved and to take a second wife.

The Constitution was classically conceived as a document limiting the powers of the government and regulating its procedure. This limit was further underwritten by the incorporation of the fundamental rights of the citizens of the United States as beyond the capacity of the government to touch. In some countries like Ireland and India the directive principles of state policy issue some directives to the state in regard to the rights of the citizens. The provision of universal adult franchise in the Constitution and amendments adding the rights to education of children and work of the adults are substantially in the nature of pronouncements not backed by any writs. They cannot be called mandates. However, separation of social reform from religion is a mandate of the Constitution. No one can get a writ against a social reform measure of the government on the ground of its conflict with religion. Whether a social reform assumed to be contrary to any religious doctrine will be undertaken by the government or not is a matter of the government's policy and nerve and not any constitutional bar.

Until the 42nd Amendment in 1976 the declaration of 'secularism' was missing in the Indian Constitution. But various articles in the chapter on Fundamental Rights prohibited discrimination on ground of religion. Most significantly, however, Article 25 that enshrined the right to freedom of religion itself made a clear distinction between the secular and the sacred when it laid down that, notwithstanding the freedom to profess, practise and propagate religion by all persons the state can regulate or restrict 'any economic, financial, political or other secular activity which may be associated with religious practice.' It is by the strength of this proviso that states have sought to control the secular affairs of the religious establishment. The Tamil Nadu government's rejoinder to the National Human Rights Commission on the Shankaracharya affair some time back (2006) that the Kanchi Mutt is not a place of worship but a residential colony housing some 25 families and no deity is illustrious of this dichotomy.

The 42nd amendment (1976) built a haze around the Constitution. The state functionaries, including judges, have failed the Constitution primarily on the argument that 'our secularism is different'. The word 'secular' in the amended Preamble (1976) was translated as *panth nirapeksha* (non-sectarian). In 1993 the judgement in the S.R. Bommai case following the demolition of Babri masjid and supersession of four state governments upheld secularism as a basic feature. The next year the Bombay High Court declared that Hindutva is secular and the Supreme Court upheld that opinion. The Supreme Court judgement on 'Hindutva' is a typical case of confusion.[7] The Uttar Pradesh chief minister, Kalyan Singh, undertook construction activities in the Babri Masjid–Ram Janambhoomi complex, violating the court order against such construction in the name of providing facilities to tourists and pilgrims visiting Ayodhya. A judge of the Allahabad

High Court, in the early 1990s, gave a ruling that Lord Ram is a part of the Indian Constitution on the ground that one of the pages of the original handwritten Constitution, decorated by drawings of the artist Nanda Lal Bose, about the cultural heritage of India, carried a picture of Lord Ram. Another judgement, delivered about 10 years later by another judge of the same court, summarily granted the Babri Masjid property to a Hindu party on the basis of his 'knowledge' that a Ram temple had been destroyed in the sixteenth century to build a mosque upon it. In May 2007 the visit of a Hindu minister's son, born to his Christian wife, to the Guruvayur temple in Kerala raised a hue and cry to which members of the government reacted by arguing that, whereas worship is a religious affair, entry into a temple is not.

Conclusion

There is no doubt that secularism has become a subject of political contention in India. It need not be if it is defined accurately. Secularism, to borrow Bhikhu Parekh's language, is indifference to religion, not equal respect for all religions. It allows members of government and persons in governmental authority to profess and practise their personal religious beliefs. It requires that persons in authority equally respect each citizen's personal religious belief. Thus secularism becomes a part of discourse on the fundamental right of citizen to freedom of conscience. Therefore no government should give financial or administrative support to any religious activity or block if it is strictly within the periphery of law. Nor should any government make a fuss about conversion. At the same time no government should shrink from undertaking social reform and economic development of all sections of the people under pressure of vested interests. In several European countries Christian Socialist parties operate within a secular framework of government because they can distinguish between state and society and read their constitutions as legal documents within the framework of rule of law and not of rule by prejudice.

Notes

1 'A Hindu . . . is he who feels attachment to the land that extends from Sindhu to Sindhu, from the Indus to the Seas – as the land of his forefathers – his Fatherland, who inherits the blood of the great race whose first discernible source could be traced to the Vedic Saptasindhus and which, assimilating all that was incorporated and ennobling all that was assimilated, has grown into and come to be known as the Hindu people, who, as a consequence of the foregoing attributes, has inherited and claims as his own the Hindu

Sanskriti, the Hindu civilization, as represented in a common history, common heroes, a common literature, common art, a common law and a common jurisprudence, common fairs and festivals, rites and rituals, ceremonies and sacraments. Not that every Hindu has all these details of the Hindu Sanskriti down to each syllable common with other Hindus, but that, he had more of it in common with his Hindu brothers than with, say an Arab or an Englishman' (Savarkar 1999: 62–63).

2 It was only Kṛṣna who, in the Gita, a highly philosophical discourse somewhat ill-fitted in the Mahābhārata, claimed his own supreme divinity. But he was not a king himself. Hindus, on the other hand, have frequently ascribed divinity to noble personalities like Rama, the king of Ayodhya and Kṛṣna.

3 I borrow the term from V.P. Luthera (Luthera 1964).

4 After the death of the first four 'righteous' Caliphs, in 661 A.D. the Caliphate moved from Arabia to the lay Umayyad ruler of Syria. It later moved to Iraq, to Egypt and, finally, to Turkey where it was abolished in 1924 by Kemal Ataturk.

5 At the time of the drafting of the Constitution, in the Constituent Assembly of India, Thakurdas Bhargava, a social worker among tribal people of Central India, and Seth Govind Das, president of the All-India Cow Protection Committee, both members of the Congress party, proposed a Directive Principle of State Policy to offer protection to cows and calves and other milch cattle for the promotion of agriculture and animal husbandry. The Assembly did not directly ban it – that would certainly be regarded as a non-secular act – but accepted the Bhargava-Das proposal (Shiva Rao 1968: 328). Not all states of India have banned it.

6 It is not that uniform civil code will always benefit the weak. The Hindu Succession Act of 1960 took away the exclusive right of the Nayar women of Kerala to ancestral property. In Meghalaya continuous effort has been on to take away the exclusive right of the matrilineal Garo and the Khasi women to ancestral property.

7 On one day (11 December 1995) the Supreme Court headed by Chief Justice J.S. Verma delivered judgement on two cases – Civil Appeal No. 2635 of 1989 (Bal Thackeray v. Prabhakar K. Kunte) and Civil Appeal No. 4973 of 1993 (Manohar Joshi v. Nitin Bhaurao Patil & Anr) – pronouncing that 'the word "Hindutva" by itself does not invariably mean Hindu religion and it is the context and the manner of its use which is material for deciding the meaning of "Hindutva" in a particular text . . . . The so-called plank of the political party may at best be relevant only for appreciation of the context in which a speech was made during the election campaign, but no more for the purpose of pleading corrupt practice in the election petition against a particular candidate' (the quote is from the second judgement). The Supreme Court found the speeches in the election meetings of the leaders of the Shiv Sena—BJP combine in 1989–91 Mumbai too generally seeped with communal propaganda to attract disqualification under the Representation of the People Act.

2

INSTITUTIONAL
COMMUNALISM IN INDIA

Pritam Singh

This chapter has three main objectives. The first objective is to draw attention to the anomalous and negative connotations of the word 'communal',
as it is used in the progressive (academic and activist) discourse around communalism and secularism in India. The second objective is to introduce a
new concept – 'institutional communalism' – as a theoretical tool to map the
true scale of religious sectarianism and communalism in the subcontinent
and to argue that the fight against institutional communalism involves not
only ideological or pedagogical struggle but also practical measures to record,
monitor and eradicate it. The third objective is to challenge the pervasive
practice of equating 'majority communalism' with 'minority communalism'.

Progressive discourse around 'the critique of communalism' in India has
focussed primarily on instances of inter-religious violence and the activities
of political and social organisations that are characterised as 'communal',
that is to say 'engaged in articulating the demands or viewpoints of one or
other religious community'. The fundamental weakness of this discourse
is that it neglects the deeper and less visible political, socio-economic and
cultural structures that give birth to sectarianism and communalism and to
sectarian and communal organisations. Furthermore, such a discourse has an
in-built bias, in that it equates what are normally referred to in the literature as majority and minority communalisms. This chapter is an attempt to
develop a critique of this discourse by delving deeper into the institutional
structures of communalism in India. I have chosen to name this deeper
structure of communalism as *institutional communalism*, drawing on the experiences of anti-racist activism and theories of institutional racism in the UK.

Communalism versus religious sectarianism: a brief interrogation of two terms

It is a strange linguistic anomaly that in the discourse on sectarianism and communalism in India, the word 'communal' has generally come to acquire a pejorative meaning, suggesting divisiveness and conflict. In the rest of the world, especially beyond South Asia, this word tends to relate to social unity and cohesion and to socially progressive and collective modes of thinking and activities: communal agriculture, communal ownership of land, communal irrigation, communal kitchen, communal leisure, communal singing and dancing and so on.[1] In all these examples, the word 'communal' suggests public sharing in contrast with private and individualistic pursuits – a positive connotation that implies cooperation and mutual tolerance.

In India, however, the word 'communal' has come to acquire an inverted and largely negative connotation – that of socially divisive and politically regressive activities. This linguistic anomaly is a legacy of India's anti-colonial struggle for national independence. During India's movement for independence, many of the legislative, judicial and administrative policies and instruments that the British rulers adopted in response to demands generally from non-Hindu religious communities for protecting the interests of these communities came to be called 'communal'. The meaning of the word 'communal' in that context was understood by the British, the minorities in question, and democratic-minded people in India as something that implied defending the democratic rights of the vulnerable or potentially vulnerable minorities with religious identities. However, the leadership of the Indian National Congress (henceforth the Congress) that hegemonised India's movement for national independence viewed any move aimed at safeguarding these vulnerable minorities with suspicion. The Congress view was that any government move or demand by a religious minority to safeguard minority interests was aimed at weakening the movement for independence by creating divisions in that movement.

Caste and religious collectivities

During the movement for national independence, similar conflict arose over protective measures for oppressed and vulnerable castes in the Hindu society. While Ambedkar and others advocated measures to protect Dalits, the mainstream leadership (including Gandhi) viewed those measures as moves to divide Hindus and the national movement (Ambedkar 2006/1943; Ambedkar 2008/1945). In order to differentiate the collectivity associated with caste from the collectivity associated with religion, the measures aimed at safeguarding the collective interests of vulnerable religious minorities came to be referred to as 'communal'. In essence, both the attempts to protect the interests of lower castes and the measures to protect the interests of religious minorities were communal, that is, they were aimed at protecting the interests of a section of society (Dalits and religious minorities) in a collective manner. However, what may have been mere terminological convenience (a simple differentiation between the nomenclatures for two collective endeavours, by naming the religiously collective endeavours as communal) has resulted over a period of time in creating a substantive difference in meaning and connotation. The Congress viewed the religious collectivity as more dangerous than the caste collectivity, because the latter, while it might create conflicts within Hindu society, did not have the potential of creating a geographical partition of the country such as that which resulted in the creation of Muslim-majority Pakistan. As a thought experiment, we can imagine that, had the country not been partitioned, subsequent conflicts over protective measures for caste collectivity would have acquired in the national or Hindu imagination more pejorative connotations than those over religious collectivity.[2] The word 'casteist' would perhaps have become more damning than the word 'communal'. The violence of Partition has resulted in the perception of communalism as a more dangerous threat than casteism in the Indian national imagination.

For the same reason that 'communal' became a derogatory word in Indian national imagination, it has a different connotation in Pakistan where the solidarity arising from religious collectivity is perceived as having contributed to the birth of the nation (Pakistan). However, even in Pakistan this somewhat positive connotation of the word 'communal' is seen in an instrumentalist fashion, namely that communal and religious solidarity created a social and political force and movement that contributed to the creation of a new nation state. In India, the word 'communal' has a negative connotation since it is viewed as resulting in the breakup of 'the unity of the Indian nation' whereas in Pakistan it has somewhat positive connotation because it is viewed as having contributed to the birth of a nation (Sayeed 1963). In both cases, nationalism is the determining force.

Casting the net further than Pakistan, if we contrast the term 'religious sectarianism',[3] which is used widely in the rest of the world to describe conflicts where religion is seen to be the source of stoking confrontations, we can identify a further problem with the Indian use of the term 'communalism'. Namely that while the former term qualifies and critiques the exclusionism of particular religious group formations, the negative connotations that have become attached to the term 'communalism' in India imply a suspicion of (a) religious solidarity in general, and (b) any group activity that emerges from religious origins. This suspicion is problematic and blinkered.

Many religious group activities that are genuinely communal in the sense of collective group activities are socially progressive, such as the practice of langar in the Sikh gurdwaras where any devotee can participate in the practice of communal food preparation activities and all devotees communally and collectively serve and partake of the food cooked in this manner. When the institution of langar was started by Guru Nanak, the first Sikh guru, in the fifteenth century and later popularised by Guru Amar Das, the third Sikh guru, it was socially revolutionary, in that it hit directly against the casteist practices of superiority and inferiority and untouchability, specifically the prohibitions on inter-dining.[4] Despite some distortions such as the reappearance of caste in Sikhism, the socially progressive aspect of Sikh langar has, by and large, continued since then. There are similar such socially progressive collective/communal activities and practices in other religious traditions too such as *shura* (consultation) and *ijma* (consensus) in Islam. India's Radha Soami faith is particularly strong in encouraging collective and communal practices regarding agricultural and industrial work, marketing practices and cooking and serving of food.[5]

Having discussed the flaws in the predominant Indian usage of the term 'communalism', we introduce the concept of institutional communalism and examine its application in the Indian context with the purpose of examining deeper structures of communalism in India beyond overt religious confrontations.

31

Defining institutional communalism

It may be useful for getting a sense of the term 'institutional communalism' to mention here that the inspiration for using this term came from the term 'institutional racism' used in Britain initially in the context of racism in the police force but eventually extended to identify racism in many other institutions. Judge William Macpherson who headed the inquiry into the death of a black teenager Stephen Lawrence used the term 'institutional racism' to characterise the systematic racism prevalent in London's Metropolitan Police Force. Stephen Lawrence was an 18-year-old black man from London, a student of architecture, who was murdered there in a racist attack while waiting for a bus on the evening of 22 April 1993. After the initial investigation, five suspects, all white, were arrested but not convicted. It emerged during the course of this investigation that the murder was racially motivated and that the handling of the case by the police and the Crown Prosecution Service was influenced by considerations of race. The public outrage at the handling of this case by the police and the prosecution service, the media campaign on the case and the public campaign led by Lawrence's parents forced the government to order a public enquiry in 1998 that was led by Sir William Macpherson. The inquiry report, published in 1999 that came to be known as Macpherson Report, concluded that the Metropolitan Police Force that had originally investigated the case was 'institutionally racist'. The systematic and institutional racism was not about one or more individuals in the police force being racist; instead it was about the entire gamut of functioning of the police force in its dealing with minority ethnic groups. The general definition of institutional racism provided by Judge Macpherson was: 'the collective failure of an organisation to provide an appropriate and professional service to people because of their colour, culture, or ethnic origin' (Macpherson 1999, Chapter 6).[6] Extending the scope of his recommendations beyond police reforms, Macpherson called for institutional reforms also in the civil services, local governments, the National Health Service, schools and the judicial system, to address issues of institutional racism. The term 'institutional racism' had been used before, most famously by Stokely Carmichael, the Black Panther, in the 1960s and 1970s in the United States[7] but Macpherson report triggered a resurgence of interest in this term and in shifting the public attention from the physically violent racist actions of individual racists to the direct or indirect complicity of the police and other institutions of the state in the day-to-day practices of these institutions. The focus on institutional racism triggered by the report helped in extending the public debates on racism beyond the criticisms of political organisations, which were considered racist such as the British National Party, to the investigations into racism in the mode of functioning of a wide variety of institutions of British society and state.

Employing the concept of institutional communalism in India, in the manner in which institutional racism has been used in the UK can offer us a new perspective on communalism and religious sectarianism that extends beyond the political activities of 'extremist' political, social and cultural organisations. One major weakness of the anti-communalism discourse in India has been the excessive focus on political activities of such organisations that are considered communal (e.g. the organisations associated with what is called the Sangh Parivar, the group of organisations that are considered advocates of Hindu majoritarian dominance in India). The same method is employed to examine political organisations that are considered advocates of any minority religious community such as Muslims, Sikhs and to a lesser extent Christians.

There can be different degrees of institutional communalism as there can be different degrees of institutional racism. It can vary from very subtle to very violent. The apartheid regime in South Africa and the institution of slavery in the United States may be considered examples of institutional racism in its most violent form. A range of activities and practices take place in white-dominated societies that are far apart from the violent form of institutional racism in the apartheid era in South Africa but these activities and practices still negatively impact upon the lives of minority ethnic groups in different ways and degrees.

One very useful characteristic of the experience of struggles against institutional racism in the UK, from the viewpoint of initiating a politics opposed to institutional communalism, is that the critique of institutional racism targets the racism practised by the dominant white race and considers the idea of 'minority racism' as of significantly less importance. Minority racism is considered less important because racism is seen not merely as 'false consciousness' or an individual mind-set but as a power relationship and, in the matrix of power in Western societies, non-white minority ethnic groups are placed in a hugely subordinate situation. Given the hugely disadvantaged location of the non-white minority ethnic groups, even if some members of these groups individually harbour any negative stereotypes about the dominant white race, it is virtually of no consequence from the viewpoint of social, economic, cultural and political dynamics in white-dominated societies. We will examine below the implications of this aspect of the political theorising and practice of institutional racism for our understanding of institutional communalism in India.

Evidence of institutional communalism in India

In the same manner that institutional racism represents the dominant power status of the white ethnic group in Western societies, institutional communalism in India represents the dominant power status of India's majority religious community, that is, Hindus. The overwhelming numerical majority of Hindus in India[8] (80.5 per cent according to the 2011 census) accords them a privileged location in the political, social, cultural and eventually economic networks while, at the same time, disadvantaging the religious minorities (Muslims 13.4 per cent, Christians 2.3 per cent and Sikhs 1.9 per cent) in these networks.[9] Hierarchical relations constituted through class, race, gender, religion, ethnicity and nationality operate through diverse ways and impact upon the precise location of individuals and groups in society and economy. Bourdieu's social capital theory[10] can provide us with a framework here, with which to encapsulate the privileged location of upper caste Hindus in India. Bourdieu defines social capital as 'the sum of the resources, actual or virtual, that accrue to an individual or a group by virtue of possessing a durable network of more or less institutionalized relationships of mutual acquaintance and recognition' (Bourdieu 1986: 248; Bourdieu and Wacquant 1992: 119)

> which provides each of its members with the backing of the collectively owned capital, a 'credential' which entitles them to credit, in the various senses of the word. These relationships may exist only in the practical state, in material and/or symbolic exchanges which help to maintain them. (Bourdieu 1986: 248–49)

A majority has an inherent advantage by virtue of being a majority, unless these advantages are counteracted and contained by other social forces. In other words, to use Bourdieu's social capital theory, a majority has accumulated social and cultural capital, and hence economic and political capital, by the simple fact of being socially and culturally positioned as a majority. Institutional communalism is, therefore, the exercise of accumulated power – the power of its social/cultural/political/economic capital – by the majority.

We can also draw from the work of psychologists researching on biases and prejudices, in order to understand the institutional bias that favours the Hindu majority in India. These psychologists show that in making judgements, the key players involved in decision-making processes do not pay attention to all the details and relevant facts that are brought to their attention and instead often look for information that is familiar, or that supports their favoured and pre-formed perspective or interest (Hambrick 2007; Kahneman 1973; Pirson and Turnbull 2011). This filtering process guided by psychological mechanisms such as biases plays a very critical role when a balanced judgement is to be formed after looking at evidence that may have contradictory aspects. In such situations of some degree of uncertainty, the bias leads to giving more weight to the opinions of those who are similar to the one making the decision and thus resulting in distortions of rational judgement (Pirson and Turnbull 2011; Tversky and Kahneman 1974; Kahneman 2011). This discriminatory behaviour pervades in all decision-making processes that are related to racism, communalism, casteism, sexism and ageism. Through my work with the equal opportunity initiatives in my university for many years,[11] I learnt about a well-observed global phenomenon that in the selection and recruitment process, the members of selection committees sometimes consciously but most often unconsciously tend to favour individuals who are like them thus building an inherent bias in the selection process. In a white- and male-dominated society where white and the male tend to dominate selection committees, discrimination against women and minority ethnic groups gets built into the system. To recognise this in-built bias is the first step to deal with it with the purpose of weakening, neutralising or eradicating it. Equal opportunity legislation and training, despite many shortcomings especially in training, become the instruments of weakening it.

The journey towards neutralising and eradicating the bias is a long and arduous one.

In India with nearly 81 per cent share of the population being Hindu and most institutions of power being dominated by upper caste Hindus, there is an inbuilt bias towards privileging of Hindus but almost non-existent institutional mechanisms to counteract this inbuilt bias. Apart from the affirmative action in the form of reservations for Schedule Castes and Tribes that has been a positive force in neutralising upper caste dominance, there is nothing in India on the pattern of equal opportunity legislation, monitoring and accountability that tracks systematic bias and discrimination against religious minorities. The National Minorities Commission constituted as late as in October 1993 – more than 43 years after the formation of the Indian republic in 1950 – remains a mere paper tiger without the power and institutional infrastructure to track systematic in-built bias against religious minorities, leave aside neutralising this bias.

Institutional communalism in India, that is to say Hindu majoritarian bias, pervades the Indian Constitution, bureaucracy, security forces, parliamentary institutions, judiciary, prisons, academic institutions, health services, media and the cultural and art organisations. The exact nature and extent of institutional communalism in these institutions is uneven, and deserves further detailed investigation. There is, however, a reasonable amount of evidence and research already in circulation, which indicates the pervasiveness of Hindu–communalist bias in a range of institutions in India. I outline these in the following discussion.

Constitution

I have previously challenged the existing consensus or near consensus among Indian academics and opinion makers about the secularism of India's Constitution and, through a scrutiny of various clauses in the Constitution, have demonstrated the existence of strong Hindu bias in that claimed secularism (Singh 2005). My conclusion was that India's Constitution

> has several elements of Hindu bias in it. The symbolic insertion of 'Bharat' in the opening article naming the country; the

provision for strong centralisation supportive of Hindu nationalism; the active intervention of the state to consolidate Hindu
identity through reform of the Hindu religion; the definition of
'Hindu' supportive of Hindu assimilative agenda towards Buddhists, Jains and Sikhs; cow protection; pre-eminent status for
Hindi in the Devanagari script and special importance for Sanskrit are all features of the constitution which make its secularism seriously Hindu-tainted. (Singh 2005: 921)

Bajpai (2002, 2009/10, 2011) points to the weakness of minority rights in
the Indian Constitution and Chiriyankandath (2000) demonstrates the
compromised nature of Indian secularism due to the impact of religion,
particularly Hindu religion, in the making of the Constitution.

Judiciary

Crossman and Kapur (2001) have examined several judgements and
judicial interventions of India's Supreme Court in cases that required
consideration of religious issues and have demonstrated (especially in
Chapter 2 of the book *The Supreme Court Hindutva Judgements*) the
prevalence of Hindu bias in the working of this highest judicial institution of India. Similarly Sen (2010) examines a range of cases that
had a religious component in them and demonstrates that the Supreme
Court's responses to them have contributed to 'homogenisation of religion' and nation that is favourable to the Hindu worldview and insensi-
tive to pluralism and religious minorities. Vrinda Grover (2004, 2006)
demonstrates systematic Hindu bias in the working of the police and
judiciary in the way evidence regarding the massacre of Sikhs in 1984
in Delhi was collected (or not collected) and interpreted. Congress,
the ruling party at the time of the anti-Sikh carnage, is widely believed
to have protected the guilty perpetrators of the massacre. The significance of Grover's work is that it highlights how the majoritarian Hindu
bias in the institutions of the police, investigation agencies and judiciary is not limited to periods of Congress party rule at the Centre but
transcends specific political party control of state power at any point
of time. It is due to this institutional communalism, embedded in the
agencies of the state, that even during the regime of the non-Congress

parties controlling the power at the Centre, the victims of the Delhi massacre could not get justice (Kaur 2004; Mitta and Phoolka 2007). The resurgence of the recent Sikh resentment against the acquittal of Sajjan Kumar, a prime suspect in the organisation of anti-Sikh violence in Delhi in 1984, by a Delhi court has been primarily ignited by the fact that the judge in this case did not respect and accept the eye witness accounts of women whose family members had been killed during the violence and who had testified in the court that they had seen Sajjan Kumar leading the mobs that killed their family members (*The Hindu* 2013).[12]

Another recent example of institutional communalism in India's judicial decision-making institutions came to prominence in the case of a Punjabi militant Devinder Pal Singh Bhullar who was arrested in a case of car bombing that had caused several deaths in 1993 and who was awarded a death sentence by the trial court in 2001 and endorsed by the Delhi High Court in 2002. The Supreme Court on 26 March 2002 dismissed by a split decision (2–1) Bhullar's appeal against the death sentence. The presiding judge Justice M.B. Shah gave his decision in favour of acquitting Bhullar because of the central flaw in the lower courts' decision in awarding death sentence purely on the basis of his confession in police custody, which he had retracted when produced in court. However, his two other colleagues, Justices Arijit Pasayat and B.N. Agrawal, overruled Shah by not only convicting Bhullar but also sentencing him to death. They cited extraordinary arguments for their decision that a 'proof beyond reasonable doubt' should be 'a guideline, not a fetish', and that procedure is only 'a handmaiden and not the mistress of law'. Reporting on the case, Mitta argued that 'the majority verdict in the Bhullar case testifies to the damage done by terror ideology to judicial objectivity' (Mitta 2011).

The standard procedure, if there is a dissenting judgement in a decision on the death sentence, is normally to reduce the sentence to life imprisonment – but the dissenting judgement of Judge Shah was not shown to the President of India, who refused to commute Bhullar's death sentence to life imprisonment (*The Hindu* 2013a). The culmination of the whole process leading to the very harsh decision on Bhullar is linked to accumulation of biases, prejudices and dislikes against the Sikh militant Bhullar in the whole machinery involved in the decision making concerning the first verdict of death sentence against him and then the rejection of his plea for commutation of this sentence to life imprisonment.[13]

Another example of institutionalised Hindu bias in India's judiciary was revealed by Justice S.S. Sodhi, a former chief justice of Allahabad High Court, in a public meeting in Chandigarh. Justice Sodhi revealed that 'no Sikh Judge was trusted to deal with Sikh terrorist cases' (*The Tribune* 2013).

A more glaring case of majoritarian mind-set and institutional communalism became evident in the Supreme Court decision to award death sentence to Afzal Guru, a Kashmiri militant who was secretly hanged on 9 February 2013. The bench deciding his case said that the death sentence was necessary in order to satisfy 'the national conscience', which is a surrender of the legal reasoning to a structure of biases (Peer 2013).

Security services

Manisha Sethi (2013) demonstrates brilliantly the systematic bias in the working of intelligence agencies and police in their dealings with the minority Muslim population. Her quotes from two police officials are worth repeating here:

> In cases of terror attacks or communal riots, if the police goes after the perpetrators of the violence, and they happen to be mostly Muslim, you cannot, in the name of secularism, expect the police to act in proportion to their population. (Prakash Singh, former Director General, Border Security Force)

> There is nothing like Saffron terrorism. It just doesn't exist in the Hindu pantheon. (M.N. Singh, former Commissioner of Police, Mumbai)

Since there is no evidence that there was any protest at these remarks or official contestation of them by anyone in the police force, these views can reasonably be taken as representing a wide consensus in the Indian police's perceptions regarding Muslims and Hindus.

It is very difficult to get hard data on the representation of different religious communities in the inner core of the Indian state, namely the intelligence agencies. A human rights activist who shared with me some confidential information he was able to gather was of the view that there

PRITAM SINGH

were many layers of secrecy associated with different intelligence agencies of the state and that it was an unwritten rule that more secret an agency was, the less likelihood of non-Hindus being given a job or role in it. Other information that has come to light seems to confirm this view. Subhash Gatade (2008), writing on the emergence of Hindu terror groups, notes that one problem in investigating these groups is 'the near absence of Muslims or Sikhs in the different intelligence wings of the government'. Datta (2006) in an article titled 'Muslims and Sikhs Need Not Apply' pointed out that barring Intelligence Bureau (IB), which has a handful of Muslim officers, none of the other wings of intelligence have a single Muslim officer in its ranks. According to him,

> From 1969 till today – RAW's [Research and Analysis Wing, perhaps the most secret agency] current staff strength is about 10,000 – it has avoided recruiting any Muslim officer. Neither has the National Technical Research Organisation (NTRO), a crucial arm of external intelligence. The Intelligence Bureau (IB) with 12,000 personnel has been a little more open. It has a handful of Muslim officers, the senior most is a Joint Director.

In 2012, for the first time a Muslim officer Asif Ibrahim, a former history student of Delhi's Jawaharlal Nehru University, was made the director of IB.

Forced by a petition to the Supreme Court, the Army has admitted that bodyguards to President of India are recruited only from Hindus (Rajputs and Jats) and it seems since a considerable part of India's Jat population that is in Punjab is Sikh by faith, the Jat category has been extended to include Sikh Jats also (*The Tribune* 2013a).

Media

Analysing the media coverage of the Punjab crisis in the 1980s, I have documented extensively that Doordarshan (Central government-owned TV channel), All India Radio (AIR) and the mainstream English language media displayed deeply embedded institutional communalism in systematically pandering to Hindu biases, prejudices and sentiments in reporting and commenting on Indian Army's Operation Blue Star action

40

at the Golden Temple – the holiest Sikh shrine – in June 1984 followed by the massacre of Sikhs in October 1984 after the assassination by Sikh bodyguards of Indira Gandhi, the then Indian prime minister who had ordered the army action at the Golden Temple (Singh 1984, 1985a, 1985b). Patwant Singh (1985) also demonstrates how in the media reportage of Punjab, the inherent bias due to the majoritarian Hindu control of the Indian media led to distorted reports and commentaries that perpetuated pre-existing prejudices against the Sikhs and led to distorted information being fed to the citizens of India.[14] In more recent years, since the massacre of Muslims in Gujarat in 2002, the Kargil war conflict with Pakistan and the global rhetoric on 'war on terror', the majoritarian bias in media and popular culture especially in Indian cinema is particularly directed against the Muslim minority (Kumar HM 2013).

What I have outlined thus far is merely the tip of the iceberg – a few examples to initiate a debate on embedded Hindu bias and institutional communalism in India. A thorough and collective examination is required, not only of state institutions (civil services, security forces, judiciary and prisons) but also of non-state institutions (corporate world, non-governmental organisations [NGOs]) and the ideological apparatus (universities, research institutes and media establishments). A critique of organisations and institutions beyond those organisations that are popularly perceived to be overtly 'communal' (such as the Sangh Parivar), which is to say, a critique of the deeper structures of communalism at work within the Indian state, would give us a much more complex understanding of institutional communalism.

Criticism of equating 'majority and minority communalism'

Theoretical and political work against institutional racism has highlighted one aspect that is crucial to the further work on institutional communalism, namely that racism, if any, of minority ethnic individuals or groups against the dominant white racism is of very little significance and any energy devoted in the direction of exploring and critiquing minority racism (sometimes referred to by white racists as 'reverse racism') is a diversion from the central task of fighting racism. The central core of racism is not just about racially charged beliefs and attitudes but also the power to put into practice those beliefs and attitudes in a way that it has differential impact on the lives of members of different races. Many institutions in the Western world have been characterised as racist because of the 'culturally sanctioned beliefs, which, regardless of intentions involved, defend the advantages whites have because of the subordinated position of racial minorities' (Wellman 1993: X). Therefore, there is no substance in what is claimed as minority racism or reverse racism because even if some individuals or groups in minority-ethnic groups harbour prejudices against the dominant white race, they would not be able to cause any substantial disadvantage to the dominant group because they do not possess the power to oppress the dominant group. This does not mean that marginal cases of harassment of the individual members of dominant white race by some members of any minority racial group cannot take place. However, what is crucial is that the minority racial groups do not have institutionalised power to systematise the harassment of their members of the dominant racial group.

Similarly one can say that in fighting sexism, any talk of gender biases by women against men, which is sometimes referred to as reverse sexism, is almost a meaningless exercise. This does not mean to say that there does not exist any stereotyping of members of the white ethnic community by some members of minority ethnic groups or that that there is no prejudice by some women against men. However, given the structures of power in race and gender relations, prejudice by minority ethnic individuals against whites and by women against men have virtually no role to play in shaping the political and social dynamics of everyday life. In fact, one can go further and say that if there were no racism (i.e. dominance by white ethnic groups), there would be no retaliatory, however fragmentary, racism by minority ethnic individuals and groups. Similarly, if there were no sexism in society, there would be no resentment among individual women against men as a gender group. If there are any racist attitudes and behaviour among minority ethnic groups or if there is any sexist stereotyping of men by any individual women, it is solely the offshoot of race and gender oppression in society.

In India, there has been one strain of thinking in the discourse on communalism that not only lays emphasis on providing evidence of what is called 'minority communalism', it even equates minority communalism with majority communalism, and, in fact, sometimes goes even further

than that in articulating that majority Hindu communalism is a retaliatory response against minority communalism.[15] The central flaw in this
argument is that it does not begin by acknowledging that in the structure
of power relations between the majority Hindu community in India and
the minority religious communities (Muslims, Christians, Sikhs, Buddhists, Jains), there is a huge inequality. By equating two unequals, the
discourse of equating majority and minority communalism ends up by
further reinforcing the power of majority communalism and thus sharp-
ening unequal power relations.

There are two distinct strains of arguments that tend to equate
majority and minority communalism, and both are flawed. One strain
of thought derives its inspiration from the ideology of Indian nationalism. Votaries of one unified Indian nationhood view both majority and
minority nationalism as dangerous for the project of merging diversities
of India into one nationhood (Chandra 1984). However, in this narrative, since only the minority communalism is viewed as having the
potential to cause division of the country, this is viewed as more dangerous for territorial integrity of the nation. This narrative does view
majority communalism also as dangerous for the country precisely for
the reason that it might increase the alienation of the minorities to
the point that a minority might be pushed to seek secession. Its criticism of majority communalism is therefore merely derivative because of
the implications of majority communalism for minority communalism.
Since it considers that majority communalism by its very nature does
not endanger country's territorial integrity, majority communalism is not
the focus of its attack. It might view majority communalism as dangerous
from the angle of viewing the possibility of majority communalism growing into authoritarianism or even fascism but not from the viewpoint
of the threat of majority communalism causing breakup of the country.
Its focus of attack, therefore, remains on minority communalism. Posing
minority and majority communalism as equals in this nationalist framework amounts in reality to be more anti-minority communalism than
anti-majority communalism. This perspective, therefore, eventually ends
up endorsing the unequal power relations between the majority Hindu
community and the various religious minorities in India. It fails to recognise, acknowledge and respect that attempts by members of minority
communities at solidarity are defensive mechanisms to reduce or negate

the disadvantages the members of the minority community suffer as a result of the privileging solidarity of the members of the majority community, which is aggressive and domineering. The defensive solidarity of the minority communities, as a form of social capital, arises 'out of the situational reaction of a class of people faced with common adversaries' (Portes and Sensenbrenner 1993: 1325). To criticise the attempts at solidarity by the members of the minority community by giving them derisory terminology of minority communalism is to make them more vulnerable to the disadvantages suffered as a consequence of the privileged positioning of the majority. It would be similar to condemning women forming solidarity/self-supporting networks as sexism by women.

The second strain of thought that equates minority communalism and majority communalism comes from the secularist perspective. From the standpoint of secular fundamentalism, any kind of religious grouping is undesirable irrespective of the fact whether it is from a minority or majority community. This strain of thought on the face of it sounds very principled but since it also ignores the structural power inequality between a majority religious community and a minority religious community, its exercise of equating minority and majority communalisms amounts to acceptance of the existing structural inequality. In the context of racism and struggle against it, no one would seriously think that a principled anti-racist in Western countries would be one who rejects the idea of racism and, therefore, does not recognise the existence of majority and minority racial groups and considers them both equally repugnant. Such an anti-racist by refusing to recognise the actual practice of institutional dominance of white ethnic groups would be, in fact, contributing to the perpetuation of the dominance of the white ethnic group.

It may be argued that minority communalism is not as meaningless or powerless as 'reverse sexism' or 'reverse racism'. Even if it is accepted that minority communalism is not as weak as sexism by some women or racism by racial minorities, it is undeniable that minority communalism is hugely weak in comparison with the power of majority communalism. Therefore, even if it is recognised that minority communalism also poses dangers, the discourse that equates majority and minority communalism remains dangerously flawed because of the denial by this discourse of institutional power that is vested with majority communalism.

The framework of institutional communalism alerts us to both the spread of tentacles of Hindu dominance in a very wide set of institutions as well as the depth of Hindu domination in these institutions. It brings to light the huge inequality between the power of the majority Hindu community and the religious minorities. The vulnerability of two of India's known religious minorities – Christians and Sikhs – is highlighted by the empirical reality of both these communities constituting merely about 2 per cent each of India's population. Even the Muslim minority, which is the biggest religious minority in India, constitutes only about 13–14 per cent of India's population. This overwhelming numerical superiority of Hindus in India adds to the salience of the conceptual framework of institutional communalism and its use in understanding the structural inequality in power relations between the majority religious group and the minority religious groupings.

A consistent struggle against institutionalised Hindu communalism can only be waged from an egalitarian perspective and not from an Indian nationalist and secularist perspective. The Indian nationalist perspective eventually ends up becoming biased against minority communalism in spite of its formal adherence to equi-distance from both forms of communalism while the secular perspective, though principled at a formal level, also ends up propping up the dominance of majority communalism through its refusal to acknowledge the inequality between communities organised through the social force of religion. The egalitarian perspective is also secular but its strength lies in acknowledging unequal power relations between the majority community and the minority communities. The theoretical perspective of equal opportunities, despite various flaws, has the strength of recognising the unequal power relations between communities or groups based on different identity markers – religion, race, gender, disability, age and sexual orientation. The framework of institutionalised racism has specially highlighted the structures of unequal power relations between the mainstream white majority and non-white ethnic minorities. This framework has also helped to shape up policy tools to weaken, reduce and eradicate racism. Adopting the theoretical framework of institutional communalism in India also has the similar promise in weakening Hindu communalism and eventually all forms of religious sectarianism.

One big difference between race and religion is, however, important to mention. Racial modes of thinking and practice have no positive social aspects to it while religious modes of thinking and living have many positive humanistic aspects to it. From the angle of unearthing and eradicating institutional communalism, it is only the sectarian dimension of religious modes of thinking and living that need to be subjected to critique and not the humanistic dimension of religion. We should attempt to retrieve the progressive connotations of the term 'communal', not only by focussing our critique on divisive religious sectarianism and majoritarianism but also by engaging with the socially progressive and collectively oriented dimensions of religious thinking and practice.

Conclusions

The concept 'institutional communalism' that has been developed here is an attempt to extend the use of the concept 'institutional racism' used in Western societies to the Indian context. The meanings of the word 'communal' and 'communalism' as used in South Asia and India have been probed and the limitations of this terminology have been highlighted.

The lens of institutional communalism allows us to see beyond the surface level communal activities of political and social organisations to the deeper roots of communalism embedded in the working of diverse range of public, semi-public and private institutions in Indian society. In the same way as the tool of institutional racism highlights the racism of the majority white community because of the power the white mainstream community enjoys in Western societies, the tool of institutional communalism helps us to highlight the communalism of the majority Hindu religious community because of the power it enjoys in India. The important implication that follows from this is that as in the case of anti-racist theorising and practice, the focus is on critiquing majority racism; the focus on anti-communalism theorising and practice has to be the critique of majority Hindu communalism in India. Racism as a social phenomenon exists, in its current form, because of the supremacist thinking, behaviour and practices in the dominant white community in the West. Similarly communalism in India exists, in its current form, because of the supremacist thinking, behaviour and practices in the dominant Hindu community in India.

The fight against institutional communalism in India alerts us to the bigger challenge than merely inflicting electoral defeats on the Hindu communal parties and organisations. Causing electoral defeats of Hindu communal parties and organisations remains an important anti-communalism strategic task and needs to be seen as a part of eradicating institutional communalisms. However, even if such parties are defeated electorally but institutional Hindu communalism remains pervasive in varying degrees in India's constitution, judiciary, civil services, electoral and parliamentary institutions, security forces, prisons, academia, media, corporate business and even NGOs, it will continue as a social, cultural and politico-economic force to disadvantage the lives of minority communities in India. Thinking from the perspective of institutional communalism not only alerts the anti-communalism practitioners in India to the massive challenge they face but also to the need for devising practical devices to monitor communalism in the everyday working practices of a vast range of institutions in India. There is a lot to learn from the equal opportunity initiatives in many Western countries in the way racism, sexism and other forms of discrimination are monitored, recorded and evaluated, accountability is fixed, and progress is continuously measured. It is important to do the pedagogical and ideological work against communalism but it is even more important to use practical tools to confront and defeat institutional communalism because when power interests are involved as they are in institutional communalism, mere ideological preaching has very limited effect. Those who exercise power through institutional communalism need to be confronted and defeated by challenging these institutions themselves on a continuous basis.

(*Acknowledgements*: I am thankful to James Chiriyankandath, Meena Dhanda, Rohini Hensman, Bhabani Nayak, Manisha Sethi and especially Tanya Singh for comments on earlier drafts of this article. The usual declaimer applies.)

Notes

1 Marx uses the terms 'communal labour' and 'communal property' in the sense we are referring to the word communal: ' . . . let us take communal labour

47

in its spontaneously evolved form as we find it among all civilised nations at the dawn of their history . . . At present an absurdly biased view is widely held, namely that *primitive* communal property is a specifically Slavonic, or even an exclusively Russian phenomenon. It is an early form which can be found among Romans, Teutons and Celts, and of which a whole collection of diverse patterns (though sometimes only remnants survive) is still in existence in India. A careful study of Asiatic, particularly Indian, forms of communal property would indicate that the disintegration of different forms of primitive communal ownership gives rise to diverse forms of property. For instance, various prototypes of Roman and Germanic private property can be traced back to certain forms of Indian communal property' (Marx 1981/1859: 33). He also uses the concept of 'communal labour- time': ' . . . as Gray presupposes that the labour-time contained in commodities is *immediately social* labour-time, he presupposes that it is communal labour-time or labour-time of directly associated individuals' (ibid.: 85).

2 As an indication of how the Indian/Hindu nationalist leadership perceived the threat of Dalit assertions and caste divisions, it will be useful to remember how Mahatma Gandhi viewed this threat when India's partition was not as yet on the cards. In a statement of 21 August 1932, which is a record of his conversation with Vallabhai Patel, another leading Indian nationalist/upper caste Hindu leader, Gandhi said, 'The possible consequences of separate electorates for harijans fill me with horror . . . [They] do not realise that the separate electorate will create divisions among Hindus so much that it will lead to bloodshed. "Untouchable hooligans" will make common cause with "Muslim hooligans" and kill caste-Hindus' (*Collected Works of Mahatma Gandhi*, Volume 50, p. 469). Gandhi went on fast to death to oppose separate electorate for the 'untouchables' and achieved his objective through what is known as Poona Pact by blackmailing Ambedkar to sign the Pact for abandoning the struggle for separate electorate for the Dalits. According to Anderson (2012: 41): 'Under colossal public pressure, and physical threats to him and his community, if he stood firm [on the demand for separate electorate for Dalits], Ambedkar yielded to Gandhi's blackmail.'

3 It may be useful to clarify that the term 'religious sectarianism' has not only been used in relation to conflicts between sects of the same religions such as Shia-Sunni or Catholic-Protestant but also in relation to conflicts between two different religious communities. Examples of such religious sectarian conflicts are between Jews and Muslims in Israel and Palestine, Muslims and Christians in Egypt, and Muslims and Buddhists in Myanmar.

4 See Chapter 4, 'Historical Conduits of the Political Culture of Punjab' in Singh (2010) for a more detailed discussion of this.

5 See Juergensmeyer (1991) for more details.

6 A similar kind of institutional racism has been identified in the German police's investigations into neo-Nazi terror groups. For over a decade now,

there has been a consistent pattern of bomb attacks and murders where a majority of the victims were of Turkish origin. '. . . in spite of the indications of a racial motive for the serial murders, the police and security services insisted at the time that their prime suspects were rival Turkish gangs or drug runners' (Peel 2013: 4). Thinking and activities based upon biases, prejudices and stereotypes are central to both institutional racism and institutional communalism.

7 I am thankful to Tanya Singh for very valuable information on the use of the term 'institutional racism' by black American theorists in the early twentieth century and by anti-racist/black activists in the UK.

8 It is a demonstration of the institutional power of upper caste Hindus that despite consistent opposition by sections of Dalit communities to their inclusion in the category of Hindu, they continue to be counted as Hindus. This exercise of institutional power by upper caste Hindus to keep enumerating the Dalits as Hindus is used by the upper caste Hindus to continuously reinforce their claims to be an overwhelming majority community in India.

9 See Harriss-White (2003) for a detailed empirical, ethnographic and theoretical investigation of religious dimension in the working of Indian capitalist economy and the privileging of Hindu upper castes in India's capitalist economy. Wright (1981) and Ali (1992) have argued that the privileged location of upper castes Hindus in India's state apparatus (especially after the 1947 partition of India that led to migration of many Muslim entrepreneurs to Pakistan) has led to the Indian state helping upper caste Hindu capitalists in their business ventures, and that this has contributed to the weakness in the growth of Muslim capitalist class in India. See also Rehman (2010); Arvinder Singh (1999: 152–53) has cited data from the Centre for Monitoring the Indian Economy that shows that out of the 10 largest corporate businesses in Punjab in 1994, only one was Sikh-controlled while by population size, the Sikhs were more than 60 per cent of the population (Singh 2008).

10 I am thankful to Shirley Velasquez and Oxford's Capitalism Study Group for very fruitful discussions on Bourdieu's work.

11 See Pearl and Singh (1999).

12 For a general mapping of embedded Hindu communalism in the working of the police that also contributes to judicial disempowerment of minorities, see Vijapur and Haque (2006) and for more specific examination of police prejudice against Muslims, see Khan (2006).

13 An international human rights campaign supported by Germany from where Bhullar had been earlier deported for the trial in India led eventually to the Supreme Court commuting the death sentence to life imprisonment in view of the long delay in deciding the mercy petition and Bhullar's mental illness.

14 Patwant Singh was once a part of India's elite especially in the world of architecture and art but the Indian army's attack on the Golden Temple and the

anti-Sikh carnage in Delhi turned him into a sharp critic of the Indian political, judicial and media establishment. For my tribute to him and his work, see my obituary of him and that of Ram Narayan Kumar, one of the finest human rights campaigner in India, who also reported extensively on the Hindu bias in police, bureaucracy, media and judiciary in dealing with human rights violations of India's Sikh minority (Singh 2009).

15 The Hindu communalists in India do not use the terminology of reverse communalism in the same way as the racists use 'reverse racism' and sexists use 'reverse sexism' but they use the terminology of 'appeasement of minorities' to convey a similar idea of favours being granted to or won by religious minorities. This language is as useless as 'reverse racism' and 'reverse sexism'.

3

THE PHILOSOPHY OF NUMBER[1]

Dilip Simeon

The Communists are further reproached with desiring to abolish countries and nationality. The working men have no country. We cannot take from them what they have not got. (Marx and Engels 1973: 124)

The foundation of power is somewhere other than this or that person or this or that dynasty, which could be said to incarnate it. If God is absent, there are only human beings left, and the matter of sovereignty – its foundation – can only be elucidated among them. Sovereignty is a human not a divine matter. (Mairet 2010: 53–54)

But now our requirements have changed, and the facts have changed behind us. (Mantel 2012: 238)

Introduction

It is difficult to judge which is the more grievous of our predicaments: the acceptability (for a large number of Indians) of mass murder as a fact of life or our unwillingness to understand communalism outside of a communal lens. To put it differently, many people consider the theft of money to be a greater evil than the assassination of large numbers of people, and even when we try to understand genocidal events, most of the time we end up with a variant of the proposition that 'my murderers are better than yours'. And in a country where even atheists are cast as Hindu, Muslim or Sikh and so on, an obsessive awareness of religious identity tends to colour all discourses, even theoretical ones, about communalism – 'my communalists are not as bad as yours', or even, 'my communalists are not communalists at all, yours are'. Despite the terrible tragedies that have convulsed South Asia over the past century, it appears we are no closer to an understanding of the most intractable issue in modern Indian history than we were seven decades ago. Our consciences and minds are held in a vice-like grip, and the very vocabulary of our utterances only generates misconception, self-deceit and further animus. Incessant violence and hatred have resulted in a nihilist situation.

In the period between the two assaults on the Babri Masjid, there took place a political conversation in the office of the Indian Peoples' Front, a front organisation (now defunct), of the CPI (Marxist-Leninist). A prominent leader of the ML party was hosting a discussion on contemporary issues with public intellectuals. The conversation veered to the matter of Advani's 1990 *Rath Yatra* – Advani's arrest had led to the downfall of the V.P. Singh government. The *yatra* had been obliged to skip Chhatisgarh, on account of the resistance of the Chhatisgarh Mukti Morcha led by Shankar Guha Niyogi, who was later assassinated. I asked the leader why, when Advani's pilgrimage of hate could be turned away from Chhatisgarh by strong workers resistance, the CPI (ML) did not turn it away from the areas in Bihar where it had its strongest mass movements. The answer was symptomatic of the leftist common sense about communalism. He replied that if the party had done so, the 'people would have assumed we were siding with one community against the other'. For this theoretician, the issue was (by implication) not one of upholding lawful government or the constitutional obligation to protect historical monuments; rather, what was happening was a conflict between communities. It did not call for a defence of democracy against mob violence, or an exposure of the claims of communal groups to 'represent' entire communities, it was a Hindu–Muslim issue, and the best way out of it was to get 'community leaders' to sort it out amicably. Since the communist position on bourgeois democracy is deeply ambivalent, its position on fascism is equally compromised. However, Indian communists have not theorised fascism at all, so the comrades' position reflected the stance of an entire spectrum of left opinion on communalism.

My attempt in this chapter is to place some fresh ideas on this debate. If there is a political and philosophical corollary to these ideas, it is a plea for moderate speech. Extreme positions and hyperbolic utterances have become commonplace these days and very often emanate from the heart of the establishment. It is doubtful whether meaningful communication is taking place on burning questions ranging from public security, political violence and police reform, to women's rights, education and criminal justice. Activists of mainstream political parties have been known to engage in hooliganism, and attacks on the freedom of speech and expression have become the norm. It is arguable that the Indian Constitution is under threat, not only from declared insurgents, but equally from the actions (and inaction) of persons sworn to uphold it. The important questions are not reducible to party politics, and answers to them cannot be found in partisan manifestos. It is not a party but a platform of political moderation and social democracy that is lacking. What we need to question are common sensical notions, the vocabulary in use by all protagonists, the concepts that rule without challenge in the domain of ideas. These concepts include *nation*, *majority* and *minority*. Let us begin with a quick look at a little known report from one of the most violent and tragic periods in Indian history.

A line in the ground

In September 1947, two Indian communists presented a report to Jawaharlal Nehru, which was later published under the title *Bleeding Punjab Warns*. They began with a mention of one of their comrade-witnesses, 'Baba Gurmukh Singh, veteran revolutionary who had put in 27 years in imperialist prisons and whose blood was boiling at the way Punjab was reduced to bloody shambles' and continued:

> What happened in the Punjab cannot be called a riot. It was a regular war of extermination of the minorities, of the Sikhs and Hindus in Western Punjab and of Muslims in East Punjab. It cannot be compared to Calcutta or Noakhali, Bihar, or even to Rawalpindi for in all these cases it was mobs of one community that took leading part in killing, looting and burning the minority in the area, their communal passions being roused to a pitch of frenzy and savagery. In the Punjab, however, in the recent biggest killing ever seen, it was the trained bands equipped with firearms and modern weapons that were the main killers, looters and rapers. These were the storm troops of various communal parties such as National Guards of the Muslim League in

the Western Punjab, and the Shahidi Dal of the Akalis and the Rashtriya Swayamsevak Sangh of the Mahasabha in the Eastern Punjab. They were actively aided and often actually led by the police and the military in committing the worst atrocities . . . in violence and in brutality, in the numbers killed (which Syt Shri Prakasha, India's Ambassador to Pakistan places at 1½ lakhs) in the use of plenty of modern deadly weapons, in the devastation spread over 14 districts of the Punjab and in the way in which the police, the military and the entire administration was geared not to stop the riots but to spread it – the Punjab tragedy is without parallel. (Dhanwantri and P.C. Joshi)[2]

The report describes numerous instances of atrocities carried out by the militias of various parties, as well as the extensive material support (including rifles, hand grenades, sten-guns, mortars and jeeps) given to them by the Hindu, Muslim and Sikh princely states of Punjab, including Patiala, Jhind, Nabha, Faridkot, Malerkotla, Bahawalpur and Kapurthala. It describes these states as 'the hotbeds . . . of cold deadly preparations for a war of extermination'. Whereas the Congress 'became more and more tongue-tied as it moved nearer and nearer acceptance of division', it reported the Rashtriya Swayamsevak Sangh (RSS) as having taken over the towns, 'and roused the spirit of retaliation on the communal slogan of Akhand Hindustan by force'. The report names 'financiers and blackmarketeers of the towns' as patrons of the RSS, and 'the most reactionary toady section of big landlords' as backing the Muslim League National Guards.

This account is only one of the myriad stories of the systematic mass murder that accompanied the birth of the two nation-states that had been incubated in the last decades of the British Empire in India. Independence had been preceded by much bloodshed. Every decade since the 1890s had witnessed communal violence. By the 1940s the deliberate instigation of violence had begun. The Calcutta killing of 1946, in which 5,000 to 10,000 people were killed, and up to 15,000 wounded, was a turning point. Precise figures for the numbers killed in 1947–48 are difficult to pin down, and could be half a million or more, with a further 13 million refugees, roughly evenly divided amongst Muslims and non-Muslims.[3] The bulk of the casualties, as well as the refugee population, were Punjabis.

This violence was not a marginal phenomenon, or a sudden and spontaneous outburst of communal frenzy. As Lionel Baixas argues

> It was on the contrary at the very heart of the event. Nor was it merely a consequence of Partition but rather the principal mechanism for creating the conditions for Partition. Violence constituted the moral instrument through which the tension between the pre-Partition local character of identity and its postcolonial territorial and national redefinition was negotiated. Violence operated as the link between the community and its new national territory.

It was what 'gave it its organized and genocidal dimension as it was meant for control of social space so as to cleanse these territories from the presence of other religious communities' (Baixas 2008: 2). The crux of the matter was the cleansing of territory, or the transfer of population, as it was then known. The birth of the nation-states of India and Pakistan took place amidst genocide.[4] The process was governed by the arithmetic of the nation-state, an institution defined in terms of a natural majority and a problematic minority. It is this vocabulary and the politics generated by it that was absorbed and upheld by all actors on the political stage, including the communists.

Nation and state: the new arithmetic

In a provocative essay on the ideological lineage of fascism, the historian George Mosse observed that the French Revolution 'put its stamp upon a novel view of the sacred: it created a civil religion which modern nationalism made its own, and fascism, whatever its variety, was, above all, a nationalist movement' (George Mosse 1989: 5).[5] Nationalism has always covered a range of aspirations, from the yearning for social liberation on the part of oppressed people to the desire for sovereign control over a territory by an incipient ruling class. It can unfold along a democratic trajectory, but it can also be perverted when the *demos* (people) of democracy is defined in narrow and exclusive terms, thus making space for communal hatred and political illiberality. The socialist movement in its origins had proclaimed an internationalist stance, summed up in Marx's call to workers of all countries to unite. In late nineteenth century Europe, Marx and Engels recognised the complexities arising from the oppression of Ireland and Poland and from the trajectories of German unification. After all, it was an incontrovertible fact that the contemporary world was dominated by multinational entities such as the Ottoman, Tsarist, Hapsburg, Hohenzollern and British empires. The analysis of nationalism was inevitably complicated by the need to take account of the democratic aspirations of the oppressed subjects of these empires.

Nationalism is a phenomenon almost impermeable by language. This is not least because of the desire of social scientists to pin a definition on something that is inextricably linked to historical accident, whim and sentiment – factors that cannot be grasped by axioms. The US president Woodrow Wilson's Fourteen Points used the words *nation* and *nationality* interchangeably, and the phrase 'opportunity of autonomous development' to denote what was later to be termed 'self-determination'. (The latter slogan was a political imperative influenced by Russian social-democracy, which sought to rally oppressed peoples to the side of the working class in the struggle against Tsarist autocracy.) In 1929, Karl Kautsky suggested that *nation* be used to designate the population of a state.

> The further east we go the more numerous are the portions of the population that do not wish to belong to it, that constitute national communities of their own within it. They too are called 'nations' or 'nationalities'. It would be advisable to use only the latter term for them. (Davies 1978: 6)[6]

In 1913 Stalin defined it as 'a historically evolved stable community of language, territory, economic life and psychological make-up manifested in a community of culture' – this definition dominated communist thinking for the crucial decades of the twentieth century (Stalin 1913).[7] The French social theorist Ernst Renan (1823–92) was clear that 'religion cannot supply an adequate basis for the constitution of a modern nationality'. He struggled to define it, only to conclude that 'A nation is a soul, a spiritual principle' – thereby implicitly recognising the subjective element in national consciousness (Ernst Renan 1882).[8]

As late as the 1940s however, the concept of a 'nation' did not necessarily imply a delineation of sovereignty. For a long time, it referred to an ethnically distinct people rather than a nation-state. And the term 'ethnic' could be associated with race, nationality, or religion – markers of identity by which groups identify themselves and by which others recognise it. However, over the decades nationalism has taken the form of a new civic religion, a kind of replacement for the divine right of kings. It has become the metaphysic of capitalism – the spiritual aspect of secular modernity.

Let us now examine the political language current at the time of its emergence (and that is still prevalent). This language is the vocabulary of 'majority' and 'minority' – words that carry vast meaning behind bland mathematics. It emerged in the period following the end of the Great War of 1914–18. In 1919, the League of Nations established several nation-states, a marriage of space and ethnicity that proved a disaster. This fabricated institution was the launchpad for the invention of 'minorities', entities that only came into existence because other larger groups were deemed to be natural 'majorities'. The assumption that an ethnic group needed a clearly delineated territorial space as its natural home not only threw an abstraction in the face of complex and mixed demographic reality, it invented a new 'common sense' that was bound to cause political friction amongst those denied such a space. Although the League of Nations tried to deal with the problem via the legal arrangements known as the Minority Treaties, the international order was simply incapable of enforcing them. The result was that the rising ultra-nationalist forces of the 1920s and 1930s – whose politics consisted essentially of incitement of racial hatred – could openly renege on these agreements and in any case, deploy arithmetical vocabulary to buttress their violent practices. The Fascist and Nazi onslaught on democracy could present itself as 'truly' democratic, because it represented 'the majority'. Those denied nation-states, that is, 'nationally frustrated population(s)' now became

> firmly convinced – as was everybody else – that true freedom, true emancipation and true popular sovereignty could be attained only with full national emancipation, that people without their own national government were deprived of human rights, those peoples to whom states were not conceded, no matter whether they were official minorities or only nationalities, considered the Treaties an arbitrary game which handed out rule to some

and servitude to others . . . The real significance of the Minority Treaties lies not in their practical application but in the fact that they were guaranteed by an international body, the League of Nations . . . The Minority Treaties said in plain language what until then had been only implied in the working system of nation-states, namely, that only nationals could be citizens, only people of the same national origin could enjoy the full protection of legal institutions, that persons of different nationality needed some law of exception until or unless they were completely assimilated . . . the transformation of the state from an instrument of the law into an instrument of the nation had been completed; the nation had conquered the state, national interest had priority over law long before Hitler could pronounce 'right is what is good for the German people. Here again the language of the mob was only the language of public opinion cleansed of hypocrisy and restraint'. (Arendt 2004: 347–51)[9]

With the advent of the nation-state, the state ceased to be an instrument of law and became instead an instrument of the nation. This distinction is very important, because it enables us to recognise the ideological means whereby the very basis of liberal democracy, viz. the equality of all citizens before the law, regardless of differences in ethnic origin, religious belief or sex, can be eroded. The retreat of universal democratic values before a creeping national chauvinism that speaks the language of 'glory' and 'majority rule' was a feature of the growth of Nazism in the late 1920s when, as Franz Neumann observed in his classic study of Nazism, 'in the centre of the counter-revolution stood the judiciary' (Neumann 1963 : 27).[10] We have seen such developments unfold in India as well, when judges indulge in florid metaphysical phrases such as 'collective conscience of the nation'. The distinction also provides a clue to the ease with which hooliganism in the name of 'the majority' can and does present itself as nationalism, whereas violent activities of other denominational or political groups are denounced as 'anti-national'. Thus, in the same chapter, Neumann describes how in the 1920s, courts would award the gravest punishments to left-wing cadre, while being extraordinarily lenient to Nazis. Analysing the meaning of such judgments, he goes on to say:

(The counter revolution) . . . tried many forms and devices, but soon learned that it could come to power only with the help of the state machine and never against it . . . the Kapp Putsch of 1920 and the Hitler Pustch of 1923 had proved this. In the centre of the counter revolution stood the judiciary. Unlike administrative acts, which rest on considerations of convenience and expediency, judicial decisions rest on law, that is on right and wrong, and they always enjoy the limelight of publicity. Law is perhaps the most pernicious of all weapons in political struggles, precisely because of the halo that surrounds the concepts of right and justice . . . 'Right', Hocking has said, 'is psychologically a claim whose infringement is met with a resentment deeper than the injury would satisfy, a resentment that may amount to passion for which men will risk life and property as they would never do for an expediency.' When it becomes 'political', justice breeds hatred and despair among those it singles out for attack. Those whom it favours, on the other hand, develop a profound contempt for the very value of justice, they know that it can be purchased by the powerful. As a device for strengthening one political group at the expense of others, for eliminating enemies and assisting political allies, law then threatens the fundamental convictions upon which the tradition of our civilization rests . . . (Neumann 1963: 27)

The ramifications of these developments were far-reaching. Foremost among them was the institutional justification bestowed upon the ideology of majoritarianism, that is, the belief that a nation was by definition a homogeneous entity, further that it was entitled to a national home called the nation-state, and that ethnic groups that were not part of 'the majority' were a *problem*, or a *question*. It was not enough that the inhabitants of a certain area were entitled to democratic governance and equal protection of the law. It was also deemed necessary that the inhabitants should be ethnically unified. Since in real life no such homogeneity existed, the way was cleared for projects of purification – and these came to be undertaken according to and in the name of ancient traditions, culture, religion and so on; all claiming the right to define what the nation was, or ought to be. Heterogeneity thus became a fabricated issue, and sooner or later, the *minority* or *minorities* were identified as the very embodiment of this heterogeneity. Liberal nationalists sought to protect them, chauvinist nationalists sought to intimidate them. Either way, a new form of tyranny was embarked upon, under the emblem: might is right.

Communalism and nationalism

The concept of the nation-state as defined by the dominant international order entered the Indian anti-imperialist movement almost by default. And those engaged in mobilising a conservative constituency tended to define the nation in terms of religious denomination – religion became a badge of identity rather than a source of moral or spiritual guidance. The relationship between religious revivalism, reform and communal politics is complex and deserves separate attention.[11]

Suffice it to note that in the late nineteenth century, the idea of the Hindu nation began to be articulated (the word 'nation' still referred to an ethnically distinct people rather than a nation-state). The reformist aspirations of the intelligentsia became increasingly political, and as the century progressed, outstanding literateurs took the distinctive step of naming India as naturally Hindu. By implication, Muslims began to be depicted as essentially alien.[12]

The twentieth century saw major developments in national political consciousness. These began with the Swadeshi agitation, the first mass campaign of modern Indian nationalism, which was directed against the partition of Bengal in 1905. A revolutionary terrorist movement emerged in Bengal, and elite landed interests set up the Muslim League in 1906. This was followed in 1909 by the grant of separate electorates for Muslims under the reforms of 1909 – a fateful measure that institutionalised communal categories and forms of mobilisation. An upsurge of mass nationalist consciousness took place during and immediately after the First World War, manifested in the agitations of the Home Rule Leagues and the non-cooperation and Khilafat movements of 1919–24. However, Gandhi's endorsement of the pan-Islamist assertions of a section of Muslim clergy during Khilafat strengthened the stereotypical concept of a 'Muslim interest' and gave the clergy political leverage in nationalist agitation. Composite and territorial nationalism developed schisms in the mid-1920s.[13] The period saw the setting up of the Hindu Mahasabha in 1915 and also the Lucknow Pact between the Congress and the Muslim League in 1916.

As the national movement progressed, the definition of democracy as 'the rule of the majority' became a commonplace. Although 'majority' remains an empty term until we know what we are counting, the increasingly accepted usage was that we were counting religious communities. All other features of democratic governance, such as an independent judiciary, free press and the rule of law became subservient to the phrase 'rule of the majority'. Ergo, long before independence, the popular assumption was that democracy was about numbers, rather than liberty. Religious arithmetic became the most significant factor in politics. This enabled various chauvinists to articulate their prejudices via an international legal principle. Thus, in the historical period unmistakeably stamped by the nihilist politics of Adolf Hitler, V. D. Savarkar was being quoted approvingly by the Nazi press: 'A Nation is formed by a majority living therein. What did the Jews do in Germany? They being in minority were driven out from Germany.'[14] And in one of his presidential addresses to the Hindu Mahasabha, he declared:

> just as in America, Germany, China and every other country not excluding Russia, so also in Hindusthan, *the Hindus by the fact that they form an overwhelming majority are the Nation and Moslems are but a community* because like all other communities they are unchallengeably in a *minority*. Therefore they must remain satisfied with whatever reasonable safeguards other minorities in India get and accept as reasonable in the light of the *world formula framed by the League of Nations.*[15] (Emphases added)

The language of the Muslim League in the period of its resurgence was equally suffused with *majority* and *minority* – the object being the assertion of a more acceptable status (in its view) for the 'Muslim majority' provinces. Thus, in a speech at the Aligarh Muslim University in early 1941, M. A. Jinnah, president of the Muslim League, averred that:

> As a self respecting people, we in the Muslim minority provinces say boldly that we are prepared to undergo every suffering and sacrifice for the emancipation and liberation of our brethren in regions of Muslim majority. By standing in their way and dragging them along with us into a united India we do not in

61

any way improve our position. Instead we reduce them also to the position of a minority. But we are determined that, whatever happens to us, we are not going to allow our brethren to be vassalized by the Hindu majority.[16]

Many scholars use prefixes such as 'Hindu' and 'Muslim' when speaking of communalism. Some speak only of majorities and minorities. The main problems blocking the comprehension of communalism in South Asia arise out of ideological angles of vision. On the one hand it is seen as something distinct from and opposed to nationalism. In addition, it is seen through a denominational lens, as if to conceive it as a sum of discrete entities, viz. Hindu, Muslim or Sikh communalism. It is quite appropriate to make distinctions of this kind, but such textured analyses enhance our understanding only if there is something in common among the entities to begin with. Otherwise why use the category 'communal' at all?[17]

Communalism is not an arithmetical total of assorted fanaticisms, but a singular political style with different manifestations; a generic ideology, with different expressions. In colonial India, 'communalism' referred to the idea that shared religious beliefs imply shared political interests. But Indians also possessed affiliations related to caste, region and language. As religious modes of identification were given increasing administrative and political significance by British colonial power after the 1857 rebellion, a specific ideology developed around an assumed political interest. Who were the groups making these assumptions, and when and why did their theories carry conviction? It is these questions that need exploring, answers to which may lead to a better understanding. Communalism implied a goal, not a reality, and communal ideologies imagined an ideal religious unity – it would be pointless to ask Hindus or Muslims to 'unite' if they were already unanimous.[18]

When the nation was defined in religious terms, communalism and nationalism got mixed together. Confronted with the immense complexity of identity formation in colonial India, it placed Indian thinkers and political activists in a conceptual marshland (of their own making) that generated painful consequences during colonial decline. If 'communalism' is one thing, and 'nationalism' another, then of course (from within the prevailing nation-statist perspective) the community interests of 'the

Hindus' could be represented as nothing more than a positive version of nationalism. In any case, the idea that a nation-state comprised a majority plus minorities was buttressed by reigning concepts in international law. By the late 1930s, the tortuous negotiations between the major national parties saw the Muslim League also adopting the term nation to define its interest – if 'the Hindus' were 'a nation by themselves', as V.D. Savarkar, president of the Hindu Mahasabha, liked to say,[19] so were 'the Muslims'. This was an effort to turn the tables on the Congress in the ongoing negotiations about a future constitution by rejecting the status of a minority and by insisting that the nationalism of the Congress was a thinly disguised version of Hindu majoritarianism. The assertion that there was a 'Muslim nation' in India implied that any future negotiations among the major parties would have to be an exchange between equals, rather than a parley between a minority and a majority. The locus of conflicting communal power relations was thus pushed towards the domain of international law. As far as the ideological format of the nation-state was concerned, however, nothing had changed. Another territory was to be demarcated as a national home, and new minorities created.

Communists and the nation

The British communist, Rajni Palme Dutt (1896–1974), who for many years functioned as an intellectual mentor to the Communist Party of India (CPI), wrote a book, *India Today*, in 1940, which reappeared in an Indian revised edition in 1949 (Dutt 1949). Dutt recognised the colonial 'methods of playing off Hindus and Muslims (287) against each other' and the 'modern technique of communal electorates' to place communalism in 'the forefront of Indian politics'. He noted the colonial anxiety at the officially reported 'unprecedented fraternization between Hindus and Muslims' (315). He characterised the Khilafat movement as 'in form the protest against the Treaty of Sevres to Turkey, the leading Moslem Power, but in practice the rallying point of Moslem mass unrest' (317), thus dodging the implicit query about religious symbolism and mass unrest. Dutt attacked non-violence as 'a cover conscious or unconscious, for the maintenance of class exploitation' (329). He noted that 'the attempted artificial division of the Indian people into two "nations" on the basis of religion is in reality reactionary, unpractical and contrary to the interests of democratic liberty' (430) and supported the Declaration of Rights adopted by the Indian National Congress in 1931 – declaring it to be 'correctly based on the foundation of equal democratic citizenship without distinction of caste, creed or sex' (430). However, he then took note of the 'newly emerging questions of regional or national claims to autonomy or self-determination, which in the recent period became temporarily entangled with the Hindu-Moslem issue' (430). After relating the history of Congress–League relations and Jawaharlal Nehru's arrogance in 1937, he remarked that 'the growth of the Moslem League reflected the failure of the Congress to make any serious consistent effort to reach out and appeal to the Moslem masses' (435). This observation was in marked contrast to the CPI's criticism of the Muslim mass contact programme of the Congress as a project 'rightly seen by the Muslim League as a move to destroy their organization' (Adhikari, 1943: 28).

Dutt's positions rambled and changed with fast-evolving political developments. Within India however, communists were to adopt a fateful stance. In September 1942, the senior leader and theoretician G. Adhikari placed a resolution before his party, titled 'On Pakistan and National Unity'. The resolution was ratified in 1943, and along with a lengthier explanatory report with the same title, remained the CPI position on Indian politics for the crucial period 1943–47. The documents are significant because of the way they conflate religious and non-religious identities, together with the arithmetical vocabulary of minority and majority. Thus, the resolution called for 'all-in national unity based on communal harmony', for which a united national front (UNF) was the need of the hour. It insisted that 'in Free India, there will be perfect equality between nationalities and communities that live together in India'. It then asked for the national movement to recognise 'the following rights as part of its programme for national unity':

3 (a) Every section of the Indian people which has a contiguous territory as its homeland, common historical tradition, common language, culture, psychological make-up and common economic life would be recognised as a distinct nationality with the right to exist as an autonomous state within the free Indian union or federation and will have the right to secede from it

if it may so desire. This means that the territories which are homelands of such and which today are split up by the artificial boundaries of the present British provinces and of the so-called 'Indian States' would be re-united and restored to them in free India. Thus free India of tomorrow would be a federation or union of autonomous states of the various nationalities such as the Pathans, Western Punjabis (dominantly Muslims), Sikhs, Sindhis, Hindustanis, Rajasthanis, Gujeratis, Bengalis, Assamese, Beharis, Oriyas, Andhras, Tamils, Karnatakis, Maharashtrians, Keralas, etc.

(b) If there are interspersed minorities in the new states thus formed their rights regarding their culture, language, education, etc., would be guaranteed by Statute and their infringement would be punishable by law. . .

4. Such a declaration of rights inasmuch as it conceded to every nationality as defined above, and therefore, to nationalities having Muslim faith, the right of autonomous state existence and of secession, can form the basis for unity between the National Congress and the League. For this would give to the Muslims wherever they are in an overwhelming majority in a contiguous territory which is their homeland, the right to form their autonomous states and even to separate if they so desire. In the case of the Bengali Muslims of the Eastern and Northern Districts of Bengal where they form an overwhelming majority, they may form themselves into an autonomous region – the state of Bengal or may form a separate state. Such a declaration therefore concedes the just essence of the Pakistan demand and has nothing in common with the separatist theory of dividing India into two nations on the basis of religion.

5. But the recognition of the right of separation in this form need not necessarily lead to actual separation. On the other hand, by dispelling the mutual suspicions, it brings about unity of action today and lays the basis for a greater unity in the free India of tomorrow. (Adhikari 1943: 14–15)[20]

A close reading of these documents raises fundamental issues concerning socialism and nationalism in India. My concern here is to point to the CPI's erratic conflation of nation, nationality, sub-regional and religious identity; its refusal to theorise communal politics and its resultant decision to support what it called the 'democratic core' or the 'just essence' of the Pakistan demand. Thus, it saw the Khilafat movement as a reflection of an 'upsurge of the Muslim nationalities in the East' (p. 21), although later in the text it referred to pan-Islamism as a 'reactionary separatist theory', a 'weapon of disunity' that uttered slogans of 'extra-territorial loyalty' (p. 41). It characterised the emergence of linguistic or regional demands as an expression of 'multi-national consciousness' (p. 27) and compared the British colony in India to the multi-national Tsarist Empire. It supported 'the demand of every nationality for self-determination' (p. 27) and saw its acceptance as a basis for 'revolutionary Hindu Muslim unity' (p. 38).

Adhikari's report observed that

> the guarantee by the Congress of the right of self-determination of Muslim nationalities . . . should mean for the Muslim peoples not separation from the rest of India but a more glorious and more lasting unity within a free Indian Union, in which all – Muslim and non-Muslim alike – are equal partners. (p. 44)

It stated that in 1938 the CPI had not understood 'the real nature of the communal problem', which it was now correcting (p. 29). Placing the word 'communal' sometimes in quotation marks and sometimes without, it stated that:

> To the ordinary patriot, this new aspect of the communal problem, as a problem of multi-national consciousness, has not yet become patent. We, the Communists, are able to see our way into the future by means of our theory and our ideology. By means of this, we are able to quickly see these elements in the present which are bound to develop in the future. (p. 27)

The CPI 'saw in the growth of the Muslim League not the growth of communalism, but the rise of anti-imperialist nationalist consciousness among the Muslim masses' (p. 29). It even attacked the Muslim mass contact programme of the Congress which it claimed, 'was rightly seen by the Muslim League as a move to destroy their organization' (p. 28). By this logic even communists would need to refrain from working with Muslim workers. By giving 'nationalist' credence to an assertion of communal representation, it bestowed legitimacy to similar claims emanating from Hindu nationalists. The CPI also supported the League's critique of the 1928 Motilal Nehru Report (on the future constitution) on the grounds that residual powers in a future Indian Constitution ought to vest with the states and not the Centre (p. 29). Continuing with this line of thought, it argued:

> Their (the Muslim League's) conception of the federation for a free India was a federation of autonomous and sovereign states. Why? Because the Muslim League wanted autonomy for regions in which Muslim nationalities like Sindhis, Pathans, Punjabis, Eastern Bengal Muslims lived. It was a just democratic demand. This really is the crux and kernel of all the so-called 'communal' demands raised by the Muslim League right from its inception up to the present time when they have finally been crystallised into the demand for Pakistan'. (p. 29)

The document had no analysis of communal violence either, beyond the naive reiteration that communal riots were 'engineered by goondas in the pay of dark forces of reaction' (p. 22). References to fascism were restricted to the war, wherein the USSR was on the Allied side. It is significant that September 1942 inaugurated the darkest hour for the Red Army, with the battle of Stalingrad having begun in late August. The CPI spoke about 'saving India from fascism' but only in the sense of warding off an Axis victory. 'Pakistan and National Unity' is a dense and highly confusing document. The reader can only guess at the impact it made on the communist cadre. The only awareness of the implications of mixing up regional and religious identity occurs in a paragraph referring to 'the Muslim masses' fear of oppression and exploitation by 'Hindu India'. An explanation for this 'fear' was provided thus:

> uneven bourgeois development creates conditions wherein one dominant nationality may be in a position to stifle the growth of

less developed and weaker nationalities in a free India. We saw
tiny germs of this even during the Congress Ministries . . . such
a fear is an understandable fear. (p. 38)

This formulation implied that 'the Hindus' were a 'dominant nationality'. It showed no awareness of the implication of its own arguments, viz.
that if people united by language and culture could still be distinguished
as Muslim Punjabis and Muslim Bengalis, the same could be said of
Hindu Punjabis and Hindu Bengalis. And if certain 'nationalities' could
be described as 'dominantly Muslim', why were others not referred to as
'dominantly Hindu'?

Four years later, in the midst of the traumatic violence of 1947, the communists waged a courageous but futile struggle for non-violence and communal amity. Its commentary upon the happenings in Punjab as evidenced
on the Dhanwantri Report have been noted. However, the Appeal to the
People of Pakistan (issued on 15 August 1947) in the name of 'Communists
in Pakistan' demonstrated a sad awareness (short of an acknowledgement)
of the convoluted logic of the arguments on 'self-determination' that it had
presented in 1942 and 1943.[21] On its first page the appeal recognised that
'the progressive forces' had 'not been strong enough' to defeat the policy of
the upper classes in alliance with imperialism to preach communal hatred
and foster separatism. It argued against Dominion status and the influence of the princely states and for a constitution based on 'firm democratic
principles.' And in 1948, a year after independence, it clearly regretted
its previous stance (without saying so). A 'Communist Party Publication'
printed in Bombay under the title *Who Rules Pakistan?* had this to say:

> The year of freedom that has passed thus reveals that the peo-
> ple of Pakistan, whose religious feelings were exploited by the
> vested interests to reach to posts of power, are being cheated,
> betrayed and sold in economic and political bondage to the
> imperialists . . . The fake freedom and fake leadership have been
> unmasked in the last one year . . . the people of Pakistan, like
> the people of India, have yet to liberate themselves and save
> their country from being sold to foreign exploiters . . . the Com-
> munist Party of Pakistan . . . carries on this fight for uniting the
> people in a common Democratic Front.[22]

The theoretical statements of the CPI in the 1940s show that it had not worked out the distinctions and usages of the terms 'nation' and 'nationality' and that it remained attached to the nineteenth-century concept of the nation-state. Despite its undoubtedly humanist approach towards (and work for) communal amity, and its dismay at the upsurge of communal warfare in 1947, communists adopted a confused and inconsistent approach towards communalism. It is arguable that this has continued over the decades and has had a detrimental impact upon the fortunes of the left as well as upon the political discourse of civil society in South Asia.

B.R. Ambedkar's observations on Pakistan

The arguments presented by B.R. Ambedkar in 1940 and 1945 stand in marked contrast to the theoretical sophistry of the CPI. His book *Pakistan or the Partition of India* is arguably the most substantial and well-argued contemporary analysis of the competing discourses on partition (Ambedkar 1946).[23] Relying on his own discernment rather than a set of doctrinal axioms, Ambedkar laid out the logic of communal politics. He used Ernst Renan's arguments to stress the subjective element in nationalism, made distinctions between 'nation' and 'people'; the nation as a collective passion or belief versus the nation in the de jure or de facto sense, by which we may assume he was referring to the element of sovereignty that marked the nation-state. He was clear that even the recognition that Indian Muslims were a nation was not a sufficient argument for a partition into two sovereign states. He placed great significance on the matter of communal ideologies influencing the armed forces. He presented a compelling argument against the logic of separation as well as a realistic assessment of the futility of reason as a means of preventing it. Citing examples from Canada, South Africa and Switzerland, he characterised the formation of communal parties by 'minority nations' as a 'vicious method of self-protection'. The best way of avoiding the tyranny of the majority, Ambedkar argued, was to put a 'ban on communal parties in politics' (144). Speaking of the desirability of a united non-communal party, he said Jinnah himself would have been the most qualified to lead it. Instead, he had devoted himself to a futile and harmful policy that was a perversion from the original intent of the League (144,146).

What is significant is the common sense of the times reflected in Ambedkar's vocabulary. This is visible in his ambivalent usages of the word 'nation', the frequent appearance of terms such as 'the Hindu case' and 'the Muslim case', and the numerical terminology of nation-statist demography – viz. majority and minority. Notwithstanding this, he was able to place a compelling argument from the assumed standpoint of 'the Muslim interest' against the idea of a separate nation-state. He cited the resolution of the Muslim League at its annual session held at Patna in December 1938, that decried the Federation scheme embodied in the Government of India Act, 1935 as unacceptable, whilst yet authorising its president 'to adopt such course as may be necessary with a view to explore the possibility of a suitable alternative which will safeguard the interests of the Musalmans and other minorities in India' (145). By these resolutions, Ambedkar argued:

> Mr. Jinnah showed that he was for a common front between the Muslims and other non-Muslim minorities. Unfortunately the catholicity and statesmanship that underlies these resolutions did not last long. In 1939 Mr. Jinnah took a somersault and outlined the dangerous and disastrous policy of isolation of the Musalmans by passing that notorious resolution in favour of Pakistan. What is the reason for this isolation? Nothing but the change of view that the Musalmans were a nation and not a community!! One need not quarrel over the question whether the Muslims are a nation or a community. But one finds it extremely difficult to understand how the mere fact that the Muslims are a nation makes political isolation a safe and sound policy? Unfortunately Muslims do not realize what disservice Mr. Jinnah has done to them by this policy. But let Muslims consider what Mr. Jinnah has achieved by making the Muslim League the only organization for the Musalmans. It may be that it has helped him to avoid the possibility of having to play the second fiddle. For inside the Muslim camp he can always be sure of the first place for himself. But how does the League hope to save by this plan of isolation the Muslims from Hindu Raj? Will Pakistan obviate the establishment of Hindu Raj in Provinces in which the Musalmans are in a minority? Obviously it cannot.

This is what would happen in the Muslim minority Provinces if Pakistan came. Take an all-India view. Can Pakistan prevent the establishment of Hindu Raj at the centre over Muslim minorities that will remain Hindustan? It is plain that it cannot. What good is Pakistan then? Only to prevent Hindu Raj in Provinces in which the Muslims are in a majority and in which there could never be Hindu Raj!! To put it differently Pakistan is unnecessary to Muslims where they are in a majority because there, there is no fear of Hindu Raj. It is worse than useless to Muslims where they are in a minority, because Pakistan or no Pakistan they will have to face a Hindu Raj. Can politics be more futile than the politics of the Muslim League? The Muslim League started to help minority Muslims and has ended by espousing the cause of majority Muslims. What a perversion in the original aim of the Muslim League! What a fall from the sublime to the ridiculous! Partition as a remedy against Hindu Raj is worse than useless. (146)

However, although Ambedkar was clear in his disagreement with the idea of separation, he adopted a realist stance to the demand and sought to draw out its implications:

The question that concerns the Hindus is: How far does the creation of Pakistan remove the communal question from Hindustan? That is a very legitimate question and must be considered. It must be admitted that by the creation of Pakistan, Hindustan is not freed of the communal question. While Pakistan can be made a homogeneous state by redrawing its boundaries, Hindustan must remain a composite state. The Musalmans are scattered all over Hindustan – though they are mostly congregated in towns – and no ingenuity in the matter of redrawing of boundaries can make it homogeneous. *The only way to make Hindustan homogeneous is to arrange for exchange of population.* Until that is done, it must be admitted that even with the creation of Pakistan, the problem of majority *vs.* minority will remain in Hindustan as before and will continue to produce disharmony in the body politic of Hindustan. (p. 54) (Emphasis added)

71

Ambedkar's chilling suggestion – argued at some length – that 'the only effective way of solving the minorities problem lay in exchange of population' (p. 53) was a logical argument based upon the concept of homogeneity as the accepted format of a modern nation.[24] The fact that he saw this as a feasible procedure: 'After all, the population involved is inconsiderable and because some obstacles require to be removed, it would be the height of folly to give up so sure a way to communal peace' (p. 53) is a sobering pointer to the sheer weight of the ideology of nation-states.

Sovereignty and annihilation

Colonial India's elites (including its imperial governors) discovered long ago how easy it was to inflame popular sentiment, and how communal violence was the most potent means of stalling social and political trans-formation. Communalism was and remains the Indian version of the totalitarian principle or drive in Indian politics. More specifically, it is India's fascist movement (Simeon 2013). As in Europe of the 1920s and 1930s this drive seized upon the nation-state as the ideological and insti-tutional platform upon which to enact the theatre of seizing power in the name of the nation. Undoubtedly class and traditional elite interests were at work in these processes, but fascism was and remains a mass move-ment that can and has been known to overtake the control of elites who support it (Rosenberg 2012, Vol 20, Issue 1).[25] The liberal-democratic vision of the newly established nation-states was imperiled at the out-set by the ideal of a national home for homogeneously defined nations, which provided fertile ground for the discourse of victimhood and revenge to thrive, and for its proponents to invade the public sphere with violence and hooliganism. In Europe the institutional structures and boundaries of these states had been laid down in 1919. Thus, even when the ultra-nationalist movements sought to alter these boundaries (as in Hitler's infamous imperial drive for *lebensraum*), when it came to the targeting of 'minorities', the main focus of these totalitarian move-ments was on political groups such as the communists and socialists, and ethnic ones, primarily the Jews and Romani. As regard to the former, their existence within European civilisation had for long been rendered precarious by the centuries-old tradition of anti-Semitism.

However, in late-colonial India the situation was different – here a colonised territory was undergoing a transition to independence that was complicated by contending visions and programmes of the sought-for nation-state. Here there was a plurality of actors seeking hegemony and contending for sovereignty in a highly differentiated society. The growth of totalitarian politics in India took place within a broader political terrain that included liberal and social democratic movements and ideas. Thus, the national movement and the accompanying anti-imperialist sentiment was simultaneously the ground for the crystallisation of conservative mobilisation around communal projects such as the Hindu nation and the Muslim nation. The ideological osmosis between communal groups and moderate organisations ensured that the former exercised political leverage in the latter. The binary interdependence and symbiotic nature of Hindu–Muslim communal discourse ensured that each strengthened the other and spoke the language of minority/majority to make claims upon the future constitution.

All this was accompanied by severe communal tension and violence in the 1920s and 1930s. The situation was further complicated by the advent of world wars and the machinations of a beleaguered empire. The resultant breakdown of the nationalist conversation was not a foregone conclusion, but a likely one. The communist left was so closely tied to Stalinist thought and Soviet strategic interests that it proved itself incapable of addressing the communal question in any terms other than the arithmetical discourse of the times. The attainment of a separated sovereignty by the 'Muslim majority' provinces of colonial India was a conclusion that left it in disarray, given the fact that just four years prior to independence, the CPI had advocated 'national self-determination' for these 'dominantly Muslim' areas as a step that would strengthen 'revolutionary Hindu–Muslim unity'.

One consequence of these has been the impact of sovereignty on critical thought, especially concerning the understanding of communalism. For many years, 'India' has been conceptualised as if the vast swathe that was to be renamed 'Pakistan' simply did not exist, and had never existed – its existence was wiped off retroactively from history as well. This was regardless of the fact that a powerful movement speaking the language of a fabricated monolith called 'the Muslim interest' had emerged during the Second World War and had for a while successfully co-opted certain left-wing cadre as well, with the help of the CPI. Sovereignty became a means of annihilation – not only literally, but theoretically. A movement that prided itself on its internationalism was reduced to helpless sophist pleading on behalf of one pole of communal radicalism, in ignorance of the ideological effect this might have, viz. the provision of legitimacy to the concept of a Hindu Nation. Thereafter the situation could only worsen. Today, when even high ranking members of Pakistan's elite may be assassinated for the mere suggestion that the blasphemy law needs revision, it is difficult to imagine any significant communist activism in Pakistan on behalf of an internationalist workers movement.

The idea has become endemic that the endless multiplication of sovereignty (rather than a democratic constitution that can hold heterogeneity) is a solution to social and political problems. As we have seen, by the 1940s the concept of nationhood had become irreparably tied to the sense of a communal *lebensraum*. The impact of all this, along with the conflation of ethnicity with religion, was felt amongst smaller communities as well. Thus, in a little-known reaction to what was happening in North India, a pamphlet titled 'Zoram Independent' was distributed in Aizawl, Mizoram, in May 1947, advocating independence for the Mizo hill tracts. It read:

> Every nation in the world strives for independence. India has struggled long. So have the Muslims of India for their independence. If the Mizo does not fight for their independence, they will remain slaves. We should fight for independence to avoid becoming slaves again. The fact that we speak one language (which proves that we are one people) is reason enough for us to strive for independence. All of us will be happy because then we will be working for our own future. Because of our religion alone we should be away from the Indians. All around us, different religious groups seem to form their own countries. The Burmese are Buddhists. The Indians are Hindus and the Pakistanis Muslims. Why should not we Mizos who are Christians have our own sovereign country. (Ronghaka 1985: 41–42)[26]

The marriage of ethnicity to territory was a disaster from the outset (this has been proven in the reorganised states of India's North-East as well), not only because it imposed a thoroughly impractical and formal abstraction upon the reality of mixed populations, but also because it provided legitimacy to forms of nationalist discourse that implied that minorities were a problem. In the political crises that engulfed the world between 1914 and after, many of these discourses lent themselves to 'final solutions' – the Nazi's grim euphemism for genocide. In the midst of the confusion, those who prided themselves on their scientific histori-cal insight uncritically accepted the vacuous language of majoritarian-ism and the ideological linkage between democracy and the nation-state. As a Sri Lankan comrade told me in a private conversation, 'their only way of dealing with the oppression of a minority is to convert it into a majority by handing over to it territory in which it becomes a majority which can in turn oppress the new minority.' For socialists in any case there is the broader question of the domination of capital over the world economy and the manner in which this domination is represented and reproduced as the essence of democracy. But that is a separate debate. The point at issue is not the autonomy of state power, but rather the exclusivist definition of 'the people' deemed to be sovereign.

The long shadow

In the bloodiest months of the newly independent dominions, the CPI issued a pamphlet paying 'homage to Mahatma Gandhi on his 79th birth-day'.[27] The preface spoke of how

> in his grand old age, the father of the nation has been fearlessly stirring the conscience of the nation on the most vital issues on which depends our future . . . by his personal intervention in defence of the Hindu minority in Noakhali, then of the Muslim minority in Calcutta and now in Delhi he has demonstrated how courage and confidence can be roused in the minority and a sense of shame in the majority for being misled by a handful of reactionary hate-mongers, and bonds of fraternity restored among the common people . . . let us make the nations homage to Mahatma Gandhi the culmination of a peoples peace cam-paign in which Congressmen, Nationalist Muslims, Leaguers, and all Left parties and popular organizations participate.[28]

It quoted Gandhi on the most tragic feature of the partition then unfolding:

> The transfer of population will be a fatal snare and it will mean nothing but greater misery. It is a shame for both. I claim myself to be equal servant of all. I wish India and Pakistan can unitedly make up their minds against the transfer of population.[29]

The preface ended with the hope that the Indian people would soon

> be able to declare before millions of Hindus, Muslims, Sikhs, Touchables and Untouchables, that the riot-demon stands buried and the minorities shall enjoy the protection of the living wall of the majority . . . thus alone can we defeat the anti-national communal reactionary. And play our proud role in shaping the destiny of the new world.

Here too, the most humane of aspirations was cast in arithmetical language, invoking yet again, the ideal of the homogenous nation. Even the appeal to the basic values of human decency was made in sentences that reinforced the philosophy of number, unwittingly reproducing the terrible threat that always underlay it, the danger that a mere change in the nation's mood could cause 'the living wall of the majority' to fall in a mass of destruction, carrying with it the lives and homes of millions. Ironically, communist cadres were among the few political activists in Punjab who spoke as human beings and not as members of an arithmetical category. Never was tragedy so latent in words as these moving salutations to a man whom their intellectual mentor R.P. Dutt had despised for having 'appeared throughout as the active leader of Hinduism and of Hindu revival' (Palme Dutt 1940: 437).

In 1947 however, Gandhi's efforts on behalf of suffering humanity struck a chord with the comrades, who had themselves carried a torch for human values through the nightmare of ethnic cleansing in a country that was meant to be awakening to freedom. Writes Nauman Naqvi:

> There are events in the past when the catastrophe that is to come has already come to pass, indeed when that coming

catastrophe has never ceased coming to pass. One such event is the 'Partition' of South Asia – that is, the moment of our 'freedom', our entry into modern political subjectivity, our entry into modern, historical life, pure and simple. (Naqvi 2012)

Whatever be our assessment of the historical experience of the successor states of British India, it is undeniable that a great deal was lost with independence. I refer not just to the vast scale of the killing, the uprooting of ordinary people from their homes, the framing of millions of our own as eternal enemies of each other. Along with this extraordinary violence, people (most of all in the affected areas, but elsewhere as well) also lost the sense of trust and friendship and even the capacity to disagree or be angry without dipping that disagreement or anger in the poison-well of communal hatred and communal stereotypes. What was lost was the very capacity to speak, other than as members of a majority or a minority, particles of this or that community, this or that nation. This is our plight today. This was the 'coming catastrophe' that 'has never ceased coming to pass', that lingers with us still, this was the outrage that caused Toba Tek Singh to throw his madness upon the ground and refuse a national identity. And it remains as true today as it was then, that the first step towards sanity is to see that catastrophe remains our habitation.

dil ke phaphole jal uthe seene ke daag se
is ghar ko aag lag gayi ghar ke chiraag se

Notes

1 This chapter builds upon my long-standing argument about the fascist nature of Indian communalism. It also uses material from my earlier work. The title is a phrase used by Maulana Mohammad Ali in 1911, see Tejani (2008: 170).
2 P.C. Joshi Archives, (JNU), File CPI/108, pp. 5–6.
3 The figure of one and a half lakhs dead in Punjab given by Dhanwantri in 1947 was clearly an underestimate. A new study of Punjab in 1947 cites figures ranging from six lakhs to a million, while stating that an overwhelming majority of these deaths took place in Punjab (Ahmad 2012: xli). See also (Baixas 1946–47): http://www.massviolence.org/Thematic-Chronology-of-Mass-Violence-in-Pakistan-1947–2007?decoupe_recherche=noakhali
4 The dictionary supplies the following definition of genocide: 'The (attempted) deliberate and systematic extermination of an ethnic or national group.' The

Convention on the Prevention and Punishment of the Crime of Genocide adopted by the UN in December 1948 includes intentional as well as substantial aspects. See http://www.preventgenocide.org/law/convention/text. htm#II

5 He continues: 'The general will became a secular religion under the Jacobin dictatorship – the people worshipping themselves – while the political leadership sought to guide and formalize this worship. Fascism saw the French Revolution as a whole through the eyes of the Jacobin dictatorship' (George Mosse 1989: 5–6).

6 The clear assumption here is that the nation is ethnically homogenous.

7 Section 1, http://www.marxists.org/reference/archive/stalin/works/1913/03. htm

8 The essay is downloadable here: http://ig.cs.tu-berlin.de/oldstatic/w2001/eu1/dokumente/Basistexte/Renan1882EN-Nation.pdf

9 See also Mark Mazower (1999).

10 A pdf file may be read here: http://www.unz.org/Pub/NeumannFranz-1942–00027

11 These arguments are developed in my articles Simeon (1994) and Simeon (1986). See http://www.sacw.net/article2760.html

12 For different accounts of the emergence of Hindu nationalism, see Chandra (1992), Dalmia (1997) and Sharma (2003).

13 A critical assessment may be read in Alavi (1998); also available at: http://hamzaalavi.com/?p=86. For further reading on nationalism see Hardiman (2003), esp. Chapters 2 and 7, 'An Incorporative Nationalism' and 'Fighting Religious Hatreds'. Also see Tejani, *Indian Secularism*.

14 Speech at Malegaon, 14 October 1938. Cited in Casolari, 'Hindutva 2000', pp. 218–28, at 223–24. Available online at http://www.sacw.net/DC/CommunalismCollection/ArticlesArchive/casolari.pdf

15 From Savarkar's Kanpur address in *Hindu Rashtra Darshan*, pp. 122–25; a collection of presidential speeches: http://liberalpartyofindia.org/communal/Hindu-Rashtra-Darshan.pdf; p. 123.

16 Ahmad (267).

17 Until the late 1980s, the MA syllabus for modern Indian history at the University of Delhi included a separate paper on Muslim Politics. Communal politics of other hues were under-recognised or ignored.

18 For a more detailed discussion of this theme, see Simeon (1986). See also http://www.sacw.net/article2760.html

19 On 15 August 1943, Savarkar (president of the Hindu Mahasabha from 1937 to 1943) declared: 'I have no quarrel with Mr. Jinnah's two-nation theory. We Hindus are a nation by ourselves and it is a historical fact that Hindus and Muslims are two nations' (Indian Annual Register 1943: 10 (Vol 2).

20 G. Adhikari, ed., *Pakistan and National Unity* (Bombay, 1943). Page references are from this publication. The full text of the Resolution may be read at http://www.unz.org/Pub/LabourMonthly-1943mar-00093; and an

abridged version of the Report at http://www.unz.org/Pub/LabourMonthly-1943mar-00087?View=PDF, accessed on 15 February 2015.
21 'August 15 — To the People of Pakistan: Communist Party's Appeal'; File CPI-117; P.C. Joshi Archive.
22 Communist Party Publication (Bombay, 1948), File CPI/147; P.C. Joshi Archive.
23 B. R. Ambedkar, *Pakistan, or the Partition of India* (Bombay, 1946). The first edition appeared in 1940 as *Thoughts on Pakistan*. A pdf copy of the book is available here: http://www.satnami.com/pakistan.pdf. Numbered citations of Ambedkar's views refer to the 1946 edition of this book.
24 For a detailed account of Ambedkar's views on Pakistan, see Simeon (2013).
25 A pdf copy of Rosenberg's essay is available at http://www.sacw.net/article 2756.html
26 Cited by Nag (1993).
27 'On his 79th birthday – Our Homage and our Pledge'; File CPI-117; P.C. Joshi Archive, Jawaharlal Nehru University Library.
28 Ibid., 'On his 79th birthday', pp. 1–2.
29 Ibid., 'On his 79th birthday', p. 6. Address at prayer gathering on 13 September 1947.

4

TRACING THE TRAJECTORY OF COMMUNALISM AND COMMUNAL VIOLENCE IN INDIA

Prateep K. Lahiri

Communalism in India has been an enduring phenomenon from the early years of British rule, and its overt manifestation has been in terms of clashes between communities, mainly between Hindus and Muslims, which together comprise about 95 per cent of the population. Some scholars, such as Ashutosh Varshney, describe inter-religious conflicts as 'ethnic'. They refer to intra-religious conflicts, say between Dalit and upper-caste Hindus, as 'communal'. In this chapter we opt for the popular term, used by media, and preferred in common parlance, wherein conflicts between Hindus and Muslims are described as 'communal' rather than as 'ethnic'. In this regard the following definition by Bipan Chandra seems both comprehensive and apt:

> Communalism is the belief that because a group of people follow a particular religion they have, as a result, common social, political and economic interests. It is the belief that in India Hindus, Muslims, Christians and Sikhs form different and distinct communities which are independently and separately structured or consolidated; that all the followers of a religion share not only a community of religious interests but also common secular interests, that is, common economic, political, social and cultural interests; that Indians inevitably perceive such interests through the spectacles of the religious grouping and are bound to possess a sense of identity based

on religion, i.e. religion has to become the basis of their basic social identity and the determinant of their basic social relationships. (Chandra 1984: 1)

Prior to the British rule in India, communalism had not taken on an ideological dimension. The British did not wish to see the two major communities, viz. Hindu and Muslim, united because that would be detrimental to the continuance of their rule. The policy was designed to prevent growth of pan-Indian nationalism and political consolidation that could one day become an irresistible force to contend with for the British rulers. Their motivation in resorting to the 'divide and rule policy' is well encapsulated in the views of Winston Churchill, expressed in a cabinet meeting on 2 February 1940, which is recorded as follows in the Cabinet papers:

> He did not share the anxiety to encourage and promote unity between the Hindu and Muslim communities. Such unity was, in fact, almost out of the realm of practical politics, while, if it were to be brought about, the immediate result would be that the united communities would join in showing us the door. He regarded the Hindu-Muslim feud as the bulwark of British rule in India. (Chandra 1984: 245).

On pragmatic considerations, the British perhaps preferred to extend support to Muslim communalism rather than Hindu communalism because Hindus being in majority, if united, could prove to be more dangerous to the perpetuation of colonial rule. It would be fair, however, to say that British did not, as a matter of policy, encourage violent clashes between the Hindu and Muslims – this was a fall out of the divide and rule policy (Chandra 1984).

Prior to 1857 there were very few communal riots in the modern sense of the term, and during the revolt of 1857–58 Hindus and Muslims were completely united; it is noteworthy that in these two years there were no communal riots. However, from 1858 to 1919 there were several Hindu–Muslim riots such as in Bareilly (1871), Mumbai (1893), Peshawar (1910), Ayodhya (1912) and Agra (1913), to mention a few that were noteworthy (Rai 2008).

In his personal life Mahatma Gandhi was a practicing Hindu, but in the arena of public discourse he was truly secular. His aim was to forge Hindu–Muslim unity so that the two major communities would stand firmly together in espousing the cause of independence from British rule. In order to prevent the British being able to exploit fissures in this unity, Mahatma Gandhi took up the issue of Khilafat on behalf of the Congress even though it was essentially a pan-Islamic movement, subscribed to by Muslims in India (Lahiri 2009).

Gandhi also ensured that the Indian Muslims were fully involved, as equal partners, in the non-co-operation movement. While this unity was in place in 1919–20, there were no communal clashes between these communities. The unity assiduously nurtured under the leadership of Mahatma Gandhi was rent asunder as a consequence of two events of some historical significance. One was the Moplah rebellion in 1921, which started as a revolt by the Moplahs, who were Muslims, against the British but morphed into a violent agitation targeting prosperous Hindu landlords and money lenders. The second crippling blow to the unity of the two communities was the withdrawal of the non-co-operation movement by Mahatma Gandhi, consequent to the violent Chouri Choura incident, since the Mahatma held firm to the belief that the movement could not afford to stray from the path of non-violence (Lahiri 2009).

The essence of the competing ideologies of Hindu and Muslim nationalisms is reflected in the following two statements of Jinnah and Savarkar. Jinnah had averred: 'Our demand is not from Hindus because the Hindus never took the whole of India. It was the Muslims who took India and ruled for 700 years. It was the British who took India from the Musalmans.' In 1942, he asserted that if the British handed over the government of India to the Muslim League, they 'will be making full amends to the Muslims by restoring the government of India to them from whom they had taken it . . .'(Chandra 1984: 219–220).On the basis of this convoluted logic Jinnah sought restoration of Muslim rule over India. This was his maximalist position. Savarkar said: 'Every person is a Hindu who regards and owns this Bharat Bhoomi – this land from the Indus to the seas as his Fatherland (pitrabhu) and Holy land (punyabhu) – the land of origin of his religion and cradle of his faith'.[4] Savarkar coined the term 'Hindutva' for the ideology that propagates the belief that Hindu culture is the predominant one in India and to belong to the mainstream one has to accept pre-eminence of this culture. The belief in this ideology informs the attitudes and actions of the various constituents of the Sangh Parivar to this day.

Once Mohammad Ali Jinnah had broken away from the Congress and assumed leadership of the Muslim League, the goal of Muslim nationalism was focused on partition of India to create a separate homeland for Muslims. When that goal was realized, howsoever imperfectly, with the creation of the Pakistan, Muslim nationalism lost its ideological moorings in independent India. It had to reinvent itself to take up certain sectarian issues, which appeal to only a minority among the Muslims. Thus Muslim nationalism today is a pale shadow of what existed before independence. Hindu nationalism however, after a chequered history, continues to thrive fuelled, from time to time, by certain movements organised by the votaries of Hindutva.

We need to identify the factors that perennially come in the way of the two major communities coalescing and coming together to share a common worldview, working together in harmony to further common interests and goals and the reasons for persistence of tensions informing the interactions between the two communities. Its fallout happens episodically in terms of outbreaks of clashes and riots between the communities.

First of all there is an issue of perception among the two communities about each other. Perhaps due to lack of adequate civic engagement between members of the two communities, both in rural and urban centers, there is a tendency of members of the communities to live in distinctly separate areas. In many urban centers, this has resulted in the 'ghettoization' of Muslims. This phenomenon has been exacerbated for instance in many cities and towns of Gujarat after the 2002 riots.

In such a situation because of the lack of social integration, certain perceptions about the 'Other' become ingrained among the members of both the communities and lead to stereotyping. The stereotype among Hindus about Muslims often is that (a) they are 'dirty' because of their food habits; (b) they are aggressive and religious fanatics, ready to begin *jihad* at the slightest pretext; (c) they are lecherous, ready to pounce upon and rape Hindu women, who remain uncovered by *pardah*, and so on. Besides this, orthodox Hindus particularly resent Muslims because they eat the meat of cows, which are considered sacred by most Hindus. In contrast, the Muslims perceive Hindus as (a) idol worshippers, whose religious practices are irrational; (b) their liberal attitude towards inter-action between the sexes borders on the promiscuous; and (c) they are cowardly in comparison with Muslims, deceitful and untrustworthy and so on (Lahiri 2009; Hansen 1999).

As we have mentioned Muslim communalism in India lost its momen-tum once Pakistan came into existence, since that was the objective it was focused upon prior to independence. Subsequently, therefore, the contes-tation has been between the ideologies of secular nationalism and 'Hin-dutva' and this has kept alive the tension between the two communities, particularly in the northern and western parts of the country, resulting in outbreaks of communal violence from time to time. Preachers, saints and savants such as Swami Dayanand and Swami Vivekananda aimed at reforming the Hindu society so that it conformed to the true tradi-tions of Hinduism, which, they believed, had been defiled over centuries by prescriptions and elaborate rituals that had dented its pristine qual-ity. Theirs was an eclectic vision of Hinduism. Contrarily Savarkar and later Hedgewar, the founder of the Rashtriya Swayamsevak Sangh (RSS), and Golwalkar were the ideologues who propagated a militant version of Hinduism, which conceived of a Hindu Rashtra, where 'there was no place for the pluralistic and syncretic culture of India. All those who did not belong to the Hindu race, religion, culture and language were out of the pale of national life . . .' (Lahiri 2009: 170). RSS was conceived as the instrument that would translate into reality the Savarkar–Golwalkar conception of the Hindu Rashtra. These ideals have been summed up in the constitution of the body thus:

> To eradicate differences among Hindus; to make them real-ize the greatness of their past; to inculcate in them spirit of self-sacrifice and self-devotion to Hindu society as a whole; to build up an organized and well-disciplined corporate life; and to bring about the regeneration of Hindu society . . . (Dossani and Rowen 2005: 121)

The aim with which the RSS was founded was to defend the Hindu nation or *rashtra*, which is conceived as being distinct from the state. The function of the state is to maintain peace and order, but the defence of *rashtra* implies the duty to uphold the cultural ethos of the nation. The RSS professes to be a cultural organisation, and in order to broaden its ambit and reach out to all segments of society it has encouraged the formation of several other allied organisations that are collectively referred to as the 'Sangh Parivar'.

The political party linked to the RSS is the Bharatiya Janata Party (BJP), which is the present day *avatar* of the Jana Sangh founded by Dr Shyama Prasad Mukherjee in 1951. The other affiliates of the Sangh Parivar are Akhil Bharatiya Vidyarthi Parishad (ABVP), Bharatiya Mazdoor Sangh (BMS), Vanavasi Kalyan Ashram (VKA), Vishwa Hindu Parishad (VHP) and Bajrang Dal (BD). These organisations have separate identities with clear-cut objectives to promote 'Hindutva' in different areas; for instance, the ABVP works among the students in university and college campuses, and the BMS aims to spread Hindu nationalist ideologies among the organised workers in the country. The VHP and BD propagate nationalist ideologies in broader constituencies and have been in the forefront of organising movements aimed at promoting the Hindu nationalist ideology so that it garners greater space and salience in the socio-political arena.

Since the 1950s there have been several movements, organised by the constituents of the Sangh Parivar, aimed primarily to further the cause of the Hindu right and create a Hindu vote bank. The first of these was the cow protection movement. In the cow, which is venerated by Hindus, 'Golwalkar found a symbol to unite Hindus who were otherwise divided by caste, sect, language and region . . .' (Lahiri 2009: 179). The main objective of the cow protection movement was to unite the Hindus using the cow as a symbol and also make them view Muslims and Christians pejoratively as beefeaters. This movement reached its apogee, when in 1966 a large crowd marched to the Parliament, in Delhi, demanding a ban on cow slaughter, thereby creating considerable disturbance at the venue. The movement, however, petered out after this show of strength.

Actually cow slaughter is banned in a number of states but the demand is raised from time to time as a tool for political mobilisation of the Hindus. In this respect, it has achieved its objective albeit to a limited extent.

Years later in 1986, the VHP took the initiative to organise a month-long *Ekatmata yatra/yajna* (journey/religious sacrifice for national unity). There were three main *yatras* to cross India from north to south connecting certain sacred spots such as the river Ganga at Haridwar, Kanyakumari and Rameshwaram. The third one crossed India from Gangasagar on the Bay of Bengal to the temple at Somnath on the coast of the Arabian Sea. These *yatras* relied heavily on religious symbolism, such as collecting water from all sacred rivers, lakes and distributing the Ganga water the processionists were carrying at the stoppage points on the routes. The processionists gave vent to their antipathy against other communities by shouting slogans having religious connotations and seeking to project the overweening importance of Hindu culture in the nation (Jaffrelot 1987).

Although the cow protection movement and *Ekatmata yatras* were organised by RSS and its affiliates essentially for political gains, these did not have a lasting impact. The objective of the movement to build a Ram temple at Ayodhya, at the location where Babri Masjid stood for some 500 years, which really succeeded in widening and strengthening the political base for the 'Hindutva' ideology and, concomitantly, in garnering electoral success for the BJP. Clearly, these mobilising movements, that is, for cow protection, *Ekatmata yatra* and to build a temple at Ayodhya, while ostensibly being religious and cultural were really aimed at gaining ascendency in the political sphere.

Since the movement to build a temple at Ayodhya has had a seminal influence in communalizing the political narrative in the country, it would be apposite to trace the course of the movement from its beginnings to its climax and afterwards. Way back in 1853, when Awadh was under the rule of Nawabs, on getting a false information that Babri Masjid had been destroyed by the members of the Bairagi sect, Maulavi Amir Ali gave a call for *jihad* (holy war). Nawab Wajid Ali Shah sought the intervention of the East India Company to restrain the Muslims, but the British resident deliberately declined to do so. Wajid Ali Shah then sent his troops and in the ensuing fight Maulavi Amir Ali was killed. This episode indicates that the British had no interest in resolving the matter and the dispute was allowed to fester since that time (Rai 2008).

The issue remained in hibernation for almost a century before it was revived in independent India in December 1949. Some elements interested in raking it up publicised the allegedly miraculous appearance of the idols of Ram and Sita within the precincts of Babri Masjid, at the spot where it was believed Ram had been born. The then district magistrate reported to the state government that actually a group of Hindus had surreptitiously entered the Babri Masjid under the cover of darkness and installed the idols there.

Prime Minister Pandit Nehru wanted the idols to be removed from the spot but the state and local authorities did not do so for fear of repercussions. Justice Srikrishna, who enquired into the Bombay riots in 1992–93, which occurred in the aftermath of the demolition of the Babri Masjid, has observed that the vacillating attitude of the government not only emboldened those who demanded to carry out *puja* (worship) therein but also resulted in the Babri Masjid becoming a rallying point for the Muslims (Srikrishna Commission Report 1997).

In the 1980s, the VHP took up the issue aggressively and organised the *Shri Ram-Janki rath yatra* starting from Sitamarhi in Bihar for purposes of 'awakening the nation'. There were various other *pada yatras* and *dharmasabhas* to keep the momentum of the movement alive and press for the demand to allow Hindus to worship to idols inside the Babri Masjid. On the other side, the Babri Masjid Action Committee (BMAC), headed by Syed Sahabuddin, also became active in calling for protests on behalf of the Muslims.

The VHP initiated a novel programme in which consecrated bricks were to be brought to Ayodhya from different parts of the country by volunteers to build the Ram temple. This programme generated considerable enthusiasm and received extensive media coverage. Clearly, the BJP derived political mileage from the movement and improved its tally of seats in the Lok Sabha to 85 in 1989 against only two in the previous Lok Sabha.

The unfortunate consequence of these processions converging from different parts of the country and heading to Ayodhya was that communal passions were aroused and ill-feelings generated among the communities, because of the religious symbolisms used by the processionists and the provocative nature of the slogans. This resulted in riots erupting at a number of places such as Indore, Mhow, Ratlam, Kota, Jabalpur and Bhagalpur (Lahiri 2009).

This phase of the Ayodhya movement culminated with the laying of the foundation stone of the Ram Temple on 9 November 1989. This was obviously done with the tacit support of the authorities of the state and Central government. When the Central government headed by Prime

Minister V.P. Singh decided to implement the recommendations of the Mandal Commission in August 1990, the BJP withdrew support from the government and took steps to shift the debate towards the religion and *mandir–masjid* question. A *rath yatra* led by L.K. Advani from the ancient temple of Somnath in Gujarat to Ayodhya in Uttar Pradesh was organised beginning on 25 September 1990. As historian Ramachandra Guha describes it:

> Militants of the Vishwa Hindu Parishad (VHP) flanked the van, flagging it off from one town and welcoming it at the next. At public meetings they were complemented by saffron-robed sadhus, whose 'necklaces of prayer beads, long beards and ash-marked foreheads provided a strong visual counterpoint' to these armed young men. The march's imagery was 'religious, allusive, militant, masculine, and anti-Muslim'. This was rein-forced by the speeches made by Advani, which accused the gov-ernment of 'appeasing' the Muslim minority and of practicing 'pseudo-secularism' which denied the legitimate interests and aspirations of the Hindu majority. The building of a Ram temple in Ayodhya was presented as the symbolic fulfillment of these interests and aspirations. (Guha 2007: 635)

Although the main *yatra* was halted in Bihar with the arrest of L.K. Advani following the order of Lalu Prasad Yadav, the then chief min-ister of Bihar, thousands of *kar sevaks* from different parts of the county converged at the Babri Masjid with the intention to demolish it. This was prevented by the state government with use of force. At least 20 of the *kar sevaks* died in the clash between them and the security forces. VHP activists declared these *kar sevaks* to be 'martyrs' and carried their ashes to various parts of North India, which led to communal riots (in which mainly Muslims suffered) in the towns of Aligarh, Agra, Khurja and Bulandshahar. Thus it has been said that L.K. Advani's *rath yatra* became a *rakt yatra*, a journey of blood. Finally on 6 December 1992, when a BJP led government was in power in Uttar Pradesh, notwith-standing assurances given to the Supreme Court by the government, the Babri Masjid was allowed to be demolished by thousands of *kar sevaks*, without any interference from the security forces.

Communal violence on a large scale erupted subsequent to the demolition of the Babri Masjid. Many places in northern and western India were affected by these riots and hundreds of persons lost their lives and were injured in the clashes in states such as Gujarat, Madhya Pradesh, Assam and Karnataka. The violence in Bombay was one of the worst ever. Sri Krishna Commission, which enquired into the 1992–93 riots in Bombay inter-alia, criticized organizations such as BJP, VHP, Bajrang Dal and Shiv Sena for their role in inciting violence. The commission also criticised the bias of the police against the minority community. Subsequent to the communal riots there were a series of bomb blasts in Mumbai apparently organised by Muslim dons with the intent to wreak vengeance for the sufferings of Muslims during the 1992–93 riots.

The aggressive movement for building a Ram temple at Ayodhya, the demolition of the Babri Masjid and the subsequent fallout in terms of communal violence were cataclysmic events that exacerbated the divide between Hindus and Muslims in vast swathes of the country. It also led to a polarisation of the electorate, resulting in electoral dividends for BJP, which won its highest ever number of seats (182) in the Lok Sabha in 1998 and repeated its performance in the mid-term elections of 1999. The cleavage thus created between the two communities would indeed take a long time to heal (Lahiri 2009).

The next watershed event after the demolition of the Babri Masjid and the communal violence that followed was the post-Godhra carnage in Gujarat in 2002. In these riots some 2,000 persons lost their lives. There was extensive damage to property, many religious places were desecrated and families were forcibly moved out of their homes and hearths. While both the communities suffered in these riots, the minority community suffered more both in terms of casualties and damage to their properties.

The Gujarat riots of 2002, while being one of the worst since independence, could prove to be a turning point since that was the last time any major communal conflagration has taken place anywhere in the country. Perhaps it could have been a cathartic moment for both the communities. Based on the outcomes of the general elections in 2004 and 2009, it could have been concluded that religion centric mobilising movements such as the building of a temple at Ayodhya were past their sell-by-date. However, the results of the 2014 elections force a rethink. Though it is too soon after the event, most analysts appear to conclude that the massive electoral mandate given to the BJP is more due to the governance failures of the previous regime on all fronts, rather than the people voting on ideological considerations. The BJP had indeed focused much more on the plank of development in their election campaign and the earlier core demands such as abolition of Article 370 and the building of the temple at Ayodhya were placed on the back burner.

It would be fruitful to consider the perspectives from which three eminent social scientists – Ashutosh Varshney, Steven Wilkinson and Paul R. Brass – analysed the causal factors and dynamics of the episodic clashes that have been taking place between the two major communities. Based on analysis of data, Varshney has established that communal violence in India is not as widespread as it is believed to be. It is city-centric, that is, largely an urban phenomenon and hardly affects the rural hinterland. Among cities too Varshney has identified some of them, where communal violence is endemic. He terms these urban centres as 'riot prone'. The riot-prone cities have been classified into four categories based on the number of communal riots that have occurred in these cities, their periodicity and number of deaths that have taken place. On this basis he has classified the riot prone cities into four categories and in the topmost category are the cities of Ahmedabad, Baroda (Gujarat); Meerut, Aligarh (UP); Mumbai (Maharashtra); Hyderabad (Andhra Pradesh); Kolkata (West Bengal); and Delhi. On analysing the data further, Varshney finds that these eight cities account for 45.5 per cent of the total deaths in urban India and 49 per cent of all deaths in the entire country due to riots. At the same time these cities are home to only 18 per cent of the urban population. If we add the rural population then, according to Varshney, 'riot proneness' is confined to only 5 per cent to India's population (Varshney 2005: 100–103).

Varshney's hypothesis is that the levels of prevailing civic engagement is the main determining factor that influences riot proneness in any city. According to him, there are two forms of civic engagements, viz. 'associational' and 'quotidian'. As far as associational forms are concerned, these are professional organisations, associations, trade unions, cadre-based political parties and so on. In these forms members of different communities interact and such interaction is conducive to bonding. Quotidian or everyday forms are daily interactions amongst individuals and families through jointly participating in social functions, festivals and so on. Both forms of engagement, that is, associational and quotidian promote peace and harmony between communities. To substantiate his argument, Varshney has made a paired comparison of certain cities. He has selected three from the eight most riot-prone cities and three peaceful ones for such paired comparison. In doing so he has taken up, in each pair, two cities with roughly similar Hindu–Muslim percentages of the population. We may briefly consider his analysis of one of these pairs, that is, Hyderabad and Lucknow.

There are certain striking similarities between the two cities in as much as the Hindu–Muslim population percentages have been in the same range. Both cities have Muslim rulers, Nizams in Hyderabad and Nawabs in Lucknow.

Despite these common factors the only major Hindu–Muslim riot in Lucknow took place in 1924. It remained peaceful even in the Partition years and also when there were clashes between the two communities at the peak of the Ayodhya movement and in the aftermath of the demolition of the Babri Masjid. On the contrary, Hyderabad has witnessed many riots since 1938.

> Searching for the causes of the stark contrast these two cities present in terms of their record of communal violence, Varshney has argued that historically, the dominant cleavage in Lucknow has been an intra-religious one between the Shia and the Sunni sect of Muslims, not an interreligious one. In Hyderabad, on the other hand, the mass politics that emerge in the 1930s was superimposed on Hindu–Muslim and not Shia–Sunni difference. (Lahiri 2009: 17)

In Lucknow, economic and commercial activities provide a major source of civic engagement between the two communities. The Chikan and Zardozi industry is crucial to Lucknow's economy. Almost half the Muslim population of Lucknow works as artisans in this industry, whereas the traders and entrepreneurs are mostly Hindus. Thus there is continuous engagement between the two communities that keep the wheels of the industry churning. As Varshney puts it, these two communities in Lucknow have come together in a 'mutually dependent relationship'. Both communities realise that any violence would disrupt the smooth functioning of the industry and would be detrimental to the interests of both communities. In Hyderabad, however, there is no such convergence of economic and commercial interests of the two communities. Unlike Lucknow where the dominant cleavage is intra-religious between Sunnis and Shias, in Hyderabad it is inter-religious between Hindus and Muslims.

In regard to the phenomenon of virtual absence of communal clashes in rural areas, Varshney's take is that everyday forms of civic interaction are much stronger and help in forging bonds between the two communities, even if 'associational' forms are non-existent.

While Ashutosh Varshney and Steven Wilkinson collaborated in their research of communal riots and shared certain data sets, they have taken divergent paths in identifying the causative factors of riots. The central argument given in Wilkinson's book is that electoral politics and competition is the principal causative factor for occurrence of communal riots in India (Wilkinson 2005: 6).

Wilkinson takes Gujarat riots of 2002 as a reference point and placed the states in three categories. In the first category are Kerala, Bihar and Orissa where three or more political parties compete for the minority vote. In Andhra Pradesh, Madhya Pradesh and Rajasthan since there are only two major parties, the competition for minority votes is bipolar. Gujarat is in a category of its own because, despite competition between two parties, there is no reliance on the minority vote. Wilkinson posits that the government in the first two categories have worked proactively to prevent riots. But in Gujarat the BJP government, not having a support base in the minority community and with the other parties in the state not offering enough competition, had no incentive to protect the Gujarati Muslims.

Wilkinson has made a study of riots in Uttar Pradesh and has concluded that

> polarizing the electorates through communal processions and other events, likely to divide people and increase the salience of religious identity, have proved to be a highly effective electoral strategy. Between the 1989 state elections and 1991 state elections in Uttar Pradesh, thirty-three riots took place in which 295 persons died. The precipitating event for violence in each

case was an organized Hindu nationalist attempt to disrupt a Muslim procession, to hold an anti-Muslim public meeting, or to raise the fear that Muslims were about to turn upon Hindus. (Wilkinson 2005: 49)

The riots in Agra and in Aligarh in December 1990 have been cited as examples.

On the basis of the election outcomes in Uttar Pradesh, Wilkinson has demonstrated that the vote share of the BJP went up by 24 per cent in towns affected by riots but only by 7 per cent in the unaffected towns. He has also given several examples of how, in Uttar Pradesh, political parties engineered riots for electoral gain. One incident cited is that of the sensitive city of Varanasi where in 1991, when BJP was in power, its ally VHP was allowed to take out a religious procession in the city. The processionists shouted provocative slogans while passing through Muslim localities and this sparked off riots in which 17 persons were killed and considerable damage to property, mainly of Muslims, was inflicted (Wilkinson 2005).

Paul Brass has studied in-depth the phenomenon of communal riots in certain cities, specifically Aligarh and Meerut in Uttar Pradesh. His view is that the search for causes of these riots is futile because they are the outcome of a historical evolutionary process and the dynamics of relationship between the two communities.

Hindu–Muslim riots take place in the backdrop of the communal discourse, which has been set in a historical perspective. Brass is in agreement with leftist historians, according to whom the representations of a collective 'Hindu' past, are key in contributing to the persistence of communal violence in India. Evidence exists to show that this memorialisation leads to demonization of the 'Other', who in the case of India are the Muslims (Brass 2003: 366–84).

In this backdrop Brass has developed the theory of institutionalised riot system (IRS) that exist at places where riots are endemic. IRS has been compared to a dramatic production in a theatre wherein the actors are described as 'conversion specialists' and 'fire tenders'. The fire tenders keep the fires of communal tensions smouldering and the role of the conversion specialists is to play up a trivial everyday incident so that it can result in a clash between the communities. There is merit in Brass' view that a trivial incident is often played up with ulterior motive of engen-dering riots. This so-called precipitating incident serves as a red herring, highlighted by interested parties and sections of the media, to transfer the blame for causing the riot to a particular group. As Brass puts it, it serves the purpose of 'blame displacement'. The issue of the 'precipitating incident' in riots is elaborated upon later in this chapter. To quote Brass:

> The institutionalized riot systems or networks that exist in riot-prone cities and towns comprise a multiplicity of roles . . . they include informants who carry messages to political group leaders of the occurrence of incidents that may affect the rela-tions between Hindus and Muslims; propagandists who create messages to be conveyed to particular segments of society, to the press, to the general public; vernacular journalists who publish these messages in the form of 'news', poster plasterers who place them on walls, rumourmongers who transmit them by 'word of mouth'; recruiters who collect crowds from colleges and univer-sities and goondas (thugs) to kill, loot, and burn when the time is ripe . . . (Brass 2003: 32–32)

While IRS is an interesting proposition, it cannot obviously be used as a straitjacket to fit all riot-prone centers. It has been theorised that certain riots have taken place due to clash of economic and commercial interests of the two major communities. To give certain examples of the 'economic explanation', some have ascribed the 1992–93 riots in Bom-bay and 2002 in Ahmedabad as a strategy used by real estate developers to displace Muslims from valuable lands, which could be sold at high prices. The 1928 riots in Bhiwandi in Maharashtra had been depicted organised attempt by Hindu cloth merchants to damage property of Mus-lim competitors in the region. Brass sees the economic correlation that riot has as an effect rather than a cause. His views is that 'riots occur in a communal discursive context and are almost always associated with political activities' (Brass 2003: 215).

When riots occur, economic and commercial interests of both Hindus and Muslims suffer. Hence, it is logical that neither community would like to deliberately start a riot that would be counter-productive for both. However, when a riot does happen, whatever be the trigger, members of either community sometimes try to take advantage of the situation and harm the members of the other community through looting, arson and other means.

It will be evident that it is futile to search for any single or even a multiple set of causes that would explain the phenomenon of Hindu–Muslim riots. Often, in the past, a minor incident, such as the slaughter of a cow near a temple allegedly by Muslims, or a pig being killed in the vicinity of mosque by Hindus, or the playing of music in front of a mosque and even an incident of rape of woman belonging to a particular community by a member of the other community, have apparently triggered riots involving the communities. The incident that allegedly triggers such a riot can be described as a 'precipitating incident'. Persons responsible for the riots and even the media often play up such an incident as being trigger for riots, with the ulterior motive of deflecting attention from the real causes. The example of the 1961 riots in Jabalpur can be cited where the riots were allegedly caused by an incident of a Hindu girl committing suicide after she was raped by two Muslim youths. This was reported in a very provocative manner by a local newspaper, resulting in exaggerated rumours about the incident being spread and inflaming the pent up feelings of the members of the majority community. In the riots that followed a large number of Muslims were killed and their properties damaged. Subsequently a journalist, who investigated the matter, concluded that the incident of rape was not substantiated and the girl committed suicide because, being from an orthodox family, she was not allowed to marry one of the Muslim youths with whom she was in love (Lahiri 2009).

The so-called precipitating incident is often used as ruse to cover up the real causes and it is an act of 'blame displacement' on the part of those who engineered the riots to deflect attention. The root causes are embedded in the tensions and dynamics of the relations between the two communities prevailing at a given time and place.

It is pertinent to mention that elements interested in creating disturbances and riots often resort to spreading false information or rumors through word of mouth or the media. At times when tension prevails and the communities are hostile and suspicious about each other's motivation and activities, such rumours can lead to prolongation of the conflict and escalation of violence. An example given by Paul Brass pertaining to riot that occurred in Aligarh in 1990 is worth

citing in the context. In December 1990, there was a communal conflagration in Aligarh when a mob of Hindus had attacked a train and
killed a number of Muslim passengers. Two days after this incident leading Hindi newspapers, *Aaj*, *Dainik Jagaran* and *Amar Ujala* published a
news item reporting the death of many Hindu patients at the hands of
the Muslim doctors at the AMU Medical College Hospital. This was a
completely false story but it was widely publicised in North India. This
rumour served the purpose of taking the attention away from the killing of the Muslim passengers in the train and led to vengeance attacks
of Muslims, because of the alleged incident of killing of Hindus at the
hospital (Brass 2003). When dealing with such situations, it is necessary for the authorities to be extremely alert and use whatever means
possible to counter such rumours and inform the public at large of the
actual facts.

Indeed there can be no generic explanation to satisfactorily cover the
varying situations leading to incidents involving communal violence.
Hansen has summed up the situation very well thus:

> Many of the communal riots in contemporary India, especially
> those occurring in what police records often term 'trouble spots'
> with a long record of such ritualized violent encounters with
> the other community, do not appear as pathological parentheses
> in a sea of normality. They are, rather, points of condensation
> where the everyday knowledge, events, and interactions that
> may take the form of 'joking relationships' or minor irritants
> which in themselves cannot constitute a major insult, suddenly
> coalesce with other older myths and narratives of enmity and
> violence into chains of equivalence, re-constructing the peren-
> nial enmity and antagonism between the groups. The provok-
> ing event is often teasing girls, fighting among youths, or police
> brutality that in combination with a communally charged atmo-
> sphere built up over some time may ignite large scale violence.
> In such areas, communal violence and enmities are regular fea-
> tures of their social and political organization, with local strong-
> men and political activists maintaining systems of organization
> and vigilance with pre-designed roles and choreography, ready
> for the next confrontation . . . (Hansen 1991: 205–6)

The reason we are so concerned about Hindu–Muslim riots is that the two communities together constitute about 95 per cent of the population of the country. While Hindus have a numerical majority, the population of Muslims, spread across most Indian states, comprises about 15 per cent of the population and this makes India the second largest Muslim country in the world. For this reason alone, so long as there is discord between the two major communities resulting in violent clashes, the issue will remain as one of the grave concerns for the body politic. However, as has been brought out, the problem of communal violence is confined to certain clearly identified locations and is not as widespread as it is often believed to be. In dealing with the socio-economic factors, which are at the root of these clashes, attention should be centered on the identified areas which are really riot prone, so that the problem can be tackled in a focused manner and overcome.

For the country to move towards an era when communal clashes become history, there are two areas that need to be tackled on priority basis. The first is to address the deprivation amongst the Muslims and take all possible measures to promote their integration in the society. The second is to move away from the politics of identity.

As far as the issue of deprivation of Muslims is concerned, the subject has been comprehensively dealt with by the Sachar Committee. The committee has found that compared to other communities the Muslims are educationally backward, and their literacy rates among both men and women is lower than the national average. They suffer in regard to enrolment in educational institutions at all levels, that is, primary, school, higher, and technical education. The education imparted in the madraasas needs to be reformed. As a concomitant of backwardness in education, Muslims are also under-represented vis-à-vis their population in employment under the local, state and Central governments. Their representation is also poor in elected local bodies, state and Central legislatures (Sachar Report 2006).

The governments and social organizations must proactively work to ensure that measures are taken for Muslims to get better integrated in the society and this will be possible only through improved access to education and fairer representation in elected bodies.

It has been found that Muslims are often discriminated against in matters relating to housing and this is one reason for 'ghettoisation' of the members of the community, mainly in urban centers and even in certain rural areas. This is a fallout of social discrimination. An awareness has to spread that isolating the community in this manner is injurious to everybody's interests and comes in the way of holistic social and economic development (Lahiri 2009).

Politics of identity in India has revolved around castes, religion and language. These identities are brought to the fore and often promoted so that vote banks are created around the identities, resulting in electoral dividends. We have seen how the movement to build a temple in Ayodhya, basically a religious issue, has been used to achieve political objectives.

At the root of the identity issue is the individual. That religion (or caste or linguistic affiliation) need not define primary or exclusive identity of an individual has been very well demonstrated by Amartya Sen while describing his own identity thus:

> I can be, at the same time, an Asian, an Indian citizen, a Bengali with Bangladeshi ancestry, an American or British resident, an economist, a dabbler in philosophy, an author, a Sanskritist, a strong believer in secularism and democracy, a man, a feminist, a heterosexual, a defender of gay and lesbian rights, with a non-religious lifestyle, from a Hindu background, a non-Brahmin, and a non-believer in an afterlife and also, in case the question is asked, a non-believer in a 'before-life' as well. (Sen 2006: 19)

In the areas of political and social discourse, the religious or, for that matter, caste or linguistic identity of an individual should not be at the fore. This will happen only once a consensus can be achieved in society not to allow the religious affiliation of individuals to influence choices to be made in fields where religion ought not to play any part. Anecdotal evidence suggests that we too are changing; for instance, to become a youth icon today Salman Khan does not have to gloss over his religious affiliation as Mohammad Yousuf Khan, popularly known by his changed name Dilip Kumar, did a generation ago. Communal conflicts will become history once all major political formations decide to eschew communitarian politics.

Besides anecdotal evidence, there are some positive indications that our society is evolving in this direction. The incidence of communal riots in the twenty-first century has been on the decline and there has not been any major riot since the violence in 2002 in Gujarat. The problem though is still alive since incidents of involving communal violence continue to occur. Numerous communal clashes have occurred in various states since 2002, most notably in Uttar Pradesh, Maharashtra, Andhra Pradesh and even Gujarat. All these can be described as minor riots. Not so the clashes between Hindus and Muslims in Muzzaffarnagar in Uttar Pradesh in August-September 2013 where 62 persons were killed, many more injured and thousands displaced. Nevertheless, even these clashes were nowhere near the dimensions of the 2002 post-Godhra riots in Gujarat.

Despite the occurrence of sporadic communal clashes, intermittently in different parts of the country, communal violence is less of a law and order concern today than say terrorism, Maoist insurgency or crimes against women. As the future unfolds we can be reasonably optimistic that with the country developing and poverty declining, incidents of communal violence too would abate. With economic expansion the minorities too are getting their share of the pie that is getting bigger by the day.

5

THE DIASPORA COMMUNITY

Martha Nussbaum*

Whereas the United States is deeply enriched by its Indian American residents;

Whereas the Indian American community and the graduates of the Indian Institute of technology (IIT) in the United States have made valuable and significant contributions to society in every profession and discipline; and

Whereas IIT graduates are highly committed and dedicated to research, innovation and promotion of trade and international cooperation between India and the United States: now, therefore, be it

Resolved, That the House of Representatives-

Recognizes the valuable and significant contributions of Indian Americans to American society;

honors the economic innovation attributable to graduates of the Indian Institutes of Technology; and

urges all Americans to recognize the contribution of Indian Americans and have a greater appreciation of the role Indian Americans have played in helping to advance and enrich American society.

H.R. (House Resolution) 227, 26 April 2005

A model minority

On a dark, rainy August day, my research assistants and I visit the dazzling Swaminarayan temple in Barlett, Illinois, about an hour northwest of Chicago, a primary enclave of the Gujarati community in the United States. For the time being one of my assistants, Shaheen Haji, a Gujarati Muslim from California, has assumed the Hindu name of

100

Meenakshi Mehta so that we can hear opinions about Muslims frankly expressed. When I introduce her under this name, the face of our guide, a young man recently arrived from Gujarat, lights up with sympathy and recognition. With the beatific smile and the intense earnestness that one associates with members of authoritarian cults, he lectures us about the sect's beliefs, telling us that its followers believe that the voice of the sect's spiritual leader is the direct voice of god. Then, pointing to the beautiful carved limestone and marble ceiling, he asks whether we know why the ceiling glows as it does. I don't know, but I fully expect a spiritual answer. Our guide's eyes light up again. 'Fiber-optic cables!' he says. 'We are the first to bring this technology to a temple.'

Was the climate of religious hatred in Gujarat made in the United States? Many people think that the Hindu Indian American community has played a significant role in funding the spread of hatred in India in general, in Gujarat in particular. They believe, as well, that young Hindu Americans, deeply influenced by the ideology of the Hindu Swayamsevak Sangh (HSS), a US branch of Rashtriya Swayamsevak Sangh (RSS), and Vishwa Hindu Parishad (VHP), are growing up full of prejudice and suspicion. To what extent are these fears well founded? And how does my guide's strange combination of ideological docility with technological sophistication contribute to the situation?

Indian Americans have, for better or for worse, the status of a 'model minority'. Among, the largest ethno-national groups migrating legally to the United States, they currently number around 1.6 million, or 0.6 per cent of the U.S. population. They are the largest subgroup of South Asian Americans, and the third largest subgroup of Asian Americans, after Chinese and Filipino Americans.[1] According to the US Bureau of the Census, they have the highest median income of any ethnic group in the United States ($60,093).[2] They also have unusually high intellectual attainments. Many are doctors, engineers and information-technology experts. Many others are hotel owners and small business owners. (Recall that Narendra Modi's original invitation to the United States was issued by the Asian American Hotel Owners Association.) Many came for graduate school in these and other fields and decided to remain. Their greater fluency in English often gives them advantages over graduate students from other parts of Asia.

Indian Americans are as diverse as India itself: Muslims, Hindus and Christians, speakers of all the major Indian languages. The largest single subgroup is probably Gujaratis, who by one informal estimate account for 40 per cent of the US Indian American population.[3] Indian Americans are perceived as (because many of them are) as success story in scientific and technological achievement, a hard-working minority that enriches America and is therefore to be praised.

There is a negative stereotype connected with these images; that of hyper-competitiveness, exemplified, for example, by the (real) Indian father, in the much-praised documentary film *Spellbound*, who pushes his son to study lists of words for hours and hours in addition to his school-work, meanwhile promising a large donation for prayer in Hindu temples and for poverty relief in India – if his son wins the spelling competition. But Mr Kadakia's excesses are, to Americans, acceptable and even lovable. This is the sort of immigrant community that Americans eagerly embrace.

Despite its success and public acceptability, however, this new minority still faces discrimination. Sikhs, for example, were often harassed after 9/11, because ignorant Americans confused their turbans with those of the Taliban. The hostility towards polytheism that runs straight through the history of Anglo-Indian relations can found in the United States, too, if in a milder form. Meanwhile Indian Americans who are Muslims face yet other problems, being linked ignorantly to Arab Muslim terrorism. Indian Americans are only beginning to make an impact on US politics at the national level: one congressman from California in the 1950s (Dalip Singh Saund, first elected in 1956), several candidates more recently, but no current members of the House or Senate. Both of these bodies have an India caucus, but chaired by people who have no close connections with India. None of the top 100 research universities has yet had an Indian American president.

A primary reason for this lag is that Indian Americans were for the most part excluded from the United States until the 1960s. The Immigration Act of 1924 and, later, the Nationality Act of 1952 allowed virtually no immigration from India under their 'national origins' quota systems, which restricted immigration to an annual quota based on proportions in the population in 1890. From 1820 to 1960 only 13,607 people emigrated from the Indian subcontinent, and many of these did not remain in the

United States. The Immigration and Nationality Act of 1965 made the regime far less discriminatory, with each country permitted a quota of at least 20,000 per year. So immigration of Indians in large numbers is a relatively recent phenomenon[4].

Thus the 'diaspora community' occupies an insecure position – praised for its financial contribution to American success, but not honoured by the highest rewards that America gives its own. In this situation, it is natural that a search for identity would focus on a close tie to the motherland, all the more since many immigrants have family members who still live in India and think of their success as a way of contributing to its prosperity.

What, however, shall be the basis of their diaspora identity, given the community's internal linguistic and cultural diversity? The idea of Hindutva in its most innocuous form, that is, the idea of Hinduness, just being Hindu, offers an attractive answer to this question for many Indians. Consciousness of being Hindu is already greater in the United States than in India, where being Hindu is the unmarked majority thing to be. Membership in organisations such as the VHP-US and the HSS seems attractive as a way to feel solidarity with other community members and to bring up children who are conscious of their Hindu roots. HSS *shakhas* exist in most major US cities and many towns and suburbs. Typically they provide much more by way of community organisation and outreach than do organisations sponsored by the Indian government. When our local consul-general in Chicago started an Indian–American Friendship Association in 2003 – partly in order to provide a cultural alternative to the HSS and VHP, bringing Indians both Hindu and Muslim together with a diverse group of Americans around ideas of peace and non-violence – he had no funds to do the work, and despite his great energy the association got off to a slow beginning. His successor, closer in ideology to the HSS and VHP, let the association lapse, preferring to pursue those other connections. The Indian Muslim Council views the new Chicago consul-general not as an open enemy of Muslims but as someone who is surely not interested in fostering inter-religious friendship.[5]

Are there sinister connections between the HSS/VHP in the United States and violence against Muslims (and Christians) in India? The diaspora community is wealthy. It sends a lot of money back to India. It has been alleged that some of these funds, given in the United States for purposes of welfare and poverty relief in India, are often diverted to support violence against Muslims and other highly sectarian activities. At the same time the Hindu Students Council, a VHP-linked group, has been charged with supporting disruptive activities on US campuses against professors who teach Hinduism. And the Swaminarayan sect, a sect of Hinduism that originated in Gujarat, has rapidly grown in wealth and popularity throughout the United States, fuelling suspicion that it might also be a source of anti-Muslim sentiment and funding.

Are any of these suspicions well grounded?

The IDRF: funding hate?

When people in the United States make donations to charity, they naturally want to get the charitable deduction. Although some of the larger charitable organisations in India are registered as charities in the United States, many such organisations are not. Umbrella charities have therefore come into existence, US agencies that, rather like the United Way, distribute money to a wide range of charitable status. One of the largest of these is the Maryland-based International Development and Relief Fund (IDRF). In November 2002 Sabrang Communications, a group connected with Teesta Setalvad and her excellent investigative work in Gujarat, published a report online titled, 'The Foreign Exchange of Hate: IDRF and the American Funding of Hindutva'. The report has a long list of authors, but the primary author appears to have been Biju Mathew, who holds an endowed chair in the College of Business Administration at Rider University in Lawrenceville, New Jersey.

The report sticks to primary documents, quoting what the leaders of the IDRF say about their purposes on various official documents that they are required to file with the Internal Revenue Service and comparing what they say with the record of action by the organisations in India that they fund. According to the report, very little of the money donated to the IDRF goes directly to charitable work; two-thirds channeled to organisations under the umbrella of the RSS, which often have a variety of purposes other than poverty relief. All in all, less than 20 per cent of the funds go to organisations that are not openly sectarian or affiliated with the Sangh Parivar. Sometimes poverty relief is closely connected to conversion or "Hinduisation," encouraging, usually in rural areas, to become more observant in traditional Hindu practices or to return to them if they have converted to another religion. Some of the money is used for 'purely religious' purposes. Even the welfare money that is given is frequently doled out in a sectarian way. Finally, several of the RSS organisations to which money flows are 'directly involved in large scale violence against Muslim and Christian minorities'.[6]

There are some major problems with the Mathew report, which on the whole quite alarmist, even hysterical, in tone. Like some Indians, who think of conversion as always taking place at the point of a sword, the authors clearly have a deep suspicion of conversion and of any efforts that strongly encourage people to return to Hindu practices. One should certainly deplore any use of force or coercion in the conversion process, but it seems quite another matter to deplore the use of charitable funds to make converts and to encourage religious practices – so long as donors are correctly informed. Much of the anti-Christians and anti-Muslim feeling in India today stems from the idea that a religion that makes converts cannot be peaceable. This is, of course, a false notion, and one that we should all actively repudiate – as did Nehru and the constitutional framers, who protected the right to proselytise in the Fundamental Rights section of the Constitution. It is quite disturbing to see the authors, who clearly oppose prejudice against religious groups, buying into the same prejudices that made the lives of Muslims and Christians in India difficult. Hindus traditionally do not proselytise, but there is nothing wrong with their doing so.

Nor is there anything wrong with giving money to charity for purposes of proselytisation or religious activity. Many Americans do this all the time, usually supporting their own religions. Such donations are protected by the IRS definition of charitable donation. Donations to explicitly sectarian religious bodies account for more than 70 per cent of the charitable donations of Americans.[7]

Typically, as in India, US churches use the money that donors give them in a variety of ways. If a donor insists on earmarking it for a particular kind of welfare or poverty program, it is usually possible to arrange this (as, the report concedes, it is in the case of the IDRF). Much more often, though, US churches prefer (as what organisation does not) unmarked donations, so that they can use the money at their own discretion. Donors to US religious bodies can expect, as a matter of course, that some of their money will be used for welfare programs and some for religious activities – unless they stipulate otherwise. Most people have no problem with this arrangement, because they like to encourage people to practice the religion that they themselves love.

When a government agency gives taxpayer money to or through such religious bodies, then the distinction between religious and secular activities becomes very important. A significant problem that has emerged with regard to President Bush's 'faith-based initiatives' is that churches tend to mix charitable donations on adherence to religious practices. This is highly problematic when the donor is a government agency, because constitutional ideas of non-establishment and equal protection become relevant.

The RSS does a lot of welfare work, some of it very good. Indeed, one way in which it has expanded its base is by performing better than governments and other non-governmental organisations (NGOs) at some of these tasks. But it would surprise nobody if an RSS charity were to use part of the donated money for religious uses also.

Many private schools in India are run by Christian churches, and some of these teach (or it is feared that they teach) that Hindu deities are not really gods. Even if they do not say disparaging things about Hinduism, they certainly do not focus on helping students learn about their own tradition. Some of the programmes attacked by the Mathew report as objectionably sectarian are after-school programmes designed to correct the deficiencies of the curricula at these schools.[8] Mathew has made no convincing argument against such programmes.

The authors' indignation about the alleged diversion of funds to sectarian purposes seems to be based on the assumption that for a large wealthy charity to give only, or primarily, to Hindu organisations reinforces inequalities that Christians and Muslims already suffer. The report tends to equate an activity's being 'sectarian' with its being anti-minority. The two are, however, distinct concepts.

The report is in that sense defective. It does, however, raise two very serious questions. First, has the IDRF been honest about the fact that much of the money it collects will be used for religious purposes? Has it been adequately up-front with both donors and the IRS? Second, is there evidence that the money goes to support violence? On the first matter, the report shows clearly that there are serious issues that need to be addressed by the IDRF. In its official submission to the tax code the organisation states that its purpose is 'assisting in rural development, tribal welfare, and urban poor [sic]'. No mention is made of religious purposes. Furthermore, the organisation has denied any links to the RSS and VHP. In an online 'Response to Recent Malicious Media Reports', the IDRF wrote: 'It [the IDRF] is not affiliated to any group, "ism", ideology, political party.'[9] In another online exchange, Ramesh Rao quotes a vice-president of the IDRF as saying, 'There is no relation between VHP/RSS and IDRF. Fullpoint.'[10] The report on the IDRF provides ample evidence that much of the money goes to Hindu organisations that use some of the money in religious activities. This purpose should have been mentioned in the IRS documents. And the statement that the IDRF has no connection with the RSS, though it may be formally true, seems misleading if indeed, as the report convincingly argues, much of the money goes to organisations in India that do have RSS connections. Again, there need be nothing particularly subversive about these decisions, given that the RSS does run legitimate charities. But it should be made clear to both donors and the IRS what activities of these organisations are being funded. People who do not like the RSS or who believe that the RSS is capable of channelling funds to unpleasant uses should be aware that if they give to the IDRF they may be helping the RSS. This possibility is present, and should be disclosed, even if everyone involved in the IDRF believes that people's fears of the RSS are ungrounded.

As for the funding of violence, the report itself admits that this is a very murky area, where only indirect evidence exists. The documentation shows clearly that the IDRF funds organisations in states in which communal violence has occurred. Some of the organisations in Gujarat may have been involved in the Gujarat riots. Some (e.g. the VHP and Bajrang Dal) almost certainly were. But because the state has stonewalled all investigation about the Gujarat riots, it would be very surprising if any 'paper trail' exists. If the charitable organisations named in the Mathew report deny all involvement, as they do, there is no likelihood that complicity will ever be proven.

Here an analogy may be helpful. Think about the US South in the 1950s, when only the Ku Klux Klan and a few other extremists would openly admit to favouring violence, but where the whole society was suffused with attitudes that at least ignored and often condoned violence against African Americans, attitudes that clearly affected the behavior of the police and other officers of the law. Lynchings would not have occurred as they did if the law had not been prepared to look the other way and if juries had not been inclined to favour white defendants. Muslims in Gujarat today are in a position very similar to that of African Americans in the 1950s South. In such a case if a large U.S. charity funnelled lots of money to white organisations in Mississippi, one might well wonder to what extent those organisations shared the general social attitude favouring violence and 'white supremacy'. One might think that any organisation that focused charitable giving on Mississippi was underwriting a culture of violence. In the case of Gujarat the organisation of the Sangh Parivar are more closely linked to violence than any neutral charity in Mississippi would have been thought less closely and clearly linked than the Klan, since the RSS has many legitimate charitable purposes. If I were a donor who wanted to help poverty in Mississippi without condoning segregation and associated violence, I would probably look for an organisation whose philosophy was explicitly integrationist and whose board included a significant number of African American. Similarly, were I seeking to alleviate poverty in Gujarat, I would prefer an organisation even a Hindu religious, that has gone on record in word and deed against communal violence and whose good works are acknowledged as good by Muslims alongside Hindus. To donate to Hindu organisations is not in itself problematic in the way that donation to all white organisation would be as in the Mississippi case since the Hindu religion has admirable positive values, distinct from those of other religions, while the only rationale for separating whites from the blacks is racism. Still, in a context of ongoing violence one would want to make sure that the Hindu organisation in question did not also have exclusionary and supremacist attitude.

It is difficult to think that in Gujarat any all-Hindu charity is free from the attitude that produced the massacre; these attitudes are widespread, and deeply entrenched, in Gujarati Hindu society. Associations connected with the RSS are probably less likely than others to be free of such attitudes.

The IDRF could easily dispel such suspicions by inviting onto its board prominent members of society, whether Hindu or Muslim, who have publicly condemned the violence in Gujarat and by giving these people full access to information about the organisation funded. If the IDRF wished in addition to establish that it is non-sectarian, it would be a good idea to include prominent Muslims and Christians in this group. If it wished instead to establish that it takes a sectarian but unquestionably respectable course, it could find plenty of prominent Hindus, both in India and the United States, who have gone on record as opposing violence. Surely, the IDRF has strong reasons for clarifying its position of violence in light of the evidentiary difficulties created by the breakdown of the law in Gujarat. Moreover, questions need to be pressed concerning whether the IDRF has incorrectly represented its purposes on its tax forms.

How has the IDRF replied? Unfortunately, the reply itself raises further questions. On the one hand the head of the IDRF, Dr Vinod Prakash, asked the new head of the HSS in American professor Ved Prakash Nanda to look into IDRF activities for himself. Nanda, very concerned about the allegations in the Mathew report, says of Prakash: 'He has checked out where all his money goes. Money does go to the RSS also, but then those [are] RSS schools, etc. I have asked him point-blank if there is any truth in the report. I have gone to some of the places where the money goes. When the earthquake happened I had the full account of where and how the money was.'[11] Nanda, of course, cannot say definitively that no money is spent funding violence, and he could not make a well-grounded claim about the other allegations unless he had examined all the places funded by the IDRF up close and in greater detail than investigative journalists and others who have long tried to get this information. Thus his claim that the Mathew report is 'absolutely, totally wrong' is overconfident, making him seem somewhat naive and gullible, a person who believe what he wants to believe. But at any rate, the tactic of inviting people to check things out for themselves if the right way of rebutting the charges, and Prakash is to be commended for inviting Nanda, who is evidently a person of integrity, to inspect the organisation. It would be better still where the invited monitors to include people not closely linked to the RSS(HSS) and VHP, and who have openly condemned the Gujarat violence – including, one might hope, some prominent Muslims and Christians.

Other defenders of the IDRF have chosen a much less satisfactory tactic. The Bajrang Dal website Hindu Unity.org, whose violent tirades against Muslims we have noted earlier, immediately blasted Biju Mathew, calling him 'a sympathizer of fanatic Christian Missionaries and Islamic jihad organisations in India' and a 'Communist'. Readers were urged to report to the US Immigration and Naturalization Service the 'illegal' presence of a foreign communist in the United States.[12] (Mathew has been teaching at a Rider for many years, and clearly has a legitimate immigration status.) A long online attack on Mathew, commenting on the Bajrang Dal attack, asserts that 'there is a law that disallows Communists from settling down in the United States'. (Again, although there has been no such prohibition since 1990, it is the sort of falsehood that many people might believe, given our history.) As 'evidence' of his political views, the author writes: 'Biju Mathews [sic] has contributed to the Communist Party Magazine.' The author, Sekhar Ramakrishnan, goes on to say that Mathew's 'ulterior and hidden agenda' is 'to convert Hindus in India on a large scale to either Christianity or Islam and secondly to topple democracy in India to bring about Communism'. For good measure, Mathew's participation in a rally against the Iraq War is noted.[13] Another online article, written by Mohini Surin, describes a public meeting at Hunter Collee in which Mathew and Teesta Setalvad talked about Gujarat. Mathew is now called 'the Communist Kerala Christian associate professor', as if all were equally negative epithets. The author concludes that 'there is NO persecution but too much pampering, mollycoddling and foolish appeasement of dangerous psychopathic [sic] fanatical Muslims but quite the contrary'.[14] There is much more in the same vein. Meanwhile, a pro-IDRF petition circulated by the organisation itself attracted no Muslim signature, a somewhat worrisome sign.[15]

Surely the cause of the IDRF is not helped by the cheap red-baiting tactics of its supporters; nor is it helped by the evident anti-Muslim sympathies of some of the most vociferous. In 2003 Ramesh Rao and others issued a long rebuttal to the Mathew report, first online, then in a book form, called IDRF: Let the Facts Speak, it also uses tactics that are discouraging. The authors begin by providing a good deal of data about projects funded and make some analytically sharp points about the amorphous concept of 'Hinduisation' used in the Mathew report.

But then the authors oddly devote a lot of space to defending the history and politics of the RSS, an organisation with which the IDRF has denied all ties. They seek to establish that the RSS, although it did little in the anti-British independence movement, did in some ways nonetheless contribute to the eventual success of that effort.[16]

Much of the rest of the book is devoted to personal attacks on Mathew and his co-authors. Instead of saying that some of their statements are highly speculative and unproven (as they themselves acknowledge), Rao and his fellow writers trumpet 'Lies, More Lies, and Nothing But Lies'[17] – a personal attack on the authors' scholarly integrity – despite the fact that most of the Mathew report is grounded in IRS documents filed by IDRF itself. The authors are then attacked as 'leftist', as having Pakistani connections, as having published in the official journal of the Communist Party of India (Marxist) and so on. Mathew is from Kerala, a state whose development achievements, especially in health and education, are by now proverbial in the economic literature; those achievements took place under a democratically elected communist government. The fact that Mathew would publish in their journal is about as surprising as the fact that an American would publish something in an official journal of the Republican Party.

In short, the Rao rebuttal has many of the same defects that are discernible in other Rao publications: instead of calmly presenting pertinent information that would allow readers to form an intelligent judgment, it launches digression and tirades that do little to make one think well of the IDRF, to the extent that this report has its approval.

The funding controversy involves a set of questions without clear answers. Some people of goodwill and integrity believe the accusations launched against the IDRF, and the other people of goodwill and integrity (such as Nanda) believe that they are groundless. We can only hope for a thorough investigation and, above all, for more frankness on the part of IDRF about its RSS connections. If the IDRF were to distance itself publicly from the segment of Gujarati society that condones violence against Muslims, and were to include on its board prominent critics of communalisation, these steps would reassure donors that all was well. Meanwhile one solution for Indian Americans of goodwill, suggested by Ved Nanda of the HSS, is to focus a large proportion of charitable giving on US poverty, of which there is plenty, contributing to one's new community in ways that are easy to trace because they are local.

Forming a diaspora identity

Indian Americans are a remarkably diverse group. Their linguistic, regional, cultural and religious heterogeneity makes it difficult to bring them together, in the United States, around any common national identity platform. And yet Indian American parents of children born in the United States naturally want to take their children somewhere to learn about their cultures and their history. A small, highly heterogeneous minority surrounded by the dominant culture, with no opportunities for their children to learn the family's native language (whether Hindi, Bengali, Gujarati, Malayalam or some other) in public schools and all too few opportunities to study the history and traditions of India in English, will naturally fear a loss of identity. But whereas Italian Americans, Irish Americans, Polish Americans, Greek Americans and many other immigrant groups have cultural organisations expressive of national identity, there is no large organisation for Indian American that offers this minority identity without at the same time offering a religious identity. The need for such an organisation is widely felt, but any such enterprise is difficult to start up, given the variety of communities that would need to be brought together. The Indian consulates of major US cities would be a natural choice for such a role. However, they have no funds for this sort of activity, they have to compete with already strong and well-funded organisations established along communal lines, and the fact that the consul-generalship changes every five years must surely dissuade career civil servants from launching such ambitious enterprises.

Consuls-general are not political appointments, but their careers can depend in subtle ways on their relationship with political parties. Under the BJP government it would perhaps have been unwise to show strong support for an inter-religious national organisation. Even so, when Surendra Kumar arrived as consul-general in 2000, he worked hard to foster good connections with the academic community, to create interesting events involving visiting politicians and judges and to find occasions for public celebration that were appealing to all religions and groups. Independence day (August 15) is always celebrated at the consulate, but Kumar added an annual celebration of Gandhi's birthday, which included panels and interfaith discussions. He also founded an India–American Friendship Association, of which I was a vice-president.

The aim of this new association, announced with much fanfare, was to offer an alternative of the more religiously based organisations in the city, bringing together a group of Americans diverse in race, ethnicity, and religion (Kumar focused on having Hispanics, African Americans and Euro-American as officers) and a similarly diverse group of Indians. But the association had barely begun to enrol members and raise money through dues when Kumar's term was up and he was transferred to Nairobi. Whether by design or accident, his successor (also named Kumar) has been less ambitious in this regard. While retaining strong ties with existing Hindu organisations and cooperating to some extent with the Indian Muslim Council, he has done nothing to bring the religions together, letting the Friendship Association lapse completely, for some reasons. (Meanwhile, even from Kenya, Surendra Kumar continues to bring the Chicago community together, as with a large gathering he organised on our campus in June 2006.)

Indian American families in Chicago, then, have nowhere to go to connect with their national heritage in a religiously pluralistic atmosphere. The Indian Muslim Council runs a wide variety of cultural programs targeted at Muslim families. The HSS and VHP offer Hindu Indians a wide range of family and youth programs. Some other groups (such as the Swaminarayan sect) focus on a particular regional community: children in the youth groups run by this sect at its various centers in the United States learn both the Gujarati language and Indian history, with a focus on Gujarat and the life of Swaminarayan, the seventeenth-eighteenth century Gujarat saint who began the movement. Sometimes these different groups hold inter-faith activities. A growing interest in cricket in the suburbs does bring people together across communal and even national lines, with Pakistani Americans playing alongside Indian Americans. But by and large national identity is structured as a part of religious identity.

Organisations vary greatly in the degree to which they promote or discourage inter-religious cooperation. A relatively unhelpful group has been the Hindu Students Council (HSC), an organisation founded in 1990 (with headquarters in New Jersey), with chapters on the campuses of about 75 US colleges and universities. This group, which claims to be a site where people can learn about Hindu heritage and culture, melds national identity with Hindu identity, suggesting that the two are inseparable. The HSC has close links to the VHPA (the US wing of the

VHP); it is mentioned on VHPA websites as if it is part of the organisation. Many VHPA websites openly refer to the HSC as one of its projects
to carry out its work for the 'protection' of Hindu culture. One explicitly
lists the groups as part of its own organisational structure in America.[18]
HSC chapters have taken political stands, supporting the VHP on issues
such as the building of a Ram temple at Ayodhya. Mona Mehta of the
University of Chicago, one of the founders of a new alternative group of
student organisations, writes:

> The version of Hinduism that is 'dished out' to HSC members is
> highly problematic, simplistic, exclusivist and upper caste in its
> orientation . . . HSCs glorify Hindutva, refer to Indian culture
> as Hindu culture and present a simplistic version of Indian his-
> tory as one of a glorious Hindu civilization that was faced with
> constant onslaughts at the hands of 'foreigners' such as Muslims
> and Christians.[19]

The vast majority of Indian American students who join the organisation know too little about the different positions on these issues to criticise such politicised formulations; nor do they typically know about the
group's VHP links. The organisation does not encourage critical discussion. And it has taken highly political positions on campuses themselves,
such as the protest at Emory University against the presence of Paul
Courtright in the Department of Religion; other protests against visiting
lectures by Courtright have also been led by HSC on other campuses. It is
very likely that many student members would not support these activities
if all the various arguments and positions of the HSC were thoroughly
and accurately presented to them.

Mehta and many other students of Indian origin (mostly graduate students) have supported the foundation of alternative youth groups that are
progressive and pan-South Asian. These include Chingari, which means
'spark' in Hindi, 'forum for discussion, reflection and action on social,
political and cultural issues concerning the South Asian diasporic experience in North America';[20] OY! (Organizing Youth), a volunteer-based
organisation for South Asian youth, focusing on economic justice;
the New York City-based Youth Solidarity Summer (YSS), which
trains young South Asian activists to work on social justice issues; the

Chicago-based SAPAC (South Asian Progressive Action Collective); and the New York City-based SAALT (South Asian American Leaders of Tomorrow), 'dedicated to ensuring the full and equal participation by South Asians in the civic and political life of the United States'.[21] It is to be hoped that such groups will introduce a spirit of friendship and public discussion into lives of young Indian Americans.

Meanwhile the HSS, the US arm of the RSS, has received a lot of anxious criticism in recent years, focused on communal violence in India. In competing to attract American members, the HSS has become aware of its problematic public image and apparently has decided to try to put itself about the fray. In a very interesting development, its leadership was assumed in 2002 by a noted human rights scholar, Ved Prakash Nanda. Nanda, born in the Punjab in 1934, studied law in Delhi before coming to Chicago for a master of law at Northwestern University and a doctorate in law at Yale University. He is currently Vice-Provost for Internationalization and a university professor at the University of Denver School of Law. He has been president of the World Jurist Association and the World Association of Law Professors. He has published widely on international law. He also works in aviation and space law, international human rights and comparative law.[22] He recently served on the American Bar Association Task Force on Reforming the UN Commission on Human Rights.

Nanda is, then, an eminent and widely respected scholar. His views do not appear to be at all ideological. What he writes in the area of international law is thoughtful and balanced. His position in US politics would seem to be that of a thoughtful liberal. Recently he has been very vocal in urging intervention in Darfur and has published a number of newspaper articles, discussing the history of international law on genocide and crimes against humanity.[23]

Nanda is a person of high intellectual and ethical quality. He is personally warm, flexible with a good sense of humour, and not at all interested in defending a rigid party line. He apparently agreed to assume the leading role in the HSS out of deep concern about the bad publicity surrounding it. Very likely the same reason led the HSS to seek him out: he is someone whose connection to the RSS/HSS is spiritual rather than political, and he cares about rescuing its spiritual values from the bad press it has received for its political connections. At the same time, as head of the organisation he has to walk a delicate line. There are evident limits to what he can say in his official capacity.

Nanda has a history that might have led him to hate and fear Muslims. Like Gurcharan Das, he is a child of Partition, who had to flee his home during the violence. With the help of some Muslim friends, the family (which had lived in a Muslim area) was able to board a train to Jammu, and then walked 300 miles, eventually arriving in Delhi. He tells me that he acquired no animosity to Muslims as a result of the experience. Although he was brought up as a Hindu during childhood, he was not particularly religious. Later he began going to the RSS *shakha* in Delhi. He regards the central values of the *shakhas* as cultural: Hindus need to understand their own past and its major texts.

One part of Hindu tradition that Nanda admires is Gandhi's non-violence, and he regards Gandhi's assassination as horrible. When I asked him whether in general he thinks it unfortunate that 'some people connected with RSS would espouse violence', he replied, 'I do, very strongly.'[24]

Nanda views the RSS as a large organisation with tremendous internal variety. Some people go to extremes that he repudiates: 'There can be people who can be seen as going to an extreme . . . after looking back and saying for hundreds of years we have been under foreign rule and Muslims have been at times cruel rulers.' Others are bad communicators; during our conversation he frequently mentioned 'misunderstanding'. He also stressed that there are people in the organisation who were 'very uncomfortable with the violence' in Gujarat. He himself strongly condemns that violence. When I asked whether leading figures in the RSS had publicly condemned the violence, at first he said they had, but when pressed he backed off, saying only that they did not condone it. When I mentioned the equivocal character of Vajpayee's Goa speech, he backed off even further, saying, 'I think unfortunately you are right in that India and the Indian situation, from my perspective here, at times, I can't read it very well.'

As for the US situation, Nanda insisted, in a lecture at the University of Chicago in November 2005, that the HSS has officially condemned the Gujarat violence. When asked to supply dates and specific quotations, however, he responds that the organisation does not keep good records. He is able to vouch only for his own statements: 'For the record, after these tragic events in Gujarat I frequently spoke out in private conversations and public gatherings denouncing the violence on the part of both Hindus and the Muslims. HSS, too, has always deplored communal violence' (Nanda 2006c). These statements are inadequate: they equate the roles of Hindus and Muslims, and they convict Muslims of perpetrating violence when there is no evidence that they did so. Similarly inadequate is Nanda's insistence that the tactics of people who attack American scholars of Hinduism have 'perhaps been inarticulate and harsh'.[25] After all, we are talking about death threats and physical violence. At the University of Chicago in November 2005, Nanda offered his personal apology privately to Paul Courtright for what Courtright had experienced at the hands of the Hindu right and stated publicly that he had offered an apology. Throughout the meeting, at which he was the only representative of the Hindu right, he behaved with great civility and even warmth to those who disagree with him. One might say that he is simply playing a double game. It seems more likely, however, that he is decent who knows that there are limits he cannot transgress if he wants to continue to lead the organisation, and who continues to believe that the organisation, at least in its US incarnation, is on balance of force for good.

Recently, under Nanda's leadership, an HSS affiliate, the Hindu Education Foundation (HEF), has taken a leading role in seeking changes in California sixth-grade textbooks that teach the history of religions. All parties to this controversy agree that there were some inaccuracies that ought to be corrected. The HEF, however, also wants to suppress references to the caste system, to historical inequities in the treatment of women, and to migration of Hindus into India. In effect they seek the imposition of the problematic Hindu-right version of history. Opposed by the overwhelming majority of scholars in the United States who work on South Asian history, the group eventually lost on all these issues after some very divisive hearings.[26] On this issue, Nanda appears not to have exerted a moderating influence. He is correct in his claim that many Hindus in the United States are extremely sensitive to any portrayals of their religion that they consider derogatory – given the history of denigration of Hindu polytheism as barbaric and as basically equivalent to untouchability and sati – and in his assertion that voices from the community must be listened to respectfully.[27] Serious listening, however, should not lead to any compromise in the presentation of historical truth, as best we know it.

In the end, Nanda's position involves a certain amount of wishful thinking. He loves the spiritual and cultural values of the organisation and he wants it to be best it can be. He is satisfied that in the United States these good aspects are predominating. But when a problem arises, he does tend to see the world through rose-tinted glasses – believing Vinod Prakash's account of the IDRF on the basis of the incomplete evidence and believing that what is happening in India is a result of miscommunication rather than bad ideology.

> I think RSS have been such poor communicators . . . Because I know them and I know what is in them, their ideology. You are absolutely right that their ideology is seen by people who are very thoughtful and understand nuances, and they felt that their ideology is full of hate and Muslims and Christians are not welcome. And the point is that they can't articulate and present their viewpoint in a way that people would understand them. I feel sad about that.

Nanda refers frequently to difficulties in the Hindu Indian 'psyche', based on a long history of subordination and 'a kind of inferiority complex and not having your own identity and then finally saying that we have got to stand up to it. So that is where the difficulty comes'. And it seems to his more considered, more nuanced, view that the failure of the RSS to put forward the spiritual values that Nanda himself embraces is attributable to this kind of psychological wound, which leads to violent wishes.

> You can't say that everyone who sees them and feels their hatred are all wrong and the RSS is totally right. But at the same time I have known them having seen what they profess, and not being able to articulate it and project it is the sad part. And that's why I feel that here are some remnants in the psyche that I talked about.

Whatever the complications of his views about the RSS, Nanda seems to be providing strong and positive leadership for the HSS in America. He emphasises the importance of the values of inter-religious cooperation, non-violence and sex equality as key parts of what is taught in the US *shakhas*. He himself travels a lot, giving many speeches to local organisations. He speaks often to Muslim groups also, although he acknowledges with regret that there are no organised inter-faith activities including Muslims.

The Hindu right is comparable to the US South, torn between explicit appeals to racism and a more inclusive politics. First, a time comes when politicians begin to realise that an open appeal to hatred and division is not acceptable. (Vajpayee and Advani seem to have reached this moment.) Next, we would expect that over time a 'New South' would come into being – that is, politicians who really do not believe in sectarian animosity would gradually take the place of those who conceal their animosity behind code words. There are no clear examples of this next generation among BJP leaders in India. In the United States, however, Nanda (albeit not a young man) is an example of what this 'next generation' of Sangh Parivar public figures might be. He obviously has difficulty dealing with the ambiguous statements and the questionable behavior of the older generation, but his own direction is clear. The evident tension between his personal commitments and his most important Hindu diaspora organisation is far from clear and that its internal politics are complex.

Swaminarayan Hinduism

In Barlett, Illinois, my research assistants Shaheen (aka Meenakshi) and Emily and I tour a temple carved in Gujarat and shipped in countless containers to Chicago, its ceiling glowing with light supplied by fiber-optic cables. We are in the heart of one of the most powerful subcommunities in the diaspora, the Swaminarayan sect of Hinduism, which organises the local Gujarati community.

The Swaminarayan sect arose from the achievements of a distinguished Hindu holy man, Sahajanand Swami (1781–1830), who was born near Ayodhya but spent most of his life in Gujarat. In religious terms, the sect is a part of the *vaishnava* wing of the *bhakti* movement, a devotional type of Hinduism focused on spirituality rather than on ritual practice. Its two main subdivisions focus on Vishnu and on Shiva; the *vaishnava* movement focuses on Vishnu. Mahatma Gandhi was from a Gujarati *vaishnava* family, and the Swaminarayan movement shares many of Gandhi's ideals, in particular his emphasis on non-violence.

Although his version of Hinduism was devotional and emphasised spirituality, Sahajanand Swami was also a dedicated social reformer. A leading scholar of the movement describes him as 'the last of the medieval Hindu saints and the first of the neo-Hindu reformers'.[28] He was very strongly opposed to repressive practices connected with women. Together with British governor John Malcolm, he led a crusade against female infanticide, which was widespread among the upper castes. (By one early nineteenth-century estimate, 20,000 infant girls were killed every year in two regions of Gujarat. The sex ratio among the upper castes was wildly skewed, with about one female to five males in these two districts.)[29] Sahajanand travelled widely preaching against this custom. He taught that infanticide was forbidden because it involved three moral wrongs: murder of a member of one's family, child murder and murder of a woman, who deserved protection. He even offered money to help families pay dowry expenses. (Female infanticide was banned by law in 1870.) Sahajanand also worked to improve the social standing of widows, to discourage the practice of widow self-immolation and to foster female education.

On caste issues, Sahajanand was also progressive; though not entirely rejecting the caste system, he did much to undermine its rigidity and strictness. Although his first successor was a Brahmin like himself, the next was a lower-caste layperson. Men from non-Brahmin caste began to be initiation as *sadhus* (priests), and today people from many castes belong to the sect, both as followers and as *sadhus*. According to a current member of the sect, 'people at the temple are unconcerned with anyone's caste background . . . Even in our youth group meetings we are taught that caste discrimination is bad'.[30] In Gujarat, where Hinduism as a whole remains deeply caste-driven, the sect – at least in its BAPS (Bochasanwasi Shree Akshar Puroshottam) version – provides a marked contrast.

Sahajanand's progressivism, however, did not challenge the traditional view that men should have the controlling role in religion. His views about the separation of the sexes during ritual were much more conserva-tive than those of more traditional Hindus.

During his lifetime Sahajanand was already seen as an incarnation of God, and his message of religious devotion attracted a large fol-lowing. Swaminarayan priests or *sadhus* lead a celibate and otherwise ascetic life. Among other things, they are not allowed to touch money or to look a woman straight in the eye or stand close to one. (This is the reason given for keeping women at quite a distance from the sacred images during worship, even in the United States.) Lay followers must take five vows: to espouse non-violence; to avoid intoxicating drink or drugs (including tobacco); to avoid adultery; to practice honesty and truth telling (in business affairs, for example) and not to eat or drink anything from a defiling caste. This last prohibition has now softened, both in India and in the United States, to a requirement that followers not defile themselves or others. In US temples today, traditional Hindu rules regarding food and even marriage have also been abandoned.

The sect has grown, along the way producing some internal splits. (The BAPS segment is by far the largest of the three existing sub-divisions.) It now has temples all over the world. In India the movement is concen-trated in Gujarat; other strong areas include London, East Africa and the United States. The Chicago temple, which opened in 2004, occu-pies 30 acres; its elaborately carved Italian marble and Turkish limestone (worked in India and shipped to the United Sates) must have cost mil-lions. The wealth of the community supporting the sect is conspicuous, both here and in other larger temples, for example in Edison, New Jersey, New York City and Houston.

Yet this devotional sect, known for its asceticism, reforming tenden-cies, and emphasis on non-violence, is today widely suspected of having some connection with the violence in Gujarat. Over the years, in part because of the important role of the Patel clan in both temple and poli-tics, there has come to be at least a perception of a close link between the Swaminarayan sect and right-wing Gujarati politics. Given the com-plexity of Gujarati civil society, it is difficult to assess the validity of this perception. Certainly, the sect is admired and praised by state politicians of all stripes, at both national and state levels. It is therefore not surpris-ing that the BJP, Gujarat's leading party, would also praise it. On account of the sect's statements discouraging conversion (its leader, the current Pramukh Swami, urges people from all religions to become better in their own religion, not to convert), it has become associated in the public mind with opposition to Islam and Christianity, the two proselytising religions in the area.[31] There is nothing sinister about the remarks themselves, however; they seem to be directed against coerced or insincere conversion. The public perception that links Pramukh Swami with communal tensions has a flimsy basis. On the other hand, the high visibility of leading BJP politicians' connections with the sect – both L.K. Advani and Narendra Modi appear as prominent guests at the sect's public events, and members of the group play a prominent role in BJP fund-raising – continues to arouse concern among people eager to stop communal violence (Williams 2004: 131–37). Swaminarayan *sadhus* say that they are a purely religious organisation and have no political views: the only link with BJP politicians is that 'we are Hindus and they are Hindus, so we are linked together' (Williams 2004: 131–37).[32] Politicians come to the festivals because they want Pramukh Swami's blessing. Interviewed in 1999 by scholar Raymond Brady Williams, Pramukh Swami stated: 'We don't have any political ties with them but only relations with respect to religion and spirituality.'[33]

The government seeks the goodwill of the sect, but the sect must also retain the goodwill of the government, to get building permits, obtain land and so forth. The sects has conspicuously avoided making any statements about Gujarat would implicate the party in power. Pramukh Swami has publicly condemned the violence and urged peace and reconciliation. Devotees were urged to aid anyone in distress; prayers for all the victims were offered; an interfaith memorial ceremony was held, including Muslim and Christian leaders, on the premises of the temple complex in Gandhinagar, the capital of Gujarat. Celebration of an important festival was cancelled in order to offer prayers for the victims at 9,000 BAPS centers around the world. Pramukh Swami met with local political and social leaders to discuss how to avoid further violence.[34] Nonetheless, the sect did not condemn the actions of police and government. Its even-handed deploring of the plight of 'victims' is all too even-handed. Many small and relatively powerless NGOs also remained publicly neutral. The admirable Self-Employed Women's Organisation incurred widespread criticism for its failure to denounce

Modi and for its leadership's continued willingness to work with him. This choice, however, can be explained by the extreme vulnerability of the organisation and its members, who would be at risk of violence had their leadership condemned the violence. It is not clear that the neutrality of BAPS can be similarly justified, given its enormous wealth and social influence.

In the United States, the link between the Swaminarayan movement and the Hindu right is even less clear. The Hindu Students Council helped to organise an international gathering of 2,000 students from 50 countries in July 2003, the 'Global Dharma Conference', with support from the VHP; this meeting was hosted by the large Swaminarayan temple in Edison, New Jersey, and Pramukh Swami gave the closing address via a satellite link. The RSS supported the event, but so, too, did many other organisations, including Jain, Buddhist, Sikh and Native American organisation[35] (though not Muslim or Christian organisations). The event was pluralistic up to a point and focused on ethical values. Nonetheless, the close linkage between the HSC and the VHPA has many people construe the event as indirectly exclusionary.

On balance, it seems likely that the Swaminarayan sect is a rather passive force for peace, and that the Gujaratis who are both affiliates of the sect and supporters of Narendra Modi derive the values of communal division that animate Gujarati civil society from another source, not from any malign teaching by the sect. The sect's practices of isolating (and implicitly denigrating) women are certainly unhelpful in the context of both the US and the Indian democracies, and its emphasis on absolute obedience to the words of Pramukh Swami surely reinforces the devaluation of critical and independent thinking that is all too prominent in Gujarat. Other closer connections to the Hindu right are widely suspected but difficult to find.

We went to Bartlett hoping to find some answers to these questions, but we discovered little. The temple seems to be managed by a large number of young men brought in from Gujarat, who describe themselves as volunteers. We got no sense of how they make their living; perhaps the temple gives them room and board in exchange for their work. Our guide's rigid, unmotivated smile troubled us, suggesting a kind of cultic obedience that Americans typically associate with authority and the abnegation of critical independence. He told us a lot about non-violence and the unity of all religions, and he showed us displays of major events in Indian history, which replicated the orthodox Hindu-right line in every detail (the Indus Valley civilisation was Hindu, there was no migration from outside and so forth). It is an old maxim of textual criticism that agreement in truth does not show a common origin, but agreement in error does. An interesting variant on orthodoxy, however, was the prominent place given on the wall picturing great Hindu artists, to the Sufi Muslim poet Kabir and the Rajput queen Mirabai, who left her husband and home to sing holy songs. We liked the creative books for little children that taught the Gujarati language and told engaging versions of the leading texts of Indian literature (including not only the canonical epics, but Sanskrit drama as well). Shaheen (aka Meenakshi) even thought of buying, since she learned to speak Gujarati from her grandmother but cannot read or write it. No ideology of hate seems to be circulating via those books, at any rate. Nor did we hear any anti-Muslim remarks.

Our guide tried hard to paint a positive picture of the sect's views and treatment of women, telling us that their relegation to the back of the temple was a mark of the great respect the *sadhus* have for them. He himself treated us quite respectfully, though cautiously once he knew that 'Meenakshi' spoke Gujarati and that I (dressed in a cotton salwaar bought in Ahmedabad) had done women's development work in Gujarat. When we discussed matters of communal conflict, however, the guide, so eloquent about fiber-optic cables, clammed up completely. (Part of the time he was being supervised by an older man, who spoke Gujarati but seemed to speak no English, and followed both him and us around the temple.) He told us that he had still been in Gujarat in 2002, so I observed that living through so much communal tension must have been difficult. He responded that the common people get along fine; it is just politicians who exploit these issues for their own gain – exactly the line espoused by the Bollywood movie *Dev*. 'Would you, then', I asked, 'say that Narendra Modi was partly responsible for what happened?' At this point his face took on a genuine expression, one of embarrassment, and he said quickly, 'I don't know about these things.' (It was shortly after this that the older man began to follow us around, as if the guide had summoned him through some other fancy technology.) Later, when we were discussing activities for families,

I asked whether they had joint activities with the HSS. 'HSS?' he said, as if he did not understand the word. I told him that the HSS has a *shakha* close by, in Villa Park, which meets every week. (I had learned this from scholar Shridhar Damle, who lives there.) Did they team up to do joint activities? Our young man simply pretended utter confusion at this point, as if he had never heard of the HSS.

The sect must know of the nearby presence of an active chapter of the HSS. Moreover, there is nothing sinister about having a connection with the HSS or about jointly organising activities for families and children. The local Gujarati community is likely to be involved in both groups. So why was our guide so eager to pretend he knew nothing about it? Clearly, the sect wants to avoid being enmeshed in political controversy or fielding questions about its political role.

Historically, the HSS has a more troubling set of ideological commitments than the Swaminarayan sect. Today it is possible that a reversal is under way. The HSS is at least under leadership that appears to be moving the organisation towards self-criticism and change. In contrast, the values of obedience that animate the Swaminarayan sect militate against self-examination. Although its values of peace and harmony are admirable, the Gujarati sub-community that it serves is in particular need of critical thinking, even in its US incarnation (which issued the invitation to Narendra Modi). The Swaminarayan sect's tremendous wealth and burgeoning influence suggest that it could play a more active and positive role than it has as yet in promoting interfaith respect and the condemnation of politicians who do not exemplify its own highest values.

The US diaspora community is and will remain an important part of Indian politics. Its wealth, high educational and scientific achievements, and close attachment to India all make it an important source of both resources and emotional energy. This community has the potential for great good, particularly in the areas of poverty and disaster relief. It also has the potential for harm, if it is not sufficiently attentive to the sources of violence in Indian politics and civil society. People of goodwill can end up supporting things that they do not know they are supporting. Attitudes that may or may not lie at the heart of RSS values and traditions may get reinforcement from people who would very likely repudiate those attitudes if they were laid out clearly. Young people who want a way of connecting to their roots when they go off to college may end up unwittingly supporting a highly politicised organisation that does a lot to undermine communal harmony and engages in questionable tactics against scholars whose ideas leaders do not like.

The diaspora community has one huge problem: the lack of an institutional structure for minority-national consciousness that is not, at the same time, a sectarian religious structure. As long as the prominent civil society organisation are Hindu or Muslim, community consciousness will remain polarised, and perhaps even more polarised than in India, where people see different groups every day and cannot help having the idea that their country is pluralistic and diverse. If an HSS *shakha* or a Swaminarayan temple is the only India you know, your sense of India will be narrower in consequence.

The problem of communalisation is probably not going to abate, given the preponderant influence of Gujaratis, both economically and numerically, in the diaspora community. To invite Narendra Modi to address a major convention is to issue a challenge to US pluralism – which the US State Department answered in the correct way. The episode suggests that the Gujarati community has insulated itself too much from critical thinking and democratic openness.

Such difficulties within the diaspora community can be addressed only by creative and active leadership, leadership that is willing to take an unequivocal stand on issues such as the abuse of power and the breakdown of the rule of law in Gujarat and the abuse of the Internet in threat against scholars. Consul-generals can do more than most have done, as the activities of Surendra Kumar show, but leaders of existing organisations also need to do more to foster genuinely pluralistic inter-faith activities and a spirit of internal criticism. This should clearly be Nanda's next step, and it is to be hoped that his members will support him in taking that step.

More could also be done by the Indian government itself as the nation moves towards closer relations with the United States in the aftermath of Manmohan Singh's highly successful visit to this country in June 2005. India–US relations currently focus on science and technology and on the nuclear issue. A much deeper set of ties could be fostered, including concerted action against religious violence and prejudice in all its forms. When I spoke to Sonia Gandhi in June 2004, she talked about fostering outreach programs in the United States that would bring news of the Gujarat violence, and communal tensions generally, to a diverse US audience. Basically, she was hoping that I would jump start such a movement, either through the university or through our consulate.[36] Surely the government of India itself has a role to play here even at a distance, and its outreach efforts. If the government can establish links with leaders of the US community who care about such issues, perhaps Surendra Kumar's India–American Friendship Association can be restarted, this time on a national scale, as a forum for public debate, intellectual exchange and social mingling.

The same issues that are central in thinking about education in India are central when we think about the children of the diaspora: critical thinking, knowledge of the world and the imagination of otherness. These capacities do not grow automatically, and they have enemies: dogmatism, fanaticism, ignorance, false ideology and emotional obtuseness. The future of the US community will be determined by the outcome of the struggle between these two sets of forces. As Ved Nanda says, there are those 'remnants in the psyche' that sometimes prevent people from living up to the best in them.

Notes

* Reprinted by permission of the publisher from Martha C. Nussbaum, *The Clash Within: Democracy, Religious Violence, and India's Future*, pp. 302–329. Cambridge, MA: Harvard University Press.

1 H.R. 227, 26 April, 2005.

2 Raymond Brady Williams, in conversation and in articles cited below.

3 For this history, see Williams (2001: 224–225)

4 Conversation with Rasheed Ahmed, Indian Muslim Council, United States, November 2005.

5 http://www.proxsa.org/newsflash/index.html.

6 www.generousgiving.org/page.aep?sec=28&page=211.

7 Yvette Rosser, quoted in Rao (2003: viii–ix).

8 http://www.idrf.org/reports/indiapost/ResponseToOutlook.html.

9 Ramesh Rao, sulekha.com, 15 June 2002.

10 Interview with Ved Prakash Nanda, August 2004.

11 http://www.aletrnatives.ca/article1049.html.

12 "Biju Makes Front Page of Bajrang/VHP Site," http://insaf.net/pipermail/ insafny_insaf.net/2003-January/000018.html.

13 http://www.hvk.org/articles/1203/34.html.
14 Ibid.
15 Rao et al., IDRF, chap. 6.
16 Ibid., 69.
17 See http://www.vhp-america.org/whatwhpa/orgcomponents2.htm.
18 Mona Mehta, e-mail attachment, 31 July 2005.
19 The group's website is http://www.chingari.org.
20 Mona Mehta, e-mail attachment, 31 July 2005.
21 Interview with Ved Prakash Nanda, August 2004.
22 See biography in the Association of American Law Schools directory of law teachers.
23 See, for example, Nanda (2006a), Nanda (2006b).
24 Interview with Nanda, August 2004.
25 Ibid.
26 See Golden (2006), Burress (2006), Krie ger (2006).
27 Nanda (2006c).
28 Williams, *Introduction to Swaminarayan Hinduism*, 31.
29 Ibid., 28.
30 Mayank Patel, paper written for a religion course at Emory University, quoted by permission.
31 Williams (2004: 131–137).
32 Ibid., from a personal interview he conducted.
33 Ibid.
34 Patel, paper written for a religion course at Emory University.
35 I am grateful to Mayank Patel for this information.
36 And indeed, the Centre for Comparative Constitutionalism at the University of Chicago held a large conference in November 2005, with 'India: Implementing Pluralism and Democracy' is announced topic. Many non-academics came to hear Amartya Sen's keynote address, but the detailed discussion of issues such as the free press, the role of the US community and the role of education that formed the rest of the conference were attended by only a handful of non-scholars.

6

GANDHI'S CRITIQUE OF RELIGIOUS FANATICISM

Ramin Jahanbegloo

When Mahatma Gandhi arrived on the political scene of India in 1915 his non-violent and pluralistic approach to religion and politics brought him in direct conflict with the issue of communalism and religious fanaticism. So far as the question of Hindu–Muslim unity was concerned, Gandhi had to confront two major perceptions in the Indian National Congress party. On the one hand, there was a group of Hindus within the Congress party, which believed that the Indian Muslims were not sufficiently patriotic so far as the Indian nationalism was concerned. In contrast, there was a great feeling of pan-Islamism among some of the Muslims leaders of the Congress, intensified with a colour of doubt and scepticism in regard to the future of Islam in India. Viewed in this perspective, the divergence between Gandhi and communalists was very deep from the very beginning of his entrance on the Indian political scene. The reason is simple: for Gandhi the power of the nation was vested with the people, rather than religion. And the reason why Gandhi saw religion in the Indian intra-civilisational context rather in an ideological dimension was that he believed in the inherent harmony of the Indian cultural and social order, which had been disrupted by modernity.

Gandhi was a pluralist in religious matters, though he was not a relativist. His equal respect for all cultures and religions implied the idea of mutual learning and inter-faith dialogue. When Gandhi affirmed: 'I do not want my house to be walled on all sides and my windows to be stuffed. I want the cultures of all lands to be blown about my house as freely as possible' (Gandhi 1921: 170)[1] he was essentially talking about a spirit of openness in the quest for the sacred which transcends religiosity and organised form of religion. Thus, Gandhi did not privilege any one religion over another, not even Hinduism. Religion for him was a matter of soft spirituality, rather than hard rituals and hard institutions. Therefore, he proclaimed: 'For me the different religions are beautiful flowers from the same garden, or they are branches from the same majestic tree. Therefore, they are equally true, though being received and interpreted through human instruments equally imperfect' (Gandhi 1937).[2]

Gandhi's pluralist attitude towards God and spirituality developed over time through his study of different religions and his friendships with individuals of faiths other than his own. Already as a young student in London, he believed that every religion can shed light on a seeker's path. Later he realised that self-centredness in religious matters as in political matters created prejudice and misunderstanding. This is the language he used in an article in *Indian Opinion* in 1907: 'If the people of different religions grasp the real significance of their own religion they will never hate the people of any religion other than their own . . . there may be many religions, but the true aim of all is the same' (Gandhi 1938–1994: 338). Essentially, for Gandhi, the very foundation of religion is ethics. As such, Gandhi's religious pluralism is an application of his approach to ethics. For Gandhi, the only way to find God is to serve all human beings. As he puts it:

> Man's ultimate aim is the realization of God, and all his activities, social, political, religious, have to be guided by the ultimate aim of the vision of God. The immediate service of all human beings becomes a necessary part of the endeavour, simply because the only way to find God is to see Him is His creation and be one with it. This can only be done by service of all. (Bose 1957: 25)

As we can see the nuclear element of Gandhi's pluralistic thought is his idea of an ethical God, who is all-inclusive and develops love and ahimsa in every human conscience. As Gandhi explains:

> God is that indefinable something which we all feel but which we do not know. To me God is Truth and Love, God is ethics and morality. God is fearlessness. God is the source of light and

life and yet He is above and beyond all these. God is conscience. He is even the atheism of the atheist. . . He is the greatest democrat the world knows, for he leaves us unfettered to make our own choice between evil and good . . .[3]

On this basis, we could say that Gandhi's attitude towards the fellowship of all religions is founded on their shared moral values. It means the belief in a common ethical basis that transcends all religions and harmonises them. In other words, Gandhi believed in a universal religion that included all religions and negated the spirit of divisiveness and exclusion, for these could not bring peace either inwardly or in society as a whole. This is why he affirmed: 'Temples or mosques or churches . . . I make no distinction between these different abodes of God. They are what faith has made them. They are an answer to man's craving somehow to reach the Unseen.'[4]

For Gandhi, God was not a monopoly of any religion. Already during his time in South Africa, he wrote: 'The time had passed when the followers of one religion could stand and say, "ours is the only true religion and all others are false'".[5] As such, there is no trace of proselytising or dogmatism in Gandhi's proclamation of his spirituality. He truly believed in Hinduism as a religion of non-violence and regarded the *Bhagavad Gita* as the philosophical foundation of his non-violence. But his openness to other religious sources and his particular study of the *New Testament* and the *Qur'an* helped him to view Islam and Christianity as partners in his search for Truth.

Gandhi by his own confession subscribed to the *Advaita Vedantic* view of religion. Therefore, he believed that the moral aspect of Truth is universal and present in all religions. It is difficult to understand Gandhi's philosophy of non-violence and his struggle for communal harmony without some kind of idea of what he means by Truth. According to Gandhi, a Satyagrahi had to participate in Truth and Truth 'could not depend on individual impressions and decisions alone'; it had to be extraordinarily disciplined, with a 'commitment to suffer the opponent's anger without getting angry and yet also without ever submitting to any violent coercion' (Raghavan 1991: 314–20). For Gandhi, truth was not only a metaphysical category but also a moral and a political concept signifying the importance of truth in social life. In this regard, Gandhi did not dismiss the concept of truth from the sphere of action. He tried to comprehend which uses of truth cancel pluralism and which conversely warrant pluralism. Truth is a moral link between different actions and it cements the gap between political freedom and moral necessity. Therefore to adhere to truth is based on the principle that moral life is centred around truth-following. Gandhi's argument in support of this is that truth is the foundation of non-violence and he often claims that truth and non-violence are the two sides of the same coin. In other words, truth has the character of a moral imperative, which is self-imposed on the truth-seeker by his or her 'inner voice'. The inner voice cannot be fully defined in words, but it may be described as one's conscience. Gandhi refers to the inner voice as a truth force or soul force that would lead us to peaceful solution to conflicts in life. So the purpose of listening and responding to the inner voice is for practical and progressive reality transformation. Guided by the inner voice, Gandhi decided to undertake fasts as form of self-sacrifice through which he wished to arouse compassion in other people's hearts. He fasted many times to end bloodshed between Hindus and Muslims even in his last fast when he was 78. For him fasting was a political action, but also an experiment with truth. The idea of experiment with truth primarily means abiding by the principle of truth in thought, action and speech. For Gandhi an experiment with truth is always empirical and open to inspection and revision. Thus the Gandhian experiments with truth are moral practices which are undertaken in the midst of a political action. Gandhi chose politics as the field of his experiments with truth. That is why for Gandhi, truth and non-violence go together, truth as the end and non-violence as the means. Gandhi considers non-violence as a means to truth because he believes that only a non-violent person can attain truth. Here Gandhi holds that non-violence is the practical and political way to truth and leads us to the ultimate victory of truth over untruth. In other words, a Satyagrahi or a follower of non-violence does not mind sacrificing his life for the sake of truth and thus is ready to encounter any difficulty on the path of truth. Satyagraha as a political weapon also does not lose its moral grounding in view of the fact that for Gandhi morality and politics go together. Therefore, in the Gandhian philosophy of non-violence truth wears a human face and speaks to everyone in the inner voice, thus compelling each person to respond to the fundamentally political problem that the public world continually raises.

The Gandhian principle of non-violence is presented, therefore, as a challenge to fanaticism that is always necessarily implicated with the foundation of an ideologised religion. Gandhi's critique of an ideologised religion leads him to a concept of the spiritual, which finds its expression in the 'spiritualisation of politics'. For Gandhi, the aim of spiritualizing politics is constructing the future of 'human living together'. He, therefore, understood religion as a morally conscientious and socially responsible exercise of spirituality. Gandhi believed that every social and political opportunity must be made use of to forge a harmony among communities. His dialogue with Indian Muslims must be understood in this conceptual network. He sought to practically demonstrate this need of dialogue with Islam when he answered to a number of his critics in a speech at Sholapur in 1927 when they accused him of being partial to the Muslims. He said:

> You may say I am partial to the Mussalmans. So be it, though the Mussalmans do not admit it. But my religion will not suffer by even an iota, by reason of my partiality. I shall have to answer my God and my Maker if I give anyone less than his due, but I am sure that He will bless me if He knows that I gave some one more than his due. I ask you to understand me.[6]

While in South Africa where he started to work in 1893 as a lawyer for a Muslim merchant from Porbandar, Abdullah Sheth, Gandhi was able to establish close ties with the Indian Muslims. He felt familiar with the cultural identity of the Indian Muslims and shared a common life with them. 'When I was in South Africa', he affirms,

> I came in close touch with Muslim brethren there . . . I was able to learn their habits, thoughts and aspirations . . . I had lived in the midst of Muslim friends for 20 years. They had treated me as a member of their family and told their wives and sisters that they need not observe *purdah* with me.[7]

It was Abdullah Sheth who suggested Gandhi for the first time to read Sale's translation of the *Qur'an*. Gandhi's first approach to the *Qur'an* developed his basic understanding of Islam that was strengthened by a second reading during his prison time in January 1908 in Transvaal. But previous to this adventure, Gandhi had forged a broad resistance movement largely based on the participation of Indian Muslims and in alliance with the Hindus against racial discrimination in South Africa. In his very first week in Pretoria, Gandhi called a meeting at a Muslim merchant's house. 'It was a largely Muslim gathering with 'a sprinkling of Hindus'.[8] The bringing together of Hindus and Muslims in the Gandhian experience of *satyagraha* in South Africa was Gandhi's first important step towards the idea of communal harmony. This experience strengthened in him a powerful motivation in the joint commitment of Hindus and Muslims to truth and justice irrespective of their differences. By navigating easily between different religious traditions and communities, Gandhi convinced his fellow Indians of the validity of inter-faith solidarity. Gandhi had decided to affirm in South Africa that communal harmony and dialogue among religions was the only cure for violence and injustice. However, in this enterprise he was also helped by his readings of spiritual writers like Tolstoy. 'We believe' asserted Gandhi,

> Tolstoy's teaching will win increasing appreciation with the passage of time . . . He pointed out that selfish priests, Brahmins and Mullas had distorted the teaching of Christianity and other religions and misled the people. What Tolstoy believed with special conviction was that in essence all religions held soul-force to be superior to brute force . . . There is no room in religion for anything other than compassion. A man of religion will not wish ill even to his enemy. Therefore, if people want to follow the path of religion, they must do nothing but good . . .[9]

There is no doubt that Gandhi's action in South Africa and later in India was shaped by his conviction that all religious boundaries are arbitrary and false. That is why Gandhi's view of religion brought under its fold people belonging to different religions. Though deeply religious by nature, Gandhi did not believe in rituals, customs, traditions, dogmas and other formalities observed for the sake of religion. Like Rabindranath Tagore, Gandhi's religion was not confined to temples, churches, books, rituals and other outer forms. Thus Gandhi's concept of religion was not bound by any dogmatic behaviours. Gandhi was convinced that a mere doctrinaire approach in the field of religion does not help to create inter-religious fellowship. Dogmatic religions do not help to promote creative dialogue. The religions dogmas directly or indirectly breed an attitude of dislike towards other religions. Mahatma Gandhi's mission was to find a common ground based on non-violence among religions. He wanted not only to humanise religion but also to moralise it. He would reject any religious doctrine that was in conflict with morality. This is how he challenged people of faith to recognise their religious hypocrisies. Gandhi argued that a person who believes in Truth and God cannot go to a mosque, synagogue, temple or church one day and the next day foster hatred and violence. He made no exception in the case of Islam. Gandhi did not hesitate to declare that

> even the teachings themselves of the Koran cannot be exempt from criticism. Every true scripture only gains by criticism. After all we have no other guide but our reason to tell us what may be regarded as revealed and what may not be.[10]

On another occasion, Gandhi completed this argument with an observation that takes us to heart of his position on religion and interreligious dialogue: 'My effort should never be to undermine another's faith but to make him [or her] a better follower of his [or her] own faith.'[11] Gandhi knew that independence could not come about by the efforts of the Hindus alone. He, therefore, involved the Indian Muslims in the struggle. Discontent with the 'us-and-them' divisions and mutual disregard between the Muslims and the Hindus, Gandhi engaged in an open dialogue with Islam and the Muslims. He never accepted the argument that Hindus and Muslims constituted two separate elements in Indian society. That is why Gandhi's willingness to go out of his way to win over Muslims to the Congress won him many friends and admirers among the Muslims. In South Africa, 'Gandhi had needed the wholehearted support of Muslim friends who went to jail with him, lived in his communities, supported him with funds, and generally made his victories possible' (McDonough 1994: 39). On his return to India, Gandhi's increasing involvement with the Khilafat movement helped him secure a political authority in the Indian Congress and strong legitimacy in the eyes of the British Raj. Gandhi's involvement with the fierce believers in a pan-Islamic movement surprised most of his friends and followers, but 'his stance was essentially a natural progression from the status he had prized in South Africa as spokesman for Muslim grievances, and from his championship of the Ali brothers during the war . . .' (Brown 1989: 140). It is true that the Muslim leaders like Abdul Bari, Maulana Azad and the Ali Brothers had already initiated and developed the Khilafat movement when they were joined by Gandhi in April 1918, but there is no shadow of doubt that Gandhi's arrival gave a new strength to the agitation. Gandhi expressed his sympathy for the Muslims and the Khilafat movement at the Delhi Imperial War Conference in 1918 and later followed it up by a letter to the viceroy, Lord Chelmsford. 'As a Hindu', he mentioned, 'I cannot be indifferent to their cause. Their sorrows must be our sorrows.'[12] Evidently, Gandhi's sympathy for the Khilafatists was more than a simple fellowship, since he was trying to invite the Muslim leaders to join his *satyagraha* and adopt non-violence. Moreover, by joining the Khilafat movement Gandhi wanted to consolidate the fraternisation of Hindus and Muslims. As such, two years later in response to Maganlal, who was troubled by Gandhi's involvement with Muslims, he wrote: 'If I had not joined the Khilafat movement, I think, I would have lost everything. In joining it I have followed what I especially regard as my dharma . . . I am uniting Hindus and Muslims . . .'[13] Anthony Parel points out that in Hind Swaraj Gandhi employs *dharma* as an ethical equivalent for mutual assistance.[14] This, of course, was how Gandhi had approached the Muslim leaders in the Khilafat movement. He 'treated the *Khilafat* as a "*Kamadhuk*", the mythical cow that gave whatever one asked of her' (Qureshi 1999: 104). Later Gandhi explained: 'I have been telling Maulana Shaukat Ail [*sic* for Ali] all along that I was helping him to save his cow, i.e. the *Khilafat*, because I hoped to save my cow thereby.'[15] Gandhi's emergence as a strong political allied and an inspirational leader in the Khilafat movement was not, however, a simple matter of a great number of Muslims being converted to his non-violent style of action. The Ali Brothers were never totally converted to non-violence, though 'as a gesture toward Hindus, Muhammad Ali stopped eating beef; departing from age-old practice, numerous Muslim homes celebrated Eid without beef' (Gandhi: 252).

Gandhi's deliberate attachment to the Muslims and the Khilafat movement had helped him in reaching broader groups in Indian society and rising as a non-elitist leader in the Congress. However, the main line of division between Gandhi and the Khilafat leaders was that of violence. 'The Muslim violence on the Malabar coast and the incipient violence of the extremer Khilafat leaders generated fear and resentment in other communities . . .' (Brown 175). Many Muslim leaders like Shuakat Ali or Jinnah refused to accept non-violence as a moral absolute though they accepted it as a temporary strategic device to overcome the British. Jinnah was among the Muslim leaders of the Congress Party who in 1915 welcomed Gandhi on his return from South Africa, but the variations on the non-cooperation campaign produced certainly some early divergences between the two men. Jinnah, whose opposition to Gandhi's non-cooperation was well-known to the British and to other members of the Congress Party, was especially perplexed by the fact that by 1920, the Congress, like most of Muslim India, had accepted Gandhi as their charismatic leader. 'Your methods have already caused split and division in almost every institution that you have approached hitherto', proclaimed Jinnah,

> and in the public life between Hindus and Hindus and Muslims and Muslims and even fathers and sons; people generally are all over the country and your extreme programme has for the moment struck the imagination mostly of the inexperienced youth and the ignorant and the illiterate. All this means complete disorganization and chaos. What the consequence of this may be, I shudder to contemplate . . . I do not wish my countrymen to be dragged to the brink of a precipice in order to be shattered.[16]

It is true that Gandhi's Congress–Khilafat non-cooperation movement was partly responsible for Jinnah's scepticism and bitterness, but it goes also without saying that Jinnah's political style and the exaggerated 'Britishness' that he adopted in his private and public life left him little opportunity to compete with Gandhi's simplicity and transparency. It is absolutely clear that Jinnah's dream of an independent India did not go hand in hand with the Hindu–Muslim unity. Generally speaking, though Jinnah pleaded for the Muslim cause before the Congress and the Hindu community through the years 1916 to 1938, he gradually gave up the idea of Hindu–Muslim unity and advocated the exclusive cause of Muslim India in the decade before the Independence. Jinnah's correspondence with Pandit Nehru in 1938 bears clear testimony that Jinnah had reached a dead-end in his dealings with some of the leaders of the Congress. For Gandhi, the questions of Indian home rule and the Hindu–Muslim unity were not separate issues, whereas for Jinnah the opposite was true as he mentioned in response to Gandhi:

> We maintain and hold that Muslims and Hindus are two major nations by any definition or test of a nation. We are a nation of a hundred million, and what is more, we are a nation with our own distinctive culture and civilization, language and literature, art and architecture, names and nomenclature, sense of values and proportion, legal laws and moral codes, customs and calendar, history and traditions, aptitudes and ambitions, in short we have our own distinctive outlook on life and of life. By all canons of international law we are a nation.[17]

Jinnah strongly resented relating the *swaraj* movement in favour of Khilafat. He was, in the words of Durga Das, 'amazed that the Hindu leaders had not realized that this movement would encourage the Pan-Islamic sentiment' (Das 1969: 353). Gandhi, however, saw in Khilafat an opportunity to seek Muslim cooperation in the *swaraj* movement. His political intentions in doing so were more democratic than theocratic. It would be wrong, therefore, to underline, as some analysts of Indian contemporary political history do, that Gandhi was 'unwittingly responsible for jettisoning sane, secular, modernist leadership among the Muslims of India and foisting upon Indian Muslims, a theocratic orthodoxy of the Maulvis' (Karandhikar 1968: VIII). Jinnah, like Ambedkar, criticised Gandhi's insistence on the spiritualisation of Indian politics. He was against Gandhi's view of bringing religious issues into the public sphere, because he considered it disastrous and irrelevant for political matters in India. Jinnah himself, however, prioritised religion, since he was considered as a 'communalist' by many of his critics (Raouf 1944: III). In other words, in his long political career, Muhammad Ali Jinnah clearly perceived Indian self-determination in the framework of the Muslim community. As for

Gandhi, it was quite the opposite. Ever since his first writings in South Africa, Gandhi replaced the divisive view of religion by a pluralist and tolerant one by equating religion with ethics. This, of course, was how Gandhi reacted against the specter of the 'Hindu raj' and the cry of 'Islam is in danger' that widened the communal gulf in India and created the climate of hatred between the Hindus and the Muslims. For Gandhi, the difference between the Hindus and the Muslims was not confined to religion. It was due, according to him, to the lack of truthfulness and transparency in the political realm. Therefore, as a social reformer, Gandhi believed strongly in the affinity between spirituality and politics. It is not surprising that he chose to work with individuals whose primary interests were best defined in spiritual and ethical terms. He once declared that a true Muslim could not harm a Hindu, and a true Hindu could not harm a Muslim (Bhana and Goolman 2005: 143). It was probably in this spirit that Gandhi developed a friendship and a great esteem for both Maulana Azad and Khan Abdul Ghaffar Khan. In 1939, during his third visit to Ghaffar Khan, Gandhi proclaimed:

> If you dissect my heart, you will find that the prayer and spiritual striving for the attainment of Hindu–Muslim unity goes on there unceasingly all the twenty-four hours without even a moment's interruption whether I am awake or asleep . . . The dream [of Hindu–Muslim unity] has filled my being since the earliest childhood. (Tendulkar 1967: 291)

Gandhi was certainly influenced by the tolerant Islam of Ghaffar Khan and Maulana Azad and their non-fanatical reading of the *Qur'an*, but it is also true that the spiritual teachings of the Mahatma and his political pragmatism captivated the minds of these two men. Azad was 'the Muslim on whom Gandhi relied for advice' and was 'a prominent example of the communal inclusiveness of Congress' (Brown 1989: 309). In this respect Gandhi's friendships and disputes with Indian Muslim leaders remains deeply instructive for the understanding of his critique of religious fanaticism. Gandhi required Muslims to recognise that Islam like any other religion was neither the whole truth nor nothing but the truth. That is why Gandhi rejected the idea that there was one privileged path to God and he encouraged inter-religious dialogue, so that individuals could see their faith in the critical reflections of another. One of his notable innovations was the inter-faith prayer meeting, where texts of different religions were read and sung to a mixed audience. If this provides an evidence as to what sort of cultural pluralist Gandhi was, we can add that for him the sacred texts of all religions had contradictory trends and impulses; sanctioning one thing, but also its opposite. Gandhi, however, urged that people recover and reaffirm those trends that oppose violence and discrimination while promoting justice and non-violence. For him a culture or a religious tradition that denied individual freedom in the name of unity or purity was coercive and unacceptable. When some women were stoned to death in Afghanistan for allegedly committing adultery, Gandhi criticised it, saying that 'this particular form of penalty cannot be defended on the ground of its mere mention in the Koran' and he added, 'every formula of every religion has in this age of reason to submit to the acid test of reason and universal justice if it is to ask for universal assent'.[18]

Reading Gandhi today as a critique of religious violence helps us to problematise Gandhi's non-violence against forms of religious fanaticism and communalism. In other words, in order to develop a religious approach to non-violence that is dialogical and pluralistic, one needs to become fully conscious of the fact that unity between different religious communities depends on the practice of mutual understanding and inter-faith learning. Gandhi's approach to the problem of Hindu–Muslim relations in India was based on the view that it is not an ingrained and ineradicable enmity. Gandhi, it hardly needs to be repeated, believed in a plural political and religious society. Therefore, his vision of communal harmony and his critique of religious fanaticism went hand in hand with his theory of participative democracy and shared sovereignty. He wrote: 'Mutual respect for one another's religion is inherent in a peaceful society. Free impact of ideas is impossible on any other condition. Religions are meant to tame our savage nature, not to let it loose . . .'[19] Thus it could be said that in the case of Gandhi religious pluralism and struggle against fanaticism was not of mere political agenda, but a matter of faith in the dynamism and potentiality of the Indian society to tackle the evil of communalism at the structural and mental levels.

Notes

1 Gandhi, M.K., *Young India*, June 1921: 170.
2 Gandhi, M.K., *Harijan*, 1 January 1937.
3 Gandhi, M.K. *Young India*, March 1925, quoted in (Datta 1953: 30).
4 Quoted in Krishna (1969: 62).
5 Quoted in Nanda (1990: 13).
6 Gandhi, M.K., *Gandhi and Communal Problems*, compiled by Pradip Pachinde (Pachinde 1994: 5).
7 Gandhi, M.K., *Collected Works*, vol. 2, p. 52 quoted in McDonough, Sheila: *Gandhi's Response to Islam*, D.K. Print World, New Delhi, 1994, p. 17 (McDonough 1994: 17).
8 Gandhi, Rajmohan, op.cit., p. 75.
9 Gandhi, M.K., *Collected Works*, vol. 10, p. 370 quoted in(McDonough 1994: 28–29).
10 Gandhi, M.K.: *Young India*, 5 March 1925.
11 Interview with Dr John Mott, *Young India*, 21 March 1929.
12 Gandhi to Chelmsford, 29 April 1918, in *Collected Works of Mahatma Gandhi*, vol. 14, p. 377.
13 Quoted by Gandhi, Rajmohan, op.cit., p. 245.
14 See Gandhi, M.K., *Hind Swaraj and Other Writings*, (Parel 1997: 42).
15 *Young India*, 1924–1926, 1327, quoted by (Qureshi 1999: 104).
16 Quoted in Sayid (1945: 264–65).
17 Quoted in Sherwani (1969: 78).
18 Gandhi, M.K., *Collective Works*, 21, 246.
19 Quoted in Raghvan (1986: 374).

7

COMMUNAL VIOLENCE IN INDIA
Ending impunity

Harsh Mander

In the later decades of India's struggle for freedom from British colonial rule, an immense groundswell of popular support and mass mobilisation had surged behind Mahatma Gandhi. The majority of people of this land shared his vision for the new India, of a resolutely secular nation, with freedom and equal rights of citizenship for people of every faith, community, caste, class, colour and gender. There was also influential mass support for more radically egalitarian and democratic ideologies of the Left and Dalit movements. However, leaders of the Muslim League fought for and secured an independent Islamic nation carved out from Muslim majority segments of India, convinced that people of diverse faiths cannot live together with peace and equality. Extremist Hindu organisations were also implacably opposed to Gandhi's humane and inclusive Hinduism and nationalism, and one from among their ranks assassinated him just months after India became free.

The tolerant and pluralist secularism of modern India is rooted in millennia of the civilisational experience of Indian people, a civilisation in which every major faith in the world found a home, was nurtured, and evolved, alongside a rich and challenging diversity of sceptical, rationalist, atheistic and agnostic beliefs. Indian secularism entails therefore not a denial of faith, but equal respect for all faiths – including always the absence of faith – with all the symbols, philosophical trappings and ethical imperatives of these different systems of belief. It derives from an unbroken multi-hued tapestry of practice and teachings of tolerance

142

COMMUNAL VIOLENCE IN INDIA

and love, including those of Buddha, Ashok, Akbar, Kabir, Nanak, the Sufi saints and Bhakti reformers, and Gandhi. It is overlaid in its modern incarnation of democratic secularism with not just equal respect for all faiths but also the guarantee for the practitioners of these diverse faiths of equal rights and protection under the secular law of the country.

Two years after Gandhi fell to the bullets of his assassin, the Constitution of independent India – drafted by one of India's most revered leaders from a community which traditionally was subjected to the most savage caste discrimination, B.R. Ambedkar – secured further the secular, socialist and democratic foundations of the nation reborn. This secular Constitution pledged equal freedoms and rights to all citizens regardless of the god they worshipped or chose not to worship, regardless of whether they were women or men, regardless of their caste, wealth, ethnicity, the colour of their skin, and the language they spoke.[1] Although the state had no religion, the Constitution guaranteed all people the freedom to not just follow but also to propagate their own religion.[2]

The struggle for freedom was never just a battle against colonial bondage, but also one for the India that would be rebuilt when the colonial rulers left Indian soil. It is significant that many of those who gave most for the secular democratic idea of India, such as Gandhi and Maulana Azad, were deeply devout practitioners of their respective religious faiths. And foremost among those who fought for religious states, Jinnah – father of the Pakistani nation – was not a practising Muslim most of his life, and Savarkar, founder of militant Hindu nationalism, which he called Hindutva, was an avowed atheist. The battle is not, and never indeed was, between the actual teachings of any religion. It was about whether political mobilisation and institutions should be built around identity and difference, or on acceptance of, respect for and even celebration of diversity.

Despite the solemn guarantees of the Constitution of free India and the proud and shining legacy of Gandhi and the non-violent struggle that he led – dimmed a little but by means extinguished by the slaughter that accompanied Partition – pseudo-religious fascistic organisations continue to challenge the secular democratic vision for India. Their onslaughts grew more militant since the 1980s, with a resurgence of their aggressive alternate politics of difference and hate, and their propagation of a homogenised, combative, patriarchal and upper-caste version of the essentially pluralist majority Hindu faith. Since then, their mobilisation has been organised most powerfully around the symbol of a crumbling medieval mosque, the Babri Masjid, in a small town called Ayodhya, which they claim had been constructed after demolishing a temple built to commemorate the birthplace of revered Hindu deity Ram. A massive mob assault on this Muslim place of worship in the sacred Hindu town of Ayodhya resulted in its brutish demolition in 1992. As the highest courts of the country unconscionably prevaricated in their attempts to arbitrate the rival claims to the disputed site, extremist Hindu organisations continued to demand stridently that the site of the destroyed mosque be handed over for the construction of the Ram temple regardless of the decision of the courts, or independent historical and archaeological evidence. The movement to build a grand Hindu temple at the precise site of the Babri Masjid is not about competitive reverence for Ram or Allah, but an assault on the idea of secular democratic India itself, and the ancient traditions of equal reverence for all faiths, as well as the modern constitutional guarantees of equal protection and equal rights as equal citizens before the majesty of the secular law of the land.

***

Since Independence, India has seen scores of group attacks on people targeted because of their religious identity.[3] Such violence is described in South Asia as communal violence.[4] While there is insufficient rigorous research on numbers of people killed in religious massacres, one estimate suggests that 25,628 lives have been lost (including 1,005 in police firings)[5]. The media has regularly reported on this violence, citizen's groups have documented grave abuses and state complicity in violence, and government-appointed commissions of inquiry have gathered extensive evidence on it from victims, perpetrators and officials. Despite this, it has been remarkably difficult to hold perpetrators and state authorities accountable for committing, encouraging, aiding or enabling (including through deliberate inaction) such violence.

There are many who believe that the pursuit of legal justice by the survivors actually blocks prospects for reconciliation, because the testimonies of survivors would result in the arrest and trial of their disjoined neighbours. In Gujarat after the 2002 carnage, some well-meaning organisations in fact have actively and successfully brokered the negotiated return of Muslims to their villages, accepting on behalf of the victims the condition that they would not give evidence of the names of their attackers to the police or in courts. They regard such negotiated homecoming of internally displaced people on highly unequal conditions, to be processes of forgiveness and reconciliation (Mander 2006).

However, I believe that no authentic reconciliation is possible if it is built on the foundations of persisting injustice. The return of survivors transacted on the condition of abandoning all their prospects of securing justice as guaranteed under the law of the land for all citizens, for slaughter, rape, arson or loot, is not reconciliation in the sense of a restoration of trust and goodwill but it is capitulation by a crushed and hapless people. Forgiveness is authentic only if the person who forgives has the option not to forgive. In Gujarat, we are witnessing not forgiveness but abject surrender. It is interesting that Gandhi also stressed that real forgiveness can only come from a situation of strength and agency of the person who has suffered. He says that 'Abstinence is forgiveness only when there is power to punish; it is meaningless when it pretends to proceed from a helpless creature'. He illustrates this with a metaphor: 'A mouse hardly forgives a cat when it allows itself to be torn to pieces by her.'

Contemporary India has a troubled history of sporadic bloodletting in gruesome episodes of mass violence, which targets men, women and sometimes children because of their religious identity. The Indian Constitution unequivocally guarantees equal legal rights, equal protection and security to religious minorities. However, the state's record of actually upholding the assurances in the secular democratic Constitution has been mixed.

The Centre for Equity Studies is engaged in an ongoing study that tries to map, understand and evaluate how effectively the state in free India has secured justice for victims of mass communal violence. It does so by relying primarily on extracting the state's own records relating to four major episodes of mass communal violence – beginning with Nellie (1983),[6] Delhi (1984),[7] Bhagalpur (1989) and Gujarat (2001), primarily using the powerful democratic instrument of the Right to Information Act 2005. In this way, it tries to hold up the mirror to governments and public authorities and institutions, to human rights workers and to survivors themselves – of official documents, supplemented by reports of Judicial Commissions of Enquiry (which are routinely set up after major episodes of mass communal violence and typically forgotten subsequently) – to evaluate the accountability and impunity of public officials after episodes of mass violence.

International law lays down that states owe victims of gross human rights violations reparation[8], and reparation includes (1) access to justice in the form of criminal prosecution, (2) access to truth and (3) material and non-material restitution. The Indian state has substantially failed victims of mass violence on all these counts. Particularly in the massacres before Gujarat in 2002, there have been very few criminal trials relative to incidents of serious violence. The record of cases brought at least to trial has been a little better in Gujarat, only because of greater civic activism[9] not because of the efforts of state institutions to secure justice. On the contrary, the state of Gujarat has resisted efforts to ensure justice to the survivors of the brutal mass violence.

Many of those who are engaged with this study have experience of working directly with survivors of mass communal violence and learning from the narratives and experience of victim survivors. There is also a very large body of information, of reports of judicial commissions, of investigations by civil rights groups,[10] of academic research and journalism available on episodes of mass communal violence. All of these suggest a recurring pattern of structural injustice and impunity leading up to, during and in the aftermath of such mass violence. These lay out the broad hypothesis of this study, which we tried to test against the state's own records.

The study does not investigate the build-up and prevention of such episodes of mass communal violence. It investigates the access of victims to protection, and justice and reparation after communal violence actually breaks out. Our hypothesis is that many victims of mass communal violence do not succeed in registering their complaints with the police. Where the state has a shaky record in failing to protect people from mass violence, and is perceived as partisan, victims have little confidence in its ability to pursue their complaints. But the greater problem is the climate of fear and both official and non-official intimidation, which renders it difficult to register complaints after episodes of communal violence. Where victims have complained, the police is known to often refuse to register these complaints or to register complaints but deliberately leave out crucial details narrated by the victims about the events, perpetrators and witnesses. Investigation is often found to be slipshod, and large numbers of complaints are closed without the alleged perpetrators being charged with and tried for offences. Trials are long and have often been unsuccessful.[11] As with criminal trials, the process of compensating victims is also typically very protracted. Survivors and activists, also testify that securing compensation is very cumbersome, and can take many years, and rates and standards of financial assistance extended to survivors of mass communal violence tend to be far too low to enable survivors to rebuild their lives. And finally, there is scant official disclosure on the State's response to mass violence and therefore a denial of survivors to 'truth'.

In summary our hypothesis is that the Indian state has failed, in very large measure, to prosecute perpetrators, to account for its own failures, to compensate victims, and to tell citizens about what it did or did not do.

***

Communal violence and its aftermath in India has always been characterised by injustice and partisanship by state authorities. But the carnage of Gujarat in 2002 stands apart not only because of the unprecedented denial of relief and rehabilitation[12] to the survivors by the elected state government of Gujarat, but also because of the extent of the open, deliberate and defiant subversion that it witnessed of the criminal justice system,[13] with the complicity of all its arms: the police, the prosecution and the judiciary. The charge of deliberate justice subversion is of course consistently denied by the state government and indeed by the Central government that was in office at the time of the carnage. For instance, the then deputy prime minister L.K. Advani, in a television interview, dismissed the claim that there has been an extremely grave and deliberate subversion of justice in the aftermath of the Gujarat carnage (2002). He suggested that whatever failures occurred were the routine outcome of the general collapse of the criminal justice system in country and that there was nothing distinct in the experience of Gujarat. But in fact what Gujarat witnessed after 2002 was not a spectacular state failure, but a remarkable state success, because the state succeeded in achieving what it set out to accomplish, and this was the subversion of all institutions of criminal justice with the sole objective of ensuring that those guilty for the massacre are not punished.[14]

In the scathing words of the judges of the Supreme Court of India,[15] the bench of the highest court in the land gets 'a feeling that the justice delivery system was being taken for a ride and literally allowed to be abused, misused and mutilated by subterfuge'.[16] The National Human Rights Commission earlier spoke in a similar vein of 'a large-scale and unconscionable miscarriage of justice' and stressed the imperative of the restoration of 'justice and the upholding of the values of the Constitution of the Republic and the laws of the land. That is why it remains of fundamental importance that the measures that require to be taken to bring the violators of human rights to book are indeed taken.' The failures of the state government to heed its counsel ultimately moved the National Human Rights Commission to respond to what it described as the 'damage to the credibility of the criminal justice delivery system and negation of human rights of victims', by the extremely unusual step of itself filing an application before the Supreme Court for transfer of five major criminal cases connected with the 2002 carnage for their trial outside the state of Gujarat.

These damning observations about these large cases applied equally to literally thousands of cases in which justice has been cynically and efficiently subverted by state authorities in Gujarat, in the aftermath of the carnage if 2002. My colleagues and I applied to the Supreme Court that out of a total of 4,252 first information reports (FIRs) registered after the carnage, 2,208 'summary reports' were filed with the magistrate's court. This means that these cases were closed even without submitting them to trial, based on police claims that they were unable to collect any evidence against the accused, or that the crime itself did not take place. If this was not challenged, it would mean that one could kill, rape and pillage openly and would not have to even once see the inside of a police station or court room. The impunity with which the next slaughter could be executed can then well be imagined. The extent of bias of the lower judiciary is evidenced by the fact that more than 200 courts in 17 districts passed these completely illegal orders of closure. Also, more than 300 accused had been acquitted in a short time span of over a year, with very few appeals filed by the state government. The closure of cases or acquittal of the accused in more than half the cases registered after the massacre in the short space of around one and a half years, was all the more extraordinary, given the normally sluggish pace of criminal justice in our country. It was the cumulative outcome of deliberately faulty police complaints and investigation, discriminatory arrests and bail and the intimidation of witnesses and biased prosecution and judges.

Many of the cases that were closed were deliberately destroyed in this way at the stage of the filing of the police complaint, known as the FIR, itself. The accused were not named, and instead the violence was attributed to anonymous mobs. In many cases, omnibus FIRs were filed in advance by the police, clubbing large numbers of incidents involving sometimes hundreds of witnesses and accused in single complaints to render investigation completely unwieldy and confused, and in which often the victims were accused of instigating the mobs. Subsequent complaints by victims were then subsumed under the police FIRs, and the names of many of the main accused eliminated. Even those of the accused who were charged with grave crimes were released on bail frequently without opposition from the local police, enabling them to intimidate witnesses at will. Often false complaints – informally called 'cross-cases' – were filed against the few complainants who managed to get their complaints registered, to browbeat them into not pursuing their complaints. There was also a discriminatory communally motivated pattern in the persons arrested and released on bail.

Investigation in many cases was assigned to tainted police officers accused of abetting or even participating in the massacre. The observations of the Supreme Court (again made in the context of the Best Bakery slaughter) apply to the large majority of the cases: that 'the role of the investigating agency itself was perfunctory and not impartial . . . it was tainted, biased and not fair . . . without any definite object of finding out the truth and bringing to book those who were responsible for the crime'. Witnesses and survivors allege that the police did not take down their testimonies properly, deliberately omitting details and the names of the accused.

Once trials began, prosecution was frequently deliberately shoddy and partisan,[17] and it was not unusual for public prosecutors to be often openly active members of the Sangh and affiliated organisations. The accused were frequently not arrested, under the specious claim that they are 'absconding', whereas they openly walked free, threatening and intimidating the witnesses with impunity. Once again, the Supreme Court expressed anguish about the 'improper conduct of trial by the public prosecutor' and added that when 'a large number of witnesses have turned hostile it should have raised a reasonable suspicion that the witnesses were being threatened or coerced'. It added

> The public prosecutor appears to have acted more as a defence counsel than one whose duty was to present the truth before the Court. . . . The prosecutor who does not act fairly and acts more like a counsel for the defense is a liability for a fair judicial system, and courts could not also play into the hands of such prosecuting agency.

The Supreme Court reserved its gravest strictures for the trial court. It stated:

> The courts . . . are not expected to be tape recorders to record whatever is being stated by the witnesses. . . . They have to monitor the proceedings in aid of justice. . . Even if the prosecutor is remiss in some ways, it can control the proceedings effectively so that the ultimate objective i.e. truth is arrived at.

It observed significantly that truth should prevail over technicalities that protect the innocent and punish the guilty, and the confidence in courts must be restored.

> When the investigating agency helps the accused, the witnesses are threatened to depose falsely and prosecutor acts in a manner as if he was defending the accused, and the Court was acting merely as an onlooker and there is no fair trial at all, justice becomes the victim.

The injustice was further compounded by the large-scale arrest of people of the minority community, and the strenuous resistance by the police to their applications for bail. Men and even boys were charged with murder and attempted murder in cases where police fired and killed innocent people, or powerful people were sought to be charged, in order to build pressure on the victims by filing 'cross-cases' against them. All of this continues. Witnesses remain under great pressure to not give evidence against those who attacked them and destroyed their homes, even as a condition for returning to the homes of their ancestors or under threat of being prosecuted themselves on false charges. With openly biased police, courts and prosecution, criminal cases against the accused are sinking like stones in a turgid pool.

The brazenly partisan exercise of state authority is even more evident in the unapologetically discriminatory application of the draconian Prevention of Terrorism Act 2002 (POTA) exclusively against minorities.[18] Several hundred youth arrested under cases of POTA in Gujarat have been Muslims, except for one Sikh. Most of the POTA accused have languished for years in prison without bail. By contrast, despite the brutal carnage which took more than 2,000 lives, not one of the accused were booked by the state government under POTA (Mander 2003). The Central government refused to repeal POTA retrospectively, so these cases persist.

The comprehensive and wanton failure of every institution responsible for criminal justice in Gujarat – the police, prosecution and judiciary – and the deliberate denial of justice with the objective of securing freedom for those accused of the gravest crimes of massacre, rape and arson from even the processes of the legal system let alone ultimate penalties is clearly not a routine collapse. It seems reasonable to speculate that this was the outcome of systematic planned subversion of justice in a manner not unlike the planning of the massacre itself.

***

There are many groups of people, and state as well as non-state institutions who bear responsibility for the crimes and inhumanity of the Gujarat carnage and the dishonour of its aftermath. These are the elected political leadership of the government, fascistic communal organisations, the judiciary and the prosecution. I choose to focus in particular here on the special culpability of one of them – with which I have served for two decades – the higher civil services (including the police). This is a vocation whose central calling is the upholding of justice, of law, order and the protection of vulnerable people. Default in the performance of one's duty by a civil or police officer in a riot is not only the crime of a citizen who turns one's face away from injustice, because of indifference, fear or complicity. It is a crime of much graver magnitude, akin to that of a surgeon who wantonly kills his patient on the operation table.

Half a century after India shed its colonial shackles, it continues to retain a peculiarly hybrid bureaucratic framework that is in many ways essentially incongruous in a democracy. On the one hand, it holds on to many of its colonial trappings, and public servants who are not elected exercise enormous unaccountable power over several aspects of the lives of ordinary people, both at the local level and in the framing of policy and law. But, at the same time, during the decades that the state in India assumed leadership of nation-building and social justice, this same bureaucracy was charged with combating poverty and protecting the rights of Dalit and tribal people, women and the working classes. It is this that attracted many of us to the civil services.

I spent 20 of the best years of my life in the Indian Administrative Service, living with my family in remote, tribal districts of Madhya Pradesh and Chhattisgarh, I do not regret a single day. No other employment could have enabled me to see and learn so much from the resilience, struggles and humanism of people in distant corners of my land. Like many colleagues I found enormous opportunities to implement my beliefs about land reforms, laws and programmes for tribal and Dalit equity, justice and programmes to combat poverty as well as to fight corruption.

And yet, even as I worked with the opportunities that the system afforded, I could see from the start its fatal flaws and rapid corrosion as a democratic institution. It recruited many of the country's better talents, but did little to make them genuinely accountable to the people they were mandated to serve. There were and continue to be in the ranks of the civil service women and men of the highest integrity and moral courage. But increasingly there are signs of a spirit of abject, sometimes humiliating subservience, as several civil servants habitually obey without protest even illegal and unjust directions of political superiors.

In the aftermath of the grim and bloody birth of a dismembered Indian nation in 1947, the leaders of the struggle for Indian Independence had resolved to retain a powerful bureaucracy inherited from the colonial legacy of governance. Their expectation was that it would act as a sturdy bulwark, a 'steel frame' to strengthen the unification of a vast, diverse, volatile land. In the decades that elapsed after Independence, a slow but steady decline set in, not only with the growth of indifference, unaccountability, corruption, sloth, arrogance, but most dangerously, partisanship and complicity with injustice and sectarian politics. One low was hit during the Emergency from 1975 to 1977, where few stood up against dictatorship and the subversion of the entire Constitution. And with the shameful abetment of mass violence in the anti-Sikh riots of 1984,[19] the decline became precipitous in conjunction with the ascendancy of fundamentalist fascistic militant ideologies in the country. Sections of the police, civil and military administration bared their active sympathies with these divisive ideologies – ignoring that these contradict fundamentally the letter and the spirit of the secular democratic Constitution of India that they are pledged to uphold – while the large majority opportunistically aligned with these to advance their careers.

As a result, the corroded 'steel frame' dissolved and in the 'laboratory' of Gujarat in 2002, the country witnessed its complete ignoble collapse. The savage carnage in many parts of Gujarat that followed the horrific burning of a railway compartment in Godhra on 27 February 2002, and the systematic and wanton subversion of all civilised norms of relief and rehabilitation of the survivors in the bleak months that followed are testimony to the collapse and perversion of the state machinery to an unprecedented degree. The majority of state authorities in Gujarat not only actively connived with a planned and orchestrated massacre of a section of the population, specially targeting hapless women and children. In the months that followed, they abetted and assisted for the first time in the country's history the deliberate subversion of all civilised norm of relief and rehabilitation of the survivors. In other words, they enabled and assisted not only the murder, rape and plunder of legions of innocent people and their properties. They went further to assist the ruling political class of the state to prevent the organisation of even elementary temporary shelters with basic facilities in relief camps, or grants and loans to assist the destitute and bereaved survivors to rebuild their shelters and livelihoods. This brazen, merciless treatment, with state abetment, of victims of mass violence like unwanted diseased cattle, or like enemy populations, marks a new low in the governance of this nation. It heralds the completion of the unresisting transition of the civil and police administration from protectors to predators of the people.

Until the 1980s, there was an unwritten agreement in our polity that even if politicians inflamed communal passions, the police and civil administration would be expected to act professionally and impartially to control the riots in the shortest possible time, and to protect innocent lives. There were several failures in performance, and minorities were targeted in many infamous riots, but the rules of the game were still acknowledged and in the majority of instances adhered to, which is why the higher civil and police services were regarded to be the steel frame vital to preserve the unity and plurality of the country.

The 1980s saw the breaking of this unwritten compact, which has led to the corrosion and near-collapse of the steel frame. It became the frequent practice for the higher civil and police authorities to be instructed to actively connive in the systematic slaughter of one community, and to do this by delaying sometimes by several days, the use of force to control riots. Local state authorities complied, and rioters were unrestrained by state power in their mass murder, arson and plunder.

Why is the decisive and timely use of state coercive force – lathis, tear-gas and bullets by police, paramilitary and military contingents – so vital a duty of the state in a communal situation? In every other kind of public disorder – such as labour, student or peasant protests – the broad consensus across a wide section of liberal opinion is that a democratic state must never use brute force to suppress democratic dissent. Only in the rarest of cases, and with a wide range of checks and balances to prevent human rights abuse, may a democratic state apply the principle of minimum necessary use of force to restore public order and security, respecting the right of democratic dissent and the expressions of public anger against perceived injustices and grievances.

In situations of sectarian violence, the responsibility of the state is completely different from any other. A humane and responsive democratic government must apply in all such situations – of communal riots, or violence against minorities or Dalits – the principle not of minimum necessary application of force, but instead the responsible, accountable, lawful but *maximum possible* use of force that the state can muster in the shortest possible time, while always still respecting and safeguarding human rights. This is because unlike other expressions of public anger, communal violence targets almost invariably people who are most vulnerable and defenceless, it is fuelled by perilous and explosive mass sentiments of irrationality, unreason, prejudice and hatred, and its poison spreads incrementally over space and time. Its wounds do not heal across generations. The Partition of our country continues to scar our psyche half a century after its bloody passage. A whole decade of terrorists in Punjab traced their origins to the maraudings of the 1984 rioters. As I held on my lap the six-year-old boy in a camp in Ahmedabad, recounting the killings of his parents and six siblings, I felt broken by his pain that can never heal, but wondered at the same time how he would deal with his anger when he grows up. Likewise, the ashes of the horrific burnings in Godhra have stirred up their own poison. But it is important to understand that the cycles of hatred did not begin in the railway compartments of Godhra, and they will not end in the killing fields of Gujarat.

It is for this reason that every moment's delay by state authorities to apply sufficient force to control communal violence is such an unconscionable crime: it means more innocents will be slaughtered, raped and maimed, but also that wounds would be opened which may not heal for generations. Civil and police authorities today openly await the orders of their political supervisors before they apply force, so much so that it has become popular perception that indeed they cannot act without the permission of their administrative and political superiors, and ultimately the chief minister. The legal position is completely at variance with this widely held view. The law is completely unambiguous, in empowering local civil authorities to take all decisions independently about the use of force to control public disorders, including calling in the army. The magistrate is not required to consult her or his administrative superiors, let alone those who are regarded as their political 'masters'. The law is clear that in the performance of this responsibility, civil and police authorities are their own masters, responsible above all to their own judgement and conscience. There are no alibis that the law allows them.

It may be argued that this may be an accurate description of the legal situation, but the practice on the ground has sanctified the practice of political consultation before force is applied. Only to convince the reader that I speak from the experience of myself handling many riots, I could contest this with my own experience in the major riots of 1984 and 1989, where as an executive magistrate I took decisions about the use of force and in the former case calling in the army, without any consultation. I could similarly contest this with the experience of many women and men of character in the civil and police services across the country, who would similarly testify to salutary application of force, to control more difficult communal violence, without recourse to political clearances.

There can be no dispute that given the administrative and political will, no riot can continue unchecked beyond a few hours.

However, I will not substantiate this with my own experience, or those of older officers. It gives me greatest pride and hope, amidst the darkness that we find ourselves in today, to talk of the independent action taken by a few young officers in Gujarat and neighbouring Rajasthan during the 2002 crisis itself. Rahul Sharma was posted as the superintendent of police, Bhavnagar, for less than a month when Godhra killings and the subsequent massacre all over Gujarat unfolded. Following the Godhra tragedy, he deployed a strong police contingent for the Gujarat *bandh* called by the VHP the next day on 28 February 2002. Unlike the rest of Gujarat, the day passed off without much trouble in Bhavnagar. But the next day, Rahul learned that a mob of around 2,000 men armed with swords, *trishuls* (tridents), spears, stones, burning torches, petrol bombs and acid bottles, was about to attack a madrassa with around 400 small Muslim boys between the ages of 12 and 15. Rahul rushed there with a police force of around 50 people. Seeing that the force was hesitant to open fire on the armed mob, Rahul himself took the rifle from a fellow constable and opened fire. As some attackers fell to police bullets, the crowd stopped in its tracks and faded away.

Rahul then made an entry in the logbook saying that he had fired from the constable's gun to save the lives of the children. He also gave an order that any policeman with a gun not opening fire to save human lives from a violent mob would be prosecuted for abetting murder. This gave a clear signal to the police force that their leader the superintendent of police meant business, was willing to take full responsibility for his actions and was prepared to stick out his neck any distance to uphold his duties. This had an immediate effect on his force, and Bhavnagar was a town where more rioters were killed in police firing than innocent victims in actual rioting. For this, Rahul[20] was moved out from Bhavnagar in a mere month of his assuming charge. He is quoted in the magazine *Outlook*[21] as saying, 'I'm not one to run away from transfers. I take these things in my stride.'

In neighbouring Rajasthan, the superintendent of police of Ajmer, Saurabh Srivastava, with a young sub-divisional magistrate in his first charge and his small force, doused communal fires in Kishangarh on 1 March 2002, which had the potential of inflaming the tinder box of the entire state. They controlled an enraged armed mob of over a thousand men bent on attacking minorities in a pitched battle for over four hours.

It is sometimes also argued that the entire higher civil and police services have become politicised beyond repair, therefore whatever their legal and moral duties they today lack the conditions in which they can reasonably be expected to perform them. Once again, I would strongly contest this alibi. In the 20 years of my life in the civil service, I always found that despite the decline in all institutions of public life, there continue to survive democratic spaces within it to struggle to act in accordance with my beliefs without compromise. One may be battered and tossed around, in the way that young police officers who opposed political diktats to control the recent rioting in Gujarat were unjustly transferred. But in the long run, I have not known upright officers to be terminally suppressed, repressed or marginalised. On the contrary, I value colleagues, in the civil and police services, usually unsung and uncelebrated heroes, who have quietly and resolutely performed their duties with admirable character and steadfastness. Few in the civil and police services can in all honesty testify to pressure so great that they could not adhere to the call of their own conscience.

It is not that there are no costs, but then if the performance of duties was painless, there would not be many who would fail in the performance of their duties. The costs are usually of frequent transfers, and deprivation of the allurements of some assignments of power and glamour, which are used to devastating effect by our political class to entice a large part of the bureaucracy today.

When I stand witness to the massacre in Gujarat enabled by spectacular state abdication and connivance – or to the national disgrace of the subversion of all civilised norms of relief and rehabilitation – I confront the cold truth that the higher civil and police services are today in the throes of an unprecedented crisis. The absolute minimum that any state must ensure is the survival and security of its people and elementary justice. If state authorities wantonly let violent mobs target innocents without restraint – or connive with the most cynical and merciless designs to deny them the elementary means for human survival – and they continue to do this with impunity and without remorse or shame, then citizens of the country need to resolutely demand accountability and fundamental reforms. They cannot permit the collapse or subversion of the state, and

its metamorphosis from an institution for justice and security, the protection and welfare of the people, into one that victimises as state policy a
segment of its population, treating them as 'children of a lesser god'.

***

Many hoped that Independence would progressively bring an end to
violent communal strife and pogroms in India. But after 63 years of freedom, millions of Indian people continue to live with lurking fear in
their hearts: fear of violence that can snuff out their lives and loved
ones, violate their bodies, and devastate their homes and livelihoods.
Among these are persons of the Scheduled Castes and Tribes, religious
minorities, especially Muslims, and in tribal areas, Christian converts,
and linguistic minorities. I have spoken to ordinary people of Muslim
faith in many corners of the country. When they recall their lives, it
is always as life lived in the space *between* riots. Each of them nego-
tiates everyday living with unspoken trepidation that one day – any
day – everything that they love and live for can be destroyed in one brief
storm of hate. And in many tribal areas, communal organisations have
succeeded in driving a deep and dangerous wedge between people who
converted to Christianity, and others – often of the same tribe – who
have not. Scheduled Castes and Tribes have lived with subjugation and
fear of violence for centuries. And migration has fuelled fear and violence against linguistic minorities who travel to other states in search
of dignified work.

Long after the fires of torched homes, looted shops and desecrated
places of worship are doused and the blood on the streets dries; after
slaughter, rape, plunder and expulsion are accomplished; wounds rarely
heal. Survivors live out their lives haunted by the fear of recurrence, the
anguish of betrayal and the dying of hope and trust.

We have witnessed too often in this country the women, men and children attacked only because of their identity as dalits or tribals, religious
or linguistic minorities. As we have observed in this chapter, a recurring feature of most such brutal episodes of bloodletting in anti-Dalit and
anti-minority hate crimes and mass violence is that elected and selected
public officials fail to uphold their most sacred constitutional duty – to
secure equal protection to every citizen, regardless of their caste, faith or

linguistic identity. They fail not because they lack the mandate, authority or the legal powers. They fail because they *choose* to fail, because of the pervasive prejudice and bias against these disadvantaged groups that permeates large segments of the police, magistracy, judiciary and the political class.

But this enormous moral crime of public officials enabling massacre is not recognised explicitly as a crime for which they can be criminally punished. Far from it, officials who have been named as guilty of bias and worse in numerous judicial commissions of enquiry have very rarely been even administratively penalised; contrarily, guilty police and civil officers have enjoyed illustrious careers, and political leaders under whose watch such carnages have occurred have reaped rich electoral harvests of hate.

A similar culture of impunity surrounds those who instigate and participate in the killings, arson and rape. Impunity is the assurance that you can openly commit a crime and will not be punished. This impunity admittedly does arise from infirmities in and corrosion of the criminal justice system, which require long-delayed police and judicial reform. But it is important to recognise that the collapse of the justice machinery is massively compounded when the victims are disadvantaged by caste, religion or minority language. You are more likely to be punished when you murder a single person in 'peace-time' with no witnesses, than if you slay ten in broad daylight observed by hundreds of people.

We have carefully studied several major episodes of targeted violence and discovered that despite these being separated vastly by time and geography, despite the victims sometimes being Dalits, sometimes Muslims, sometimes Christians, and sometimes say Tamils in Karnataka – there is a chillingly similar pattern of systematic and active subversion of justice. The impunity of the accused begins immediately after the violence. Preventive arrests and searches usually target Dalits and minorities. Police refuse to record the names of the killers, rapists and arsonists, and instead refer to anonymous mobs. If victims assert excessively, 'cross-cases' are registered against them, accusing them of crimes. Arrests are partisan, and the grant of bail even more so. Accused persons from the dominant group find it easy to get bail in weeks, or at most months, while those caught in cross-cases are not released sometimes for years.

This openly discriminatory treatment of the accused based on whether they are from dominant or discriminated groups, is one way to coerce them to 'compromise' (Mander 2008). This means extra-legal out-of-court 'agreement' by victims to turn 'hostile', to retract from their accusations in court. To accomplish this, victims are also widely intimidated and threatened, offered inducements or threatened with exile or social and economic boycott. Police investigation is deliberately shoddy, and the majority of cases are closed even before they are submitted to trial. Those few cases that reach the court are demolished by prosecution who often do not even disguise their aim to protect the accused rather than establish their guilt, and judges who often share their bias.

Therefore, many in this country pin great hopes on a law which could help end communal violence. This Communal Violence Bill has been in incubation for an extended seven years, ever since the United Progressive Alliance (UPA) government was first elected in 2004 with a mandate to end the politics of fear, hate and division in the country. But despite two drafts by the government, in 2005 and 2010, there was wide rejection of, and disappointment with, what the government has on offer. The government versions of the law had very little in common with what secular opinion, and minority leaders, believe are essential to such a law.

Successive government drafts of the Communal Violence Bill mainly aim to greatly enhance the powers of the police, on the premise that these increased powers are needed to enable police and governments to take decisive steps to prevent and control mass communal violence. The draft bill provides for governments to declare areas in which communal violence is imminent, or has actually broken out, as 'communally sensitive' areas. In these areas, for the duration of the notification, the police would function with expanded powers, and there would be enhanced punishment for crimes committed in this area, and special courts would hear the criminal cases that arise.

The assumption of the government drafts is that if only the powers of police and governments are augmented in communally charged times and areas, they would control communal violence effectively and decisively. This assumption flies in the face of the actual experience of successive communal pogroms. Did governments in Assam in 1983, Delhi in 1984, Mumbai in 1992–93, Gujarat in 2002 or Kandhamal in 2008 fail to prevent slaughter and arson because they lacked sufficient powers? Do we really believe that these governments were *unable* to control violence because they lacked the legal muscle? Or was the truth that they did not want to control the violence, but instead they deliberately enabled the slaughter? That they wanted to reap political advantage from a violently polarised polity and were assured that they would legally be able to get away with such a crime?

If government officials and political leaders wish to act, the law as it stands is more than adequate to empower police and officials to prevent and control communal violence. No riot can continue for more than a few hours without the active will of the political leadership of governments that violence should persist and indeed spread and the active abetment of police and civil officials to prolong the slaughter and arson. Communal carnages occur because they are systematically planned and executed by communal organisations, and because governments which are legally and morally charged to protect all citizens, deliberately refuse to douse the fires, and instead allow rivers of innocent blood to flow.

As already observed, I regard such abetment of slaughter by public officials to be one of the gravest crimes possible in public life. To protect minorities from communal pogroms and mass violence, we do not need a law which adds further to the powers of police, civil authorities and governments. Ironically, such a law will achieve the exact reverse of what it claims to seek. The consistent experience of minorities is that greater powers in the hands of police would only be used against them. There is great unease with declaring regions as 'disturbed areas': in large swathes of India's North-East and Kashmir, people have lived in the shadows of similar declarations, which give extraordinary powers to security forces. These routinely lead to crushing of people's elementary democratic freedoms.

We need a very different law, not one which makes police and public officials more powerful, but instead one which forces them to be legally answerable to the people who they are responsible to serve and protect effectively and impartially. In present law, public officials can at best be charged with active conspiracy and participation in mass violence (although even this is rarely done). But the worst crimes of police and civil authorities, and those in command positions like chief ministers, are deliberately and maliciously refusing to take action to prevent and control violence. We need law to recognise such deliberate inaction – because of which killings, rape and violence continue unchecked for days and sometimes weeks – to be grave and punishable crimes against humanity.

The law also needs to recognise new crimes, especially forms of gender violence during communal carnage. The narrow definition of rape does not envisage the many forms of gendered crimes that are common in mass violence situations, such as stripping and parading women, mass disrobing by the attacking men, insertion of objects into bodies of women, cutting breasts and killing of children in the womb. The procedures for recording complaints, investigating and trials also need to be sensitive to the suppression, fear and sense of public shame, which shrouds in silence most such episodes of targeted violence against women.

In most episodes of communal violence, states are partisan also in extending relief and compensation. The survivors of the Nellie massacre of 1983 were paid a mere Rs. 5,000 for each death,[22] against a total of around Rs. 7 lakh for the families of those killed in the Sikh massacre of 1984. Such an implied hierarchy of official valuation of human lives of people of different persuasions and ethnicity is intolerable. The government in Gujarat in 2002 refused even to establish relief camps and forced the premature closure of the privately established camps. The law therefore must establish binding standards for awarding compensation after communal violence and duties relating to rescue, relief camps, rebuilding of homes, livelihoods and places of worship.

The National Advisory Council (NAC) has produced a draft law[23] to prevent communal violence and end impunity, by making public officials legally answerable to the people for their acts – and failures to act – which lead to the brutal and criminal loss of innocent lives. The NAC draft law is currently under debate, and we are sure it can be further improved in many ways. However, to discourage targeted hate crimes in future, we are convinced that what is required is a law which creates the offence of dereliction of duty of public officials who deliberately fail in their constitutional duty to protect targeted vulnerable groups. This must be coupled with the principle of command responsibility, which ensures that responsibility for failing to act is carried to the level from which orders actually flow. This public accountability is at the heart of the NAC draft bill. We are convinced that if such a law existed, the massacres at Khairlanji and

Chundur, Delhi, Gujarat and Kandhamal would have been controlled and justice better accomplished.

We also need a law that established binding duties and standards for relief and rehabilitation, because these do not exist. Indian criminal law is also based on the assumption that the state is always on the side of the victim, against the accused, and therefore primarily the rights of the accused need to be protected. The state investigates, prosecutes and also adduces evidence and appeals. The victim has limited rights in this process. The reality of targeted violence against non-dominant groups is that a biased state may, in these cases, be on the side of accused and actively hostile to the victim. This bill seeks to correct this bias, by incorporating a number of rights and protections of victims in post-conflict criminal justice.

I have spoken to victims of caste and communal carnages in many parts of the country and found that the most important reason that they cannot find closure even years later is because legal justice is not done.

> How can we forget, even less forgive, if we see every day the man who raped our daughter or killed our father, walk free; when not once has he had to even see the inside of a police station or a court? How can we believe we are equal citizens of this land?

The Right to Information changed on its head the relationship of public servants with the people, by enabling them to question them for the probity of their actions. We believe that the Communal Violence Bill must carry this further, by enabling them to ask whether they did all they should to protect all citizens against mass violence, regardless of their religious faith, gender, caste and ethnicity. Only such a law can stem the rivers of innocent blood that flow periodically across this land. Only such a law can secure secular democracy in India.

Appendix: inquiry reports

Nellie

Commission of Enquiry on Assam Disturbances ('Tewary Commission') Report

Sikh Riots

Justice Ranganath Mishra Commission of Inquiry Report

R.K. Ahuja Committee report

Kusum Lata Mittal Committee Report

Jain Aggarwal Committee Report

Justice G.T. Nanavati Commission Report

Report by Ensaaf, 'Twenty Years of Impunity; The November 1984 Pogram of Sikhs in India, Kaur Jaskaran', 2nd edition, October 2006, accessed at www.ensaaf.org/publications/reports/20years/20years-2nd.pdf

A PUCL-PUDR joint fact finding report, "Who Are the Guilty"?, accessed at www.pucl.org/Topics/Religion-communalism/2003/who-are-guilty.htm

Bhagalpur

Bhagalpur Riots Commission of Inquiry Report

Report by Special ADM, Law & Order, Bhagalpur

PUDR Report

Gujarat

Concerned Citizens Tribunal Report, accessed at www.sabrang.com/tribunal

NHRC Report 2002, accessed at http://nhrc.nic.in

Amnesty International Report

PUCL Report, accessed at www.pucl.org/gujrat-index.htm

Notes

1 Article 15, Constitution of India.
2 Article 25, Constitution of India.
3 For an interesting analysis of this, see Engineer (2004).
4 For a discussion of the term "communalism" in the Indian context, see Vanaik (1997: 33–34).
5 For elaborate discussion, see Rajeshwari (2004).
6 For details, see Kimura (2003).
7 For details, see Phoolka and Mitta (2007).
8 UN Basic Principles and Guidelines on the Right to a Remedy and Reparation for Victims of Violations of International Human Rights and Humanitarian Law.

9 Nyayagraha began its work on 2 October 2005, and has since reached out to at least 10,000 survivors of the carnage in four districts – Ahmedabad, Sabarkantha, Anand and Kheda – offering legal and moral support. About 2,000 individuals came forward to fight legal battles with Nyayagraha's support.

10 See Amnesty and Concerned Citizen's Tribunal Repot of investigation of the post-Godhra (2002) riots in Gujarat.

11 In the 1984 carnage in Delhi, also called Sikh riots, senior leaders like Sajjan Kumar and Jagdish Tytler have escaped punishment for their alleged crimes even after so many years.

12 See Relief and Rehabilitation section, CCT report VOL 3 accessed at http://www.sabrang.com/tribunal/tribunal3.pdf.

13 National Human Rights Commission report 2002, accessed at http://nhrc.nic.in.

14 PUCL Report, Violence in Vadodra, 2002, accessed at www.pucl.org/gujrat-index.htm.

15 In the *Zahira Habibiullah Sheikh v. State of Gujarat* case, better known as the Best Bakery case.

16 Best Bakery Citation : 2004CriLJ2050, (2004)2GLR1078, (2004)4SCC158, 2004(2)UJ1041(SC).

17 Writ Petition (Cri) filed by the NHRC of 109/2003 and the related Criminal Miscellaneous petition No. 3742/04.

18 Amnesty International, 'Abuse of the Law in Gujarat: Muslims Detained Illegally in Ahmedabad.' 1–2 (6 Nov. 2003), accessed at www.web.amnesty.org/aidoc/aidoc_pdf.nsf/index/ASA200292003ENGLISH/$File/ASA2002903.pdf.

19 'Who Are the Guilty?' A PUCL-PUDR joint fact finding report, accessed at www.pucl.org/Topics/Religion-communalism/2003/who-are-guilty.htm and Twenty Years of Impunity; The November 1984 Pogram of Sikhs in India, Kaur Jaskaran, Report by Ensaaf, 2nd edition, October 2006, accessed at www.ensaaf.org/publications/reports/20years/20years-2nd.pdf.

20 Concerned Citizens Tribunal Report on incidents at Bhavnagar, Gujarat, 2002, accessed at www.sabrang.com/tribunal/volI/incbhavnagar.html.

21 Quoted in *Outlook* magazine, edition 8 April 2002, accessed at www.outlookindia/article.aspx?215119.

22 Assam Relief Manual, 16 June 1976, Administrative Reforms Department, Government of Assam. Available at http://sdmassam.nic.in/download/assam_relief_manual.pdf.

23 The draft National Advisory Council law called 'Prevention of Communal and Targeted Violence(Access to Justice and Reparations) Bill', accessed at www.nac.nic.in/pdf/pctvb.pdf.

8

CONFLICT AND ATTRITION IN THE NORTH-EAST

Identity, impunity and inequality

Sanjoy Hazarika*

On 27 June 2012, the Government of India's Ministry of Tourism had this to say about the North-East in an item published in *The Hindu* titled 'Discover Adventure':

> Let the adrenaline surge through your veins with Meghalaya or the 'Abode of Clouds' and its capital city, Shillong or the 'Scotland of the East' and the rainiest rain-belt of Cherrapunjee. Mizoram is the land of highlanders with rugged terrains, gurgling streams and rivers, ideal for adventure sports and Assam rever-berates with the melody of Bhupen Hazarika, harvest festival of Bihu, colonial tea bungalows, soul stirring places of pilgrimage and ancient Ahom architectural marvels.

This syrupy, poorly written drivel came out barely a few weeks before the western part of the Assam Valley erupted in violence and bloodshed between the Bodos and the Muslims in the region, triggering a scale of displacement that has not been seen since independence, with some four lakh and more persons fleeing their homes in terror and panic and taking shelter in temporary relief camps, which became their home for several months. Over a hundred persons died in the attacks and clashes during which not just primitive weapons like *daos* (machetes) were used but also automatic weapons; those arrested for the events included at least one Bodo legislator charged with organising mobs and worse.

The valley staggers between some form of 'normalcy' and bouts of violence and suspicion. The state has more than 22 large ethnic groups, and its Muslim population is, in terms of ratio to overall population, the second largest in ratio to overall population size of any state in the country, next only to Jammu and Kashmir.[1]

People have moved back to their homesteads, although they remain tense and anxious about the future and deeply unsettled by the violence and hatred they have witnessed. In 2012 and 2014, there were times when villagers mounted vigils in the four districts of the Bodo Territorial Council (Kokrajhar, Chirang, Bongaigaon and Udalgiri) when villagers mounted 24-hour vigils outside their homes, sleeping near the gates of their homes, and working in shifts to prevent attacks by 'outsiders', quelling rumours from spreading and giving each other support.

A wide range of issues and concerns have come to the fore, which need to be reviewed both in a structural overview as well as a micro approach that dissects a number of separate but interconnected processes that have disrupted politics, society and systems. This chapter reviews two areas: the first is the lack of knowledge about the region, which creates greater disinformation and a sense of grievance, underlining the 'us and them' approach on both sides. The second is how the state has tied itself up in knots by giving security forces enormous clout but no accountability: the result is that conditions remain extremely contentious, disturbed, and basic issues remain unresolved while public outrage and a sense of helplessness grows. In the second case, we shall look at the Armed Forces Special Powers Act (Assam and Manipur, 1958).

*****

'India has no idea of what's going on in Assam', says Badruddin Ajmal, the outspoken head of the All India United Democratic Front (AIUDF), a native of Central Assam who is a member of Parliament and seeking to expand his young party's base across northern and eastern India. The AIUDF started as the Assam United Democratic Front (AUDF) but swiftly divested itself of the 'Assam' tag as possibly too restrictive for its larger ambitions.

The first is that there appears to be an unending cycle of conflict and attrition in an extremely complex and challenging humanscape. As in the past across the country, in such situations, the worst sufferers in the recent riots and violence have been the poor and vulnerable, especially women and children. Rural schools have been converted into relief camps – while giving temporary succour to a large number of people who have fled fear and bloodshed, such a situation also has taken off months from the school lives of those children who study at these institutions. In addition, hate speech and abuse of new media has created a situation where tens of thousands fled their places of work and residence in 2012, at places like Bangalore, Hyderabad and Pune, and returned to the North-Eastern region (NER). That flow was reversed and many of the young people from the NER, working, studying and living in these and other cities of the new India returned to their new homes and work places.

Over the past decades, my colleagues and I have met many people whose lives had been changed irrevocably by the decades of violence that had gripped their states.[2] In the states of Nagaland, parts of Assam, Tripura, Manipur and Mizoram especially the villagers have borne the brunt of contesting ideas and forces, and many families and individuals have stories to tell, of personal loss, of bereavement, of physical and emotional trauma. For many of them, these meetings with those who campaign for rights, the media or academics and researchers were often the first interaction with people from another part of India in their villages. These are stories that the world does not know of, has not cared to know, contributing to the silencing of voices on the margins. The telling of these stories work as a form of political intervention and empowerment, building bridges between communities and helping to open up a little known region and an alienated people.

Analysts say war and conflict are devastating to social and cultural institutions because they impact societies and individuals; every person who has survived conflict is in some way scarred by her or his experience. It takes people and society a long time to come to terms with what happened.

A young woman in Dimapur (Nagaland) who is a member of a women's association, which works like an informal, tribal panchayat where social cases relating to women are handled, shared an experience. Her village, she said, was bombed by the Indian Air Force in the 1960s. She was only a baby at the time but her mother who was running away from the burning village hid her in the hollow of a tree thinking she would come back and retrieve her when it was safe. It was three days before she could come back. The child lay inside that hollow, hungry, frightened and alone. We wondered: 'What must she have thought? What sort of impact would this have left on her?' The trauma haunted her, she said, and then as soon as she was old enough she went to join her father, who was a member of the Naga army fighting the Indian state. It was only much later that she came to terms with what had happened to her village, to herself and her father, who was killed in the course of battles with the army.

To say that women have faced violence in situations of conflict is to state the obvious, but what this means in terms of impacts is something that is still being studied. While the most obvious impact is physical or sexual violence, the psychological scarring as a result of prolonged expo-sure to brutality has an even deeper impact on their well-being. Women find themselves at the receiving end of violence from three fronts: the state, the militants and a corresponding escalation of domestic violence. The effects of violent acts like rape, sexual abuse and assault lead to emotional trauma and what is known as post-traumatic stress disorder (PTSD) – again this is something that is being understood only now. Facilities like trauma centres or counselling centres for such cases are few and totally inadequate to deal with the complexity and scale of the problem.

The psychiatrist Dr P. Ngully from Nagaland, associated with the study referred to earlier is among the very few specialists to have looked at PTSD and post-trauma stress syndrome (PTSS) in the state (Hazarika and Gill 2011). The people of Nagaland have faced confrontation and violence both from the state and non-state groups for over 50 years, and Dr Ngully says that the sight of a uniformed person evokes fear and terror among many villagers in the state. 'They have rarely seen any other face of India barring the army and the paramilitary, which they associate with harassment and violent behaviour', he said.

In fact, the respondents to the survey and interviews set out therein were posited on a set of questions developed by the National Institute of Health (US), which are internationally accepted as indicative of whether a person has suffered from or suffers from PTSD. This question-naire was made a prerequisite to the identification of the 'victims' to be interviewed under this project. This was done on the advice of two prominent psychiatrists.[3] These were the hinges that opened the doors to an unprecedented and moving outpouring of experiences, narrations and stories from victims for this report. The questions were the following:

'In your life have you ever had any experience that was so frightening, horrible or upsetting that, in the past month, you:

Have had nightmares about it or thought about it when you did not want to?

Tried hard not to think about it or went out of your way to avoid situations that reminded you of it?

You were constantly on guard, watchful or easily startled?

Felt numb or detached from others, from activities or your own surroundings?'

This approach has helped in the process of enabling women to share their experiences of coping with the realities of daily life, experiences that they perhaps would not have felt confident enough to share were it not for the fact that the research teams in both states chosen for the study were 'local' and that contacts with those interviewed were made with extensive help from friends, neighbours, civil society groups, local women's groups, local interpreters and guides.

Women, after all, are responsible in these situations as mothers of children, wives of the wounded, they are innocent victims of wars and conflicts not of their making (Sen, Hazarika and others 2008). They suffer as civilians with greater restrictions placed on them. They are assaulted, raped, humiliated, beaten and murdered during conflicts. They are displaced, turned out of their homes, disinherited, widowed and orphaned; they lose their children to bullets and beatings. Many just disappear, without a trace. Others are trafficked across state and national borders and face a nightmarish lifetime of sexual abuse and disease.

The loss that they face is not just emotional or physical but transfers into the economic and social spheres as well. Most women face a decline in social legitimacy and find themselves relegated to the fringes of society with no one to care for them or to speak on their behalf.

Since they form the bulk of the unemployed and the uneducated, they find themselves unable and ill-equipped to take on the burden of the household and as a result become completely poverty stricken. Young widows are forced to head households, even though in a patriarchal feudal set-up they have little or no access to land and property. In tribal societies the economic burden is generally considered a primary responsibility of women, and for this reason perhaps women get very little help from men or from the state in the aftermath of violence when the work of reconstruction begins. In Nagaland, for example, women do extensive fieldwork as in so many hill communities. In addition, they carry on with 'normal' life and do 'normal' chores to sustain their households – cooking, washing, fetching of water, bringing up and nurturing of children.

Other impacts of conflict include loss of livelihoods and food scarcity as a result of destruction of fields and farmlands, the destruction of basic infrastructure like roads and bridges, hospitals and shelters and schools (Sen, Hazarika and others 2008). The women are forced to take on the role of food providers and caretakers of the old and the infirm, the wounded and young. In times of war women's access to public spaces becomes even more restricted, and their mobility is further hampered by the presence of security forces and armed militias. All too often their bodies become the site of battle with both sides treating them as the spoils of war. Women who lose their 'honour' find it extremely difficult to lead normal lives and to live down the stigma. There is a total breakdown of structures, of the norms of behaviour, of what is socially sanctioned behaviour, and the results are the atrocities and human rights abuses that are reported by print, visual and audio media.

When there is a complete turning on its head of the known circumstances, the known life and exchanging it for the unknown, the uncertain, the insecure and the dangerous, how do people, especially women, who are the most vulnerable sections of society, cope? What happens when they are forced to flee, to leave the familiar environments of their villages and towns, and find themselves cut off from their tribes and cultural moorings? What dangers confront them in their new environments? These are difficult and challenging issues and troubling questions.

Continued violence, especially in the rural areas, has resulted in large-scale migration of young women and men to urban centres. Without any effective support system, they become extremely vulnerable to exploitation, violence and trafficking. The incidence of HIV/AIDS, drug abuse, alcohol and substance abuse increases substantially in such situations. The feminization of the AIDS epidemic is becoming all too apparent, and the increased vulnerability of women to HIV/AIDS in situations of conflict is an area of growing concern to social and health activists. The presence of armed forces in large numbers also increases the demand for sex workers, and young women are sucked into this and become pawns in a larger brutal network that thrives on human misery and conflict: human and drug trafficking proliferate with women and children being sent to other parts of the country. This is also as a result of the loss of other economic options and increased poverty as a result of longstanding conflict situations and their aftermath.

The state of women's health is another picture of neglect and apathy in areas of conflict. There is a lack of infrastructure, of adequate facilities, of health personnel, and most of the Centre's much-hyped health schemes remain just on paper with few being able to access these. Travels to the remote hinterland of both Nagaland and Assam showed us how the most marginalised segments of its population hardly figure in the 'Incredible India' promoted by large corporations and governments, marching, the public is informed, towards development and health for all.

Another point important to flag here is what is happening to the young people, 'the children of the conflict', who are increasingly leaving their violent homelands for education and jobs elsewhere including large numbers of students who flock to Delhi University every year. There has been a social impact of this out-migration: even vegetable sellers in areas where people from the region have settled have picked up languages of the new immigrants as part of an effort not just to make the latter culturally comfortable but also expand the dimensions and limits of their local businesses. This out-migration is significant but the social dimensions of this migration need to be reviewed: what does the movement of a large amount of human resource capital mean for small conflict-ridden states such as Nagaland and Manipur? Did these youth ever go back and if so to what?

An answer can be found in the fact that the exodus from the southern and western states during the 2012 outflow, fuelled by a hate campaign alleging brutality against Muslims in Assam by the Bodos, was brief. Within a few weeks or months, many of those who had fled to villages and towns in Assam, Manipur, Mizoram and Nagaland had returned to their adopted states and home cities. They defied and denounced, through their return, the patently false and extremely offensive campaigns through the social media. But what many remarked upon, either as they waited for trains to take them away or during the journeys back or as they stayed at home, was how little people even in relatively better educated states such as Maharashtra, Karnataka and Tamil Nadu appeared to know about the North-East. Everyone was tarred with one brush – either they were from Assam or the North-East. Protestations and efforts at defining individual ethnic status and emphasising differences drew few responses, showing that those who involved in the anti-North-Eastern campaigns based a broader discrimination on ignorance and media type.

But what has not been addressed so far are some of the issues raised in the earlier part of this chapter with regard to PTST and PTSS victims of either the violence in the Bodo Territorial Council or those who lived in stressful conditions but were not directly harmed. Few, if any of those who left for the NER or those who returned, requested or received any counselling from trained psychiatrists or counsellors. Therefore, it is difficult to assess the scale of trauma or stress that the migrants would have suffered although from interviews some had given to print, visual and audio media as well as social media including their own e-mails and short messaging service (SMS) messages, it was clear that they had suffered anxiety and various degrees of stress and fear.

This is why it is crucial that not just scholars, researchers, nongovernmental organisations (NGOs), activists, media and state governments, but also the State Human Rights Commissions, State Women's Commissions and State Child Rights Commissions, seize the window of opportunity presented by the Planning Commission's report in the 12th Five Year Plan. In a section on gender issues, the Planning Commission has, in a radical approach for a department of the Government of India, suggested not just compensation but also special facilities such as counselling and the need to provide access to such services to those in conflict situations. This needs to be followed up so these rights become accessible and do not just remain on paper. For this to happen, activists and other groups mentioned above need to develop a common strategy through a common approach to these concerns. Funding for special projects needs to be designed and accessed. It is a long struggle ahead but a path now exists, which has been carved out, for a change, with Central Government support, not opposition.

A large number of political conflicts in the NER are rooted in disputes over land, territory and natural resources. State governments need to appoint task forces manned by respected scholars, civil society leaders and researchers as well as senior officials to review and verify land records and the ownership of land so that the rights of all who are protected by law remain inalienable. There need to be public hearings and public forums involving young scholars and youth leaders, not the traditional public organisations with their set perceptions, to get their viewpoints across. These may be both significantly different to current discourse and established viewpoints.

Till date, the land rights of the Bodos especially have been observed more in the breach; yet, in this complex situation, it is difficult to see how the rights of any one group can be protected at the expense of others. Can one group, however old, and whose traditional lands these are, claim to have more enduring rights to land and settlement than newer groups, whose ownership may be half a century old at the least? These are serious issues which need serious and open discussion if dialogue is the way out of this excruciating conundrum.

Land and natural resources are finite; matters are not helped by ratcheting up the political rhetoric.

How is this to be resolved: the following can act as a rough roadmap – One of the first things to recognise in this complex situation is that the local revenue staff are among those who have been directly responsible for the illegal settlements by later migrants, for alienating Bodo and tribal land in the defined blocks and areas including reserved forests. They have been doing this with impunity for decades without punishment. So, clearly, one of the first things is to fix responsibility and throw the law at the errant staff, who would probably have done what he or she did, in connivance with senior district officials as well as politicians. Pressing forward with investigations will unravel the mess and the interconnectivity of corruption and power politics.

Can lands be restored without creating new fissures, fractures and fights? The way forward could be a transparent process based on a dialogue between community leaders involved as well as the government: state governments have to play honest broker through representatives who should be respected scholars or jurists. The land settlement process may involve a technical acknowledgement of the rights of the original owner and ensuring that he or she gets full and adequate compensation at competitive rates. But in such a scheduled area, where non-tribals are not supposed to hold property, can that guarantee any rights for the new and existing *pattadhari* and settlers. Can land purchase be done legally? Can the settler be assured that he or she will not be intimidated or threatened and that any such intimidation will be met with the full force of the law?

A new elite from among the Bodos has emerged, which that is articulate, both politically and economically powerful and thus has access, through its networks and clout, to large funds and keeping the land of the Bodos with Bodos, albeit a different class. In addition, the Bodo insurgency and the revolt by the United Liberation Front of Asom (ULFA) have withered despite occasional local media hype. Both groups are deeply divided and weakened by detentions, dialogue and surrenders as well as a sharp erosion of public support.

At this point, it is important to examine the other focus of this chapter: that the enormous powers endowed on the security forces have not enabled better governance or even improved security. The following example should suffice:

There was a critical delay in calling out the Army to deal with the acute burst of bloodshed between 20 and 25 July 2012, when violence peaked especially between Bodo and settler Muslims of Bengali origin, with the latter bearing the brunt of it. Yet, it is an issue that cuts across the gamut of Centre–state relations, raises issues of constitutionality and the law, and defines the role of the Army and defence forces in situations of civil conflict. The delay arguably led to the death of scores and the largest internal displacement in India since Partition.

After a series of attacks and counter-killings on 19–20 July, the violence was not stopped until Army columns moved in on 25 July. By then over 400,000 persons were homeless and sheltered in relief camps. The deployment of the Army was delayed; I was informed after inquiring of the Central Home Ministry and the Assam state government, because of a procedural issue.

In December 1992, the demolition of the Babri Masjid at Ayodhya
led to widespread communal riots. At the time, the Ministry of Defence
developed what a standard operating procedure (SOP) under which the
ministry reviews, calls for the Army to come to the aid of the civil administration during communal (or also ethnic and linguistic) disturbances
and decide how and when to act. The procedure is coordinated with the
nodal ministry for law enforcement, the Ministry for Home Affairs.

According to senior retired Army officers, the effort is 'to stop state
governments from calling the Army out at the drop of a hat' since they
feel that the Army must be the last resort. The Assam case, therefore,
is worth examining because it raises uncomfortable questions about the
limits of power.

A unified command structure, where civil and military organisations
coordinate their activities under the chairmanship of the chief minister,
is in place.

The Army has been in operation in the state since the early 1990s
where it is deployed under the aegis of the Disturbed Areas Act. In
turn, it can use extensive force under the Armed Forces (Special Powers) Act (AFSPA) to tackle any apparent security problem. The Disturbed Areas Act is the enabling law which ensures that the security
forces can act independently and aggressively. AFSPA, in contrast,
devolves the following sweeping powers – cordon and search, destruction of weapons dumps, arrest without warrants or on mere suspicion,
searches of private premises and even shooting to kill upon suspicion – on soldiers.

Significantly, nowhere in AFSPA does it specify that military action is
against armed insurgencies: the Disturbed Areas Act says that the Army
will come to the aid of civil authority.

> If, in relation to any State or Union Territory to which this Act
> extends, the Governor of that State or the Administrator of that
> Union Territory or the Central Government, in neither case, is
> of the opinion that the whole or any part of such state or Union
> Territory, as the case may be, is in such a disturbed or danger-
> ous condition that the use of armed forces in aid of the civil
> power is necessary, the Governor of that State ... or the Central

Government . . . declare the whole or such part of such State or Union Territory to be a disturbed area.

Thus, AFSPA can be used to combat rioting in 'aid of the civil power'. And it is not the Army which decides that: it is the government, acting through the governor, who is bound by the advice of the cabinet, the Centre or union territory administrator. So, if we follow the Assam case, this is the sequence of events – appeals by the Assam chief secretary, the deputy commissioners of Kokrajhar (the worst-affected district) and Dhubri districts to local army commanders requisitioning their services, were referred to the Ministry of Defence.

This was done, despite the fact that various major strike formations were located either in Assam or neighbouring states, not far from the areas where bloodshed was taking place. The first reference was made to the Ministry of Defence on 20 July; authorisation to deploy was given on 25 July. Five critical days were lost as mayhem ruled and fighters armed with automatic weapons on one side went on the offensive while large mobs of the other community counter-attacked, with spears and *daos* (machetes) wherever they found vulnerable targets.

Homes were burned – which meant that documents relating to land and property went up in smoke – as did money and valuables. For five days, despite the pleas of the state government, Assam burned. Luckily for many victims, land records have been extensively computerised, and they were later able to generate copies of their land deeds.

So, although many of us are opposed to the continuation of AFSPA since we regard it as a draconian and brutal law that has no place in a democratic polity and provides immunity and impunity to the armed forces (there can be no criminal prosecution of errant army soldiers without Central government sanction, something that has not happened in nearly 60 years), we cannot but point out that it is a law that exists (until such time as it is amended or repealed). It cannot be wished away. Surely, a law, and an existing law at that, overrides a mere standard operating procedure; the latter is nothing more than an administrative tactic.

We can go further: the major provisions of law relevant here are Sections 130 and 131 of the Criminal Procedure Code and relevant provisions of the Indian Penal Code. A reading of these makes clear that the Army must respond to summons from civil authority – as the latter is best placed to decide whether a situation has gone beyond the capacity of local law enforcement forces to deal with it. This is the law of the land, a constitutional mandate, which surely overrides both AFSPA, which is a creature of the night, designed in 1958 (without even naming an insurgent group) or a mere procedural order.

The Army and the Ministry of Defence – and the Ministry of Home Affairs, which at least has acknowledged the delay and has wanted the Defence Ministry to scrap the standard operating procedure – cannot take shelter under the plea of procedural delays. If any investigation into this failure has been conducted, it is not been made public, nor has culpability been fixed (at least not publicly). That is a fate similar to that of the Justice Jeevan Reddy Committee Report (of which I was a member), which reviewed AFSPA and submitted its report in June 2005. The government still has not made the Reddy Report public, despite extensive public pressure. If it can also be used to destroy illegal weapons dumps, as AFSPA provisos say, surely this can be a powerful tool to tackle illegal weapons floating around in Bodoland and which continue to strike such public fear.

The following is an excerpt from an article I wrote for *The Hindu* in February 2013, which sums up the contradiction and failure of relying on laws that reward brutality, create impunity and immunity and enshrine inequality:

At an institute that is virtually owned, funded and run by the Ministry of Defence, union finance minister P. Chidambaram did the unthinkable the other day. He virtually attacked the Army for refusing to review and amend the draconian AFSPA, if not repeal it altogether. Like a clever politician, he tossed the issue squarely into the lap of the Army and the Ministry of Defence, saying they were unambiguously opposed to any change and that you should ask the question to the armed forces and ask why are they so opposed to even some amendment to AFSPA which will make [it] more humanitarian. We have [the] Jeevan Reddy Committee report but yet if the Army takes a very strong stand against any dilution or any amendment to AFSPA, it is difficult for a civil government to move forward. (Hazarika 2013)[4]

This raises a startling issue about democracy, the rule of law and of civilian control over the military. Now that the most powerful figure in the Cabinet after the prime minister has spoken, perhaps someone will take notice. But the problem is far more complex than it appears to be.

After all, the minister did not say why the government of India has refused to publish the Reddy Committee's report or even table it in Parliament eight years after it was submitted. It remains accessible on *The Hindu's* website, the place where the report was first leaked and published verbatim in 2005. It is not that the question is simple, stark and frightening: who runs the North-East or Jammu and Kashmir or any area that is affected by insurgency? AFSPA is put in place after the area has been declared 'disturbed' under the Disturbed Areas Act, the enabling provision of law, which facilitates the summoning of the Army to the aid of civil authorities who are unable to control armed insurrection. This is the call of the state government or the Centre.

Passed in 1958 when the Naga movement for independence had just taken off, AFSPA is a bare law with just six sections. The most damning are those in the fourth and sixth sections: the former enables security forces to 'fire upon or otherwise use force, even to the causing of death' where laws are being violated. The latter says no criminal prosecution will lie against any person who has taken action under this act. In 54 years, not a single army or paramilitary officer or soldier has been prosecuted for murder, rape or destruction of property (including the burning of villages in the 1960s in Nagaland and Mizoram). In the discussions over the past days, no one has even mentioned the regrouping of villages in both places: villagers were forced to leave their homes at gunpoint, throw their belongings onto the back of a truck and move to a common site where they were herded together with strangers and formed new villages. It is a shameful and horrific history, which India knows little about and has cared even less for.

A year ago, two judges of the Supreme Court, intervening in a case where the Central Bureau of Investigation was seeking to prosecute army officers accused of murdering five villagers in Jammu and Kashmir, in what is known as the Pathribal incident, declared clearly that AFSPA's protection was limited to acts conducted in the line of duty.

'You go to a place in exercise of AFSPA, you commit rape, you commit murder, then where is the question of sanction? It is a normal crime which needs to be prosecuted, and that is our stand,' declared the bench of Justices Swatanter Kumar and B.S. Chauhan.

It's simple: you don't rape or murder 'in the line of duty'. These are aberrations to the law of military conduct with civilians. And the Army is upset that the Justice J.S. Verma Committee even suggested that military men accused of sexual assault should be tried under normal law and not be protected by the law that guarantees absolute protection: Immunity.

We need to remember two points here about AFSPA and the place where it all began – Nagaland, in 1958. Nagaland today is peaceful. It is not free of intimidation, extortion or a factional killing, but not a single Indian solider has fallen in combat here for the past five years. The state government has been asking, since 2005, for the removal of the Disturbed Areas Act. The government of India refuses to listen.

What is the greater abomination then? Is it that the Army, which is easy to blame and always in the line of fire, is stuck in a thankless task? Or is it that the civilian government which first sent them there is unable to take the political decision that will bring the boys home? Fifty-four years is a long time to have a law as revoltingly brutal and obscure as AFSPA. Now, both sides are stuck. The Army says it is like its 'Bible' and that if the act is removed it will face the prospect of fighting 'with one hand tied'. The Central government says that it can't persuade the Army to back down.

What will it take to close this sad, ignominious and bloody chapter in our nation's history? We will need to go beyond former finance minister Chidambaram's remarks – for what he was doing is to lay the blame at the door of the Army. That is not right for the civilian government is equally complicit in this. He is seeking to show that the 'civilian' government is opposed to a securitised approach and that the Ministry of Defence and the Army are isolated. But this approach does not work. Instead, it shows that the two, even when isolated, are more powerful than the rest of the government put together.

They have, after all, successfully stalled any effort to dilute or amend the act. Why did the 'civilian' government not have the courage to act in 2005 when the Reddy Committee gave its report, which not only recommended AFSPA's repeal but also proposed a legal mechanism by which the Army could be used in extraordinary situations involving national security? Our essential recommendation was that no one could be above the law; everyone must be equal before and under it.

The Centre has lost more than seven years in coming to no decision on the recommendations. Yes, internal wrangling is difficult to resolve, but how long should anyone have to wait for a resolution? Today, the situation has become much more complex because the window of opportunity provided by the Reddy Committee has virtually closed. The Army has bolted it because it does not want to be seen as the villain of the piece. It did not ask to go anywhere. It was sent to Nagaland and Manipur. But now it must, in its own interests and that of the country, get out of places where threats to national security simply do not exist, and when the Central government thinks it should leave. After all, if required, the security forces can always be summoned again.

The situation calls for statesmanship of a very high order. Atal Bihari Vajpayee showed this in 2003 on his maiden visit to Kohima when he reflected, as prime minister, on the suffering that both sides had faced and sought to reach out and seek reconciliation:

> Let us leave behind all the unfortunate things that happened in the past. For too long this fair land has been scarred and seared by violence. It has been bled by the orgy of the killings of human beings by human beings. . . Each death diminishes us . . . The past cannot be rewritten. But we can write our common future with our collective, cooperative efforts.

Former Prime Minister Manmohan Singh decided that AFSPA must be reviewed. But he did not press for its repeal or amendments because the opposition from the Defence Ministry and the generals was just too strong. The present situation demands measures no less significant from the current Prime Minister.

For we continue to ask, as we rest and wrestle with this tortuous story: how many more deaths, how many more naked protests, how many more hunger strikes, how many more committees, how many more editorials and articles and broadcasts before AFSPA goes?

Notes

1 Official census data show that about 33 per cent of the state population is Muslim and these are divided into three broad groups: Assamese Muslims, some of whom go back several centuries; Bengali-origin Muslims who have come from the former East Bengal and East Pakistan and settled here pre-independence and pre-1971 when Bangladesh was ripped out of Pakistan and finally 'Bangladeshis' who have come illegally to India since 1971.
2 Hazarika and Gill (2011). The report has relied upon this study for material used in pages 4–10). 'Bearing Witness: The impact of conflict on Women in Nagaland and Assam.' Heinrich Boll Foundation and Centre for North Eastern Studies and Policy Research, New Delhi. The report has relied upon this study for material used here (www.c-nes.org).
3 Dr Sandi Syiem and Dr Ngully. The former runs the San-Ker Rehabilitation Centre in Shillong, Meghalaya.
4 The author has drawn from his article in 'The Hindu' of Feb 12, 2013 for material and comments in this section.

9

ASPECTS OF HINDU–MUSLIM DIVIDE IN LITERATURE AND THE ROLE OF INTELLIGENTSIA

Hitendra K. Patel

The relation between state and religion had been 'turned around'[1] through the forces of colonial and postcolonial modernity. The practices of different communities came under the supervision of law and religious communities became self-conscious as community. Fuelled by the rivalries between the 'frustrated' middle classes of Hindus and Muslims and articulated effectively by the intelligentsia of both communities there emerged the ideology of communalism.[2]

Communalism began with nationalist claims but soon it tried to make a line beyond which it tried to exclude all others who do not belong to a particular religion. In a way, both – national and communal – ideologies use same resources but with different objectives – one mobilising with the intentions of strengthening the *dharam/kaum* and the other attempting to promote loyalty to a geographical area around which an emotional appeal is created and shared. The sense of geography in case of communal ideology is somewhat less pronounced. Both ideologies look towards the history for legitimacy but their takes are qualitatively different.

With this perspective when we try to prepare an account of the emerging and crystallisation of the Hindu–Muslim divide, or communalism in Hindi-speaking areas, hot bed of communal struggles, we face a knotty question – whether we should underline the pronounced caste-Hindu perspective in the writings of late nineteenth and early twentieth centuries or not. This dilemma is so complicated largely because these writers are celebrated, justifiably, as the icons; they had awakened the people of India and inspired them to think socially and nationally. A standard and appealing way has been to consider that even if there had been some communal 'tinge' or conservative streaks in their ideology, these writers collectively worked for strengthening the progressive forces. So, in the ultimate analysis, due to their efforts the literary world moved from conservative mode to progressive mode. Taking the example of great Bharatendu Harischandra, a great Hindi progressive literary critic, Ramvilas Sharma has emphasised that we must see how the progressive elements became stronger with the passage of time and Bharatendu did not end where he had begun his literary journey.[3] This is a fair argument and many of us would love to go by this argument and say that what mattered was the lasting and end result and these greats' literary achievements must be celebrated and the orthodoxies of their outlook were the limitations of the time. But, the problem is that we also have to write the history of communal divide in India, which seems to have threatened our social unity and which is still one of the biggest challenges before us. And, if one takes this project we get into this unpleasant task of examining the literature of late nineteenth and early twentieth centuries to say that this half a century had created a communal divide and in this entire process the role of the intelligentsia, the creator of nationalism, cannot be denied.[4]

At the time when nationalism was in the making (between the 1870s and 1920s), their communal consciousness was very much part of their national consciousness. The elements of communalism continued to be an assisting factor for nationalism until politics took a different turn in the mid-1920s.[5] It has been argued, further, that the ideologies of nationalism and communalism were interwoven and their discourses often overlapped and it was difficult to have a clear-cut distinction between the exponents of composite nationalism of the Indian National Congress variety and the communal 'nationalism' of Hindu Mahasabha variety till 1920s. Bipan Chandra has noted that, 'till the early 1930s, several leaders were simultaneously members and leaders of the Congress and the Hindu Mahasabha or the Muslim League'.[6] Even, after that, there existed, at least at the level of expectation, an association between the Hindus of the Hindu communal organisations and the 'Congress Hindus'. Jagat Narayan Lal, the most important Hindu Mahasabha leader from Bihar who became national general secretary of Mahasabha, wrote a letter to B.S. Moonje, a stalwart of Hindu communal politics from Maharashtra:

> This morning, I read your latest opinion in the "Patrika" in which you say that if the Congress does not openly condemn the (Communal) award the Mahasabha will have to set up its own candidates. I do not know how you are thinking (of it). . . . to me the matter seems to be very delicate indeed. I am sure, the Congress Board will not openly oppose the 'communal award'. I feel equally doubtful if the Mahasabha would succeed in returning a satisfactory number of candidates if it were to run the elections in its own name or that of any other party. In case, success is very doubtful, will it be politic to alienate the Congress Hindus whose sympathies would otherwise be with us in the matter of the award and go into the assembly with a few men who when they got up to denounce the award in the assembly would be received coldly by the Congress Hindus and opposed strongly by the Moslems and the government group which is bound to support the award of its own premier. The chances of successfully opposing the award with any degree of effectiveness are more favourable in the case of the Congressmen coming with us than by opposing them. . . . To me, it is clear that the safest course might be for us to set a few of our chosen men on independent tickets and to see that they are not opposed by the Congress and to send as many men in sympathy with us on Congress ticket as possible.[7]

In the 1920s and 1930s it was not unusual for the Hindu communal organisations to look upon the 'Congress Hindus' for support on issues which involved 'Hindu' and 'Muslim' interests. Multiple examples from the newspapers and literary writings of the 1920s can be cited from Hindi-speaking regions to support this view.[8]

Having said this, we should also try to see the other strands in the writings of the intelligentsia, which seem to take a different take on the Hindu–Muslim relationship. We also have a large number of evidences that inform that there were people who emphasised the need for Hindu–Muslim unity for their mutual benefit. Bharatendu's Ballia lecture of 1884 has been seen as earliest example of this approach among the intelligentsia. But, there were other who had expressed similar views much earlier.[9] This dual role of the intelligentsia is often underplayed and often scholars seem to look for only one ideology in their writings. It often gets ignored that these two ideologies – nationalism and communalism – faced each other and finally confronted each other they arose from the same social and intellectual bases should not be denied. The literature, which is seen as the site which created a national ideology for the readers of different languages of India, was also creating communal stereotypes that widened the divide of the Hindus and the Muslims. This issue is taken up in detail in this paper.

The intelligentsia and the widening of Hindu–Muslim divide

Modern Hindu communalism[10] originated in Calcutta in 1860s and 1870s.[11] How this Hindu communalism was linked with the emergence of communal thinking of the Hindi intelligentsia has been taken up for study by some scholars but all of them have sought to understand this with the empirical evidences of the United Provinces. Starting with Sudhir Chandra, Gyanendra Pandey and Vasudha Dalmia to Alok Rai and Francesca Orsini no one have gone deep into the Hindi sources of other regions to address the question why there was a clear drift towards communal ideology in the writings of the intelligentsia in the regions between Agra and Calcutta. This question is further complicated if we underline the fact that in the first half of the writings of northern India we hardly come across to literary evidences, which might suggest that the intelligentsia was much concerned about the barbaric Muslims and their unholy deeds. There is obviously a trend of making communal stereotypes in 1880s and 1890s Hindi writings.

Making of communal stereotypes in literature

In literature the scheme for an all-India organisation called the Maha Hindu Samiti exclusively committed to the defence of Hindus existed from at least 1860s. Rajnarain Basu in his *Bridha Hindur Aasha* outlined interests and overtly using Hindu labels. Nabagopal Mitra launched a national fair known as the Hindu Mela in 1867.[12] Rakhal Chandra Nath has documented how Hindu perspective had been in the making in Bengal at least since 1866.[13] Other scholars have argued that the second half of the nineteenth century saw the emergence of nationalism in Bengal, and the abiding theme of the heroic annals of this nationalism was the resistance of the medieval Hindu chiefs against Muslim invaders.[14] Bipan Chandra and Sumit Sarkar have described this as 'vicarious nationalism'.[15] 'The pioneer poet of vicarious nationalism' was Rangalal Bandyopadhyay.[16] Bandopadhyay's *Padmini-Upakhyan* was based on James Tod's book *Annals and Antiquities of Rajasthan*. It dealt with the story of Sultan Alauddin's lust for Queen Padmini a proud Hindu Rajput woman. When powerful Muslim Sultan defeated the Rajput king and he was about to approach the queen she sacrificed herself for the sake of dignity and took the course of *jauhar vrata* (jumping into the fire this pattern of putting barbaric Muslims against the pious and virtuous Hindus was followed in Bandopadhyay's other novel – *Karmadevi*. Dinabandhu Mitra, the writer of *Nil Darpan*, followed Rangalal's scheme of Indian history in his poem *Yuddha*. Other writers like Govindchandra Ray,[18] Anandachandra Mitra,[19] Dinanath Sen[20] and Bijaychandra Majumdar followed similar pattern.[21] Anuradha Roy has documented how a large number of novels, plays and poems were written, which depicted Muslims as invaders who were cruel and who had oppressed Hindus as rulers.[22] In the process, the idea of a Hindu nation was invented and religion (Hinduness) was made the basis of this newly invented nation. This nation thrived on the idea of a glorious Hindu past which became part of common sense of the educated people of Bengal largely due to these popular romances. In this scheme, Muslims became the outsiders of this nation.

The concept of Muslim foreignness and tyranny was a subsidiary to this concept of a Hindu nation.[23]

She rightly concludes:

Thanks to the *bhadralok* plunging deep down into mythical Aryan glory during the 1880s the Rajputs, the Marathas and the

Sikhs were all considered as Aryans by the nationalists. Vaish-
navas, Shaivas, Buddhists, Jains and Sikhs (as a matter of fact
all, except Christian and Muslims), were considered as Aryans
in these writings.[24]

In Hindi writings the negative image of the Muslims was pronounced
in the creative and journalistic writings of late nineteenth century.
Bharatendu Harischandra wrote: 'Jin Javanan tum dharam nari dhan tina-
hun leeno' [You Muslim foreigners! You have robbed us (Hindus) of (our)
dharma, women and wealth].[26]

In the writings of Pratap Narayan Mishr, another leading literary figure, this tendency of seeing along community lines is evident. He has
expressed his anguish at seeing the cowardliness of the Hindus not being
able to fight against the Muslims:

> Jahan rajkanya ke dola Turkan ke ghar janya,
> Tahan dusari kaun bat he jaha man log lajanya,
> Bhala in hijaran te kuch hona hai.
> [Where the princesses' palanquins go to the homes of Turks,
> What else can make these people ashamed?
> Can these eunuchs do anything worthy!]][27]

Any survey of the romances written on historical themes reveals that
these novels were written to support the morals of Nissahay Hindu (Helpless Hindu) by providing stories to make them feel good. A title Nissahay
Hindu sums up the mindset of the religious Hindus of the Hindi intelligentsia of the nineteenth and early twentieth centuries. This novel was
written in 1881 by Braj Ratna Das, a well-known Hindi writer, in which
the plight of the vulnerable Hindus was narrated.

There are a number of Hindi novels that were written between 1870
and 1917. The books written by Kishori Lal Goswami, Gangaprasad
Gupta and Jairam Gupta during this period are most significant. Kishori
Lal, the father of historical romances, wrote Hridaya Harini va Adarsha
Ramani,[28] Lavang Lata va Aadarsha Bala,[29] Gulbahar va Adarsha Bhratris-
neha,[30] Tara va Kshatrakulmalini,[31] Kanak Kusum va Mastani,[32] Hirabai va
Behayayi ka borka,[33] Sultana Razia beghum va Rangamahal mein halahal,[34]
Mallika Devi va Banga Sarojini,[35] Lucknow ki kabra va Shahi Mahalsara,[36]

Sona aur Sugandha va Pannabai,[37] *Lal Kunwar va Shahi Rangamahal,*[38] *Noorjehan*[39] and *Gupta Godana.*[40]

Most of these books were written with Hindu Brahmanical sensibilities using Hindu family values. The Muslims entered these stories either as cruel villains or beautiful women who were dying for their Hindu lovers. In some cases, Muslim women like Noorjehan and Razia Sultan were written about but it seems that these stories generally highlighted the intrigues at the courts of Muslim rulers rather than the qualities of these powerful Muslim women. Some other writers followed this pattern of writing. Ganga Prasad Gupta followed this pattern of writing in *Noorjehan va Sansar Sundari (1902), Veer Patni* (1903), *Kunwar Singh Senapati* (1903), *Veer Jaimal va Krishna Kanta* (1903) and *Hammeer* (1904). Jairam Das Gupta wrote *Kashmir Patan* (1906),[41] *Kishori va Veer Bala* (1907),[42] *Mayarani* (1908), *Veer Varangana va Aadarsha Lalana* (1909) and *Rani Panna va Raj Lalana* (1910).

The other more significant historical novels that depicted the greatness of the Hindus in historical times are: *Maharaja Vikramaditya ka jivan charitra,*[43] *Maharja Chhatrapati Shivaji ka jivan charitra, Veer Narayan, Jaya,*[44] *Anarkali, Barahvi Sadi ka veer Jagdev Parmar, Prithwiraj Chauhan,*[45] *Kotarani, Tantia Bheel, Panipat, Veer Bala, Naradev, Rani Bhavani, Noorjehan va Jahangir Begum, Padmini, Roothi Rani, Veer Maloji Bhonsale, Maharana Pratap Singh ki veerata, Saundarya Kusum va Maharashtra ka uday, Veerangana, Veer Bala, Jaishree va Veer Balikam Maharani Padmini, Rana Sanga aur Babar, Mewar ka uddharkarta, Maharashtra Veer, Razia Begum,*[46] *Pranapalan,*[47] *Veer Churamani, Bheem Singh, Krishna Kumari Bai, Anangpal, Rajput Ramani, Lalcheen,*[48] *Vichitra Veer, Veer Mani, Sone ki Rakh va Padmini, Rani Durgavati, Swapna Rajasthan* and *Aadarsha veerangana Durga.*

In these novels the storyline follows somewhat predictable patterns. Almost invariably the Hindu characters are struggling to achieve the ideal. Between these characters and their cherished ideals are the obstacles in the form of Muslim characters. In almost all stories the cruelty and selfishness of Muslims is invariably present. In those novels where the Muslims are to be retained for the authenticity of the story the whole situation was depicted as if all characters are engaged in intrigues against each other. The moral of the story was that Muslims are cruel, selfish, intriguing and dishonest.

A review of the theme, storyline and morals of these historical romances reveals that these novels were structured in such a way that the readers were expected to accept that the Muslims had not won the land by the force of sword but by conceit, cruelty and deceit. Their women were full of vanity and the Muslims, in general, were no match to honesty and bravery of the great Hindus. In a brilliant essay on the historical romances of Kishorilal Goswami,[49] Madhuresh, a Hindi critic, has shown how his 65 books have been informed by a communal view of the history of India between 1200 and 1757, the period he used as background of his novel.[50]

If we add the large number of works translated from Bengali to Hindi,[51] which were also historical novels, we have a substantial amount of literature produced during the 1870s and 1920s, which can be considered literature whose objective was to arouse national sentiments by pitting Hindu heroes and heroines against Muslim villains. In addition, a number of Bengali works were translated by the writers of Bihar, like Ishwari Prasad Sharma, in which the Hindu perspective was quite obvious.[52]

Conclusion

It can be said that the Hindi intelligentsia could not be free from the virus of communalism largely because the way the new and better social and political order was perceived by them had allowed Hindu way of looking at things in the late nineteenth and early twentieth centuries. In this whole process, the role of conservative orthodox elements of both Sanatani and Arya Samaj varieties have been studied but the role of colonial government and the role of Bengali intelligentsia have not been given due attention. In Bengal the communal tinge had been an integral part of all their national or *jatiya* imaginations.

As early as 1823 Ram Mohan Roy had written: 'Divine Providence at last, in its abundant mercy, stirred up the English nation to break the yoke of those tyrants (Muslims), and to receive the oppressed natives of Bengal under its protection.' With these words he set a trend. Throughout the nineteenth century, the Bengali literati harboured these sentiments and articulated them in their writings. Needless to add, that this literati consisted of Hindu upper-caste people who had access to Western education. Whatever their other differences, on the question of 'Muslim tyranny' they spoke with one voice.[53]

It can be argued that the recovery of a shared past and the memory of the shared social experiences can only be possible if a more thorough examination of the early nineteenth century intellectual history is written and the historical evidences of local language materials are studied.

Notes

1 Kaviraj (2010: 294). In this connection, we must keep in mind the basic difference between two schools of thought over the question of communalism – the colonial and the national: one taking an essentialist view and considering communalism as an integral part of Indian society and the other taking it as a development of the late colonial period. For elaboration on this see Romila Thapar, Harbans Mukhia and Bipan Chandra (1969).

2 Gyanendra Pandey has forcefully argued that communalism is a form of colonialist knowledge; it is reserved for the analysis of social and political conflicts in the 'backward parts' of the colonial and postcolonial world. He has argued that the nationalists have popularised its used in 1920s and 1930s while struggling against the colonial regime. He has made a forceful argument that the colonial and national takes on communalism are somewhat linked when he has mentioned that the nationalists like B.N. Dar, Gandhi and Ganesh Shankar Vidyarthi talked about the 'meekness', 'natural cowardness' and other kind of things as the basic differences between the Hindus and Muslims. In his view, the colonialists and the nationalists perspectives share a common ground. See Pandey (1992: 6–13).

3 For Ramvilas Sharma's views on this progressive role of Bharatendu see *Harischandra* (1966) and *Bharatendu Harischandra aur Hindi Navajagaran ki Samasyayein* (Delhi, 1989).

4 The intelligentsia had a powerful role in creating a situation wherefrom religion was seen as the basis of nationhood and thought (Sudipta Kaviraj, op. cit., p. 294). The role of the intelligentsia in the making of communalism has been a well attested area: In Bengal where this ideology was initially shaped its role has been studied by scholars like Amiya Sen, Pradip Datta, Anuradha Roy and others. In the study of the United Provinces the works of Sudhir Chandra, Gyanendra Pandey, Vasudha Dalmia, Charu Gupta and others can be seen ; For the role of the intelligentsia's role in Bihar towards this, works of Hitendra Patel and Mohammad Sajjad are available.

5 This argument had been developed by Gyanendra Pandey. Later many scholars have find merit in it and studied different areas to find somewhat similar conclusion. In case of Bihar, for example, it has been argued that the divide

between the ideologies – nationalism and communalism – was obvious only in 1920s; and even after this, communal ideology sought to remain seen with national ideology to use communal-minded Congress leaders. See Patel (2011).

6 (Chandra 1993: 149)

7 Jagat Narain Lal's letter from Bankipore, 10 June 1934, Patna, B.S. Moonje papers, File No. 37, Vol. I, 1934, 75 (Nehru Memorial Museum and Library), cited from Patel (2011: 224).

8 For more examples one can see *Abhyuday* (Allahabad), *Rasik Punch* (Calcutta) *Seva Sansar* (Calcutta) and other newspapers of this period.

9 The case of Shahamatali Khan (d. 1819) of Saran district can be cited in this context. His utterances over the need of unity among the Hindus and the Muslims and other issues go very close to much celebrated Bharatendu's Ballia lecture of 1884. His biographical sketch was included in Babu Ramdeen Singh's *Bihar Darpan* proves that even if we assume that the thoughts of Khan were not presented authentically, we must admit that as this was published in 1882, there existed the kind of thoughts that are attributed to Bharatendu. See Hetukar Jha ed., *Babu Ramdeen Singh Rachit Bihar Darpan* (first edition: 1882), Darbhanga: MKSKF, 1996, pp. 164–66.

10 It is to be noted that modern Hindu communalism is more related to modern Hinduism than Hinduism as a traditional religion. Ashis Nandy (1990) is correct in suggesting that the communalism is a modern phenomenon and political intolerance which sustains communal politics has not to do much with the religious tradition as such; rather it is created by modern ideas. A case of Ambikadatta Vyass (1858–1900) can be mentioned here: Vyass was an outstanding Sanskrit scholar, very knowledgeable scholar of tradition (he had successfully countered Dayanand Saraswati, Arya Samaj leader, in a *shastrtha* from traditional Hindu side) and a famous Hindi writer. If we closely read his famous play *Bharat Saubhagya*, we find him celebrating modern science, modern powerful state, industrialisation and so on along the lines of the British so that this *Bharat* could progress. He carried a communal outlook and his play had many passages that reveal his hatred for Muslims. One can say that writers like Vyass were mixing modern ideas with their articulation of tradition and the divide he perceived between Hindus and Muslims had much to do with modern ideas than tradition. (For details see Hitendra Patel, 'Aspects of the Ideology of Hindu Intelligentsia: A Case Study of Ambika Datt Vyass' http://www.academia.edu/736018/Aspects_of_the_Ideology_of_Hindu_Intelligentsia_A_Study_of_Ambika_Datt_Vyass_draft_paper_ (accessed on 29 May 2013). That is why the use of modern Hindu communalism is better than the use of mere Hindu communalism.

11 See Anuradha Roy (2003); (P. Chakravarty (1992).

12 (P. Chakravarty 1992: 9)

13 Rakhal Chandra Nath, *The New Hindu Movement 1886–1911* (Calcutta: Minerva), 1992. See Introduction.

14 Roy 2003: 35

15 Sumit Sarkar, *Modern India*, 84. Sumit Sarkar mentions that there was the development of 'vicarious nationalism' in Bengal. He attributes the phrase to Bipan Chandra.

16 Roy 2003: 38

17 Born: 1827; a scholar of English, Sanskrit and old Oriya; started his literary career with Iswar Gupta in *Samvad Prabhakar*; co-editor of Education Gazzete, 1855; teacher in Presidency College, 1860; joined as deputy collector and retired as deputy magistrate, 1882; wrote *Padmini-Upakhyan*, *Karmadevi* and *Shoor Sundari*; translated *Kumarsambhava*; wrote *KanchiKaveri* in Oriya, 1879; founded *Utkal Darpan*; wrote the first history of Calcutta *Kalikata Kalpalata*; died: 1887.

18 Born: 1838; wrote *Yamuna-lahari*; died: 1917.

19 Born: 1854; wrote *Kabir Swapna* (the dream of a poet).

20 Born: 1839; wrote *Bharater Sukhabasan*; died: 1898.

21 Born: 1861; wrote *Brahmabarte*; died: 1942.

22 For a detailed discussion on the writings which depicted Muslims in a poor light see Anuradha Roy, *Nationalism as Poetic Discourse in Nineteenth Century Bengal*, pp. 41–43.

23 Roy 2003

24 Roy 2003: 49

25 Jhari, K. D., 295. He elaborates further: 'Hindi Hindu Hindusthan' became the holy trinity of the literary gospel of this generation of Hindi writers. Nationalism in their intellectual scheme of things consisted in the uplift of the Hindu community and pride in and the glorification of its culture. 'A liberal, broad based nationalism was yet not in the offing' (292–95).

26 Bharatendu Harischandra, *Bharatendu Granthavali*, ed., Braj Ratna Das (Kashi, 1953), 764 cited in (Amin, 2002:26).

27 *Brahman*, 15 March 1883.

28 This novel was published in 1890 in *Hindustan*. The editor, Pratap Narayan Mishra, was the man who created the famous slogan, 'Hindi, Hindu, Hindustan'. It got published as a book in 1904.

29 It was also written in 1890 but as Pratap Narayan Mishra had left the paper it could not be published in Hindustan. It was published in 1904.

30 It was published in *Saraswati* in 1902.

31 Published in 1902.

32 This book was based on Bajirao Mastani written by Sakharam Ganesh Deuskar, the famous Maharashtrian writer born in Bihar, who wrote many Bengali books. It is difficult to know whether the original book had been as anti-Muslim as the Hindi book was. It was published in 1904. This narrative line was reused somewhat differently by a Hindi journal *Manoranjan* some 10 years later.

33 Written in 1904, published in 1905.

34 The first part of this novel was written in 1904 and the second part in the next year.

35 Written and published in 1905.

36 Published in 1906.

37 Published in 1909.

38 Published in 1909.

39 Published probably in 1909.

40 The first part of this novel was written by Devakinandan Khatri. Kishorilal wrote the other three volumes in the early 1920s.

41 The background of this novel is set in the context of the cruelty Moham-mad Azim Khan and his brother Zubbar Khan, the Muslim rulers of Kashmir, showed to the innocent Hindu people. Ultimately, the novel tells us, that Punjab's Keshari Ranajit Singh emancipated the Hindus from their rule.

42 See Gopal Rai (1968:131). In this novel, even Akbar the great was depicted as luring a princess of Mewar. Ultimately all his conspiracies failed. Gopal Rai sums up the novel by saying that its main them is the depiction of Akbar's baseness and the princess' bravery and devotion to her husband. (*kishori ki veerata aur pativratta ka chitran upanyas ka mool pratipadya hai.*)

43 This book was written by Kartik Prasad Khatri and was published from Muzaf-farpur in 1893.

44 This was also written by Kartik Prasad Khatri of Muzaffarpur in 1897.

45 Two books with the same title *Prithviraj Chauhan* were written, by Jayanti Prasad Upadhyay and Pandit Baldev Prasad Mishra.

46 This was written by Brajnandan Sahay, a famous Hindi writer of Bihar in 1915.

47 This novel was written by Siddhanath Singh and was published by Ishwari Prasad Sharma of Arrah in 1915.

48 This book was written by Brajnandan Sahay in 1921. Sensing its popularity this book was translated into Gujarati in 1926.

49 Born: 1865; a prolific Hindi writer; his father Basudev Lal was the literary guru of Bharatendu Harishchandra; Kishorilal Goswami wrote 65 books and he was acknowledged as the second most popular writer, after Devkinandan Khatri, of Hindi before Premchand came; he edited a highly popular literary magazine *Upanyas* whose every number carried one of his novels; his most famous books include *Hriday Harini, Lavang Lata, Gul Bahar, Tara, Kanak Kumari va Mastani, Hira Bai ka bahayami, Sultana Razia Begam, Shahi Malsara, Panna Bai, Lal Kunwar* and others; died 1932.

50 Madhuresh, 'Chinta, Chetna aur Sawal: Kishorilal Goswami', *Pahal* 89, July 2008, 226–40. In this essay, Madhuresh argues that, for Kishorilal Gos-wami even the popular Muslim personalities like Razia and Akbar were not really good characters. In many situations, Goswami talks of an alliance between the Hindus and the British against the Muslim.

51 For an idea of the amount of literature which was translated and published in Bihar we can see the list of books published by Khadagvilas Press, Patna.

In the period between 1889 and 1907 these important historical works were translated from Bengali to Hindi and published: *Rajsingh* (Bankimchandra), translated by Pratap Narayan Mishra, 1894. (Another translation was done by Kishorilal Goswami in 1910); *Indira* (Bankim): translated by Pratap Narayan Mishra, 1894; *Yuglanguriya* (Bankim): translated by Pratap Narayan Mishra, 1894. (Three editions were published.); *Radharani* (Bankim): translated by Pratap Narayan Mishra (improvised by Ayodhya Prasad Singh 'Hariaudh'), 1897; *Kapalkundala,* (Bankim): translated by Pratap Narayan Mishra, 1901. (Three editions); *Durgesh Nandini* (Bankim): translated by Radhakrishna Das, 1901; *Amar Singh* (Nagendranath Gupta): translated by Pratap Narayan Mishra, 1907; *Chandrasekhar* (Bankim): translated by Brajnandan Sahay, 1907; *Indira* (Bankim): translated by Kishorilal Goswami, 1908; *Devi Chaudhurani* (Bankim). For the complete list see Dhirendranath Singh 298–99).

52 Ishwari Prasad Sharma was one of the most important Hindi writers of Bihar until he died in 1927 at the early age of 34. He wrote more than 30 books. In the present context his works that helped in the creation and glorification of the Hindu past we can mention *San Sattavan ka Ghadar, Sipahi Vidroh, Shakuntala, Sati Parvati* and *Chandrakumar va Manorama*. His accounts would tilt towards the Hindu version of history given the slightest opportunity. Even when he was writing a biography of Dadabhai Naoroji, he started mourning the sad state of the Hindus.

53 Rudrangshu Mukerjee, review of *Bengal Divided: Hindu Communalism and Partition, 1932–1947* by Joya Chatterji, in *Biblio*, July 1995, 21.

10

INDIAN CHRISTIANS
History and contemporary challenges

Savio Abreu, M. Ashok Kumar and Rowena Robinson

Diversity and presence

According to the last available census data, Christians constitute 2.3 per cent of the Indian population. This figure has not changed much since the census prior to this one, showing that the Christian population remains static or even in slight decline. Legally, and in terms of census groupings, all Christians constitute an undifferentiated category. However, there are considerable differences and these in turn shape the challenges different groups face. In terms of numbers, there are perhaps just over 24 million Christians but they are spread very unevenly. Out of the Indian Christian population, 25.15 per cent of the Christians belong to Kerala, 15.71 per cent to Tamil Nadu, 4.19 per cent to Karnataka and 4.9 per cent to Andhra Pradesh. These four southern states account for 54.34 per cent of the total Christian population in India. In the North-East, the states of Assam, Nagaland, Meghalaya, Mizoram and Manipur together have 29.09 per cent of the Christians. In Goa, Christians constitute 26.68 per cent of the state population. In sum, 90 per cent of the Christian population is found in three regional enclaves: South and South-West India, the North-East and the tribal belt in Central India consisting of Chotanagpur and contiguous areas.

The northern Hindi belt has 40 per cent of India's population but only 10 per cent of its Christians. Just 0.56 per cent of Gujarat's population is Christian, 0.13 per cent of Haryana's and 0.13 per cent of Himachal

Pradesh's. At the same time, Christians are 2.4 per cent of Orissa's population, slightly over their presence all over India. Marginally over 66 per cent of the Christian population resides in rural areas; 34 per cent of the population is found in urban areas. Well over half of all Christians are from the former untouchable communities and 15 to 20 per cent of Christians are tribal in origin, while caste Christians, largely from Kerala and the Konkan coast, constitute at best about a quarter of the total population.

Denominationally, the range of Christianity available in India includes Syrian Christianity, Roman Catholicism and various forms of Protestantism and Evangelicalism. Catholics form the largest Christian group in India, nearly half of the total population. Another 40 per cent of the Christians are Protestants, while 7 per cent belong to Orthodox churches and 6 per cent belong to indigenous sects. Not only is the greater part of the Christian population found in these regions, but the south and west of India were also home to Christian traditions very early on: the Syrian Christians of Kerala, for example, can be traced to around the third or the fourth century CE., while Catholicism in Goa is no less than 400 years old. In general, Christians are better off in the North-East and in some parts of South and South-West India. The older Christian communities, such as the Syrian Christians or the Goans in south and south-west India are better off. In general, though, Christians remain insecure due to the thin spread of their population, their poverty and low asset base. Though overall Christians show very high literacy levels, in some parts of the country the situation is quite different. In Orissa, for instance, Christian literacy is only 54.9 per cent in contrast to the national average of 64.8 per cent.

All these contrasts make for a very diverse community with considerably varied forms of livelihood, access to resources or capacity to cope with external challenges including violence. It is these issues that are dealt with in the following sections of the chapter.

External challenges

Attacks against Christians

'The Indian government's insistence at the international level that existing laws and judicial decisions are sufficient to deal with egregious violations such as torture and attacks on religious minorities is very disappointing', said the draft report of the Working Group on India's Universal Periodic Review (UPR), a mechanism of the United Nations (UN) to review the human rights record of all its member states (Malhotra 2012). UN member countries that participated in India's UPR on 24 May 2012 in Geneva expressed concerns over India's right to freedom of religion and belief, anti-conversion laws and the targeting of religious minorities. The government of India's oral response during the UPR session was marked by a 'general lack of acceptance of human rights challenges in the country and a mere reiteration of domestic laws, policies and Constitutional provisions' and even on the Communal Violence Bill, the Human Rights Council took note of the government's 'uncertainty' regarding such a law that aims to protect minorities (ibid.).

Though most of the attacks on Christian missionaries and institutions in independent India had been isolated and sporadic, the last two decades have seen a spurt and a pattern of sustained attacks on the Christian community. The violence in Gujarat, Madhya Pradesh, Uttar Pradesh, Orissa and the attacks on churches in Karnataka have shaken the Christian community and led their leaders to re-emphasise the need for a pan-Indian Christian unity leaving aside all other differences of caste, class, region, rites and denominations. 'Mr. Prime Minister, long ago we left our fathers and our homes. We have worked without fear in distant forests and villages. Now, for the first time, we are feeling afraid', Sister Dolores, the National Secretary of the Catholic Religious in India, the association of priests and nuns in India, told the former prime minister Vajpayee at a meeting with him in 2000 (Dayal 2000: 9).

Due to the constant targeting of Christians a sense of fear has entered because of which many in the church leadership are afraid to speak out, lest their patriotism be questioned or their institutions singled out. Fear and a sense of uncertainty and vulnerability have now begun to creep into the self-consciousness of the Christian community as it increasingly sees itself as an insecure and embattled minority community. Sajan George, president of Global Council of Indian Christians, while documenting cases of attacks against Christians all over India mentions that out of 405 cases of Christians being persecuted from January 2006 till May 2007, over 325 involved Christians of Dalit background. So while the Christian community as a whole is feeling vulnerable and insecure, the Christians belonging to the lower socio-economic strata are affected the most by these anti-Christian attacks and forms of persecution. At the same time the increased attacks on Christians are seen by extremist and fundamentalist Christian groups as a divine sign to go on the offensive and intensify their proselytising activities. Persecution and attacks embolden them to fulfill their desire of bringing into being a 'Christian India' in the near future.

The increasing number of attacks on Christians is quite definitely part of a hate campaign by the Sangh Parivar and other right-wing Hindutva forces targeting Muslims and Christians throughout India. This hate campaign questions the roots of Christianity branding it as a foreign religion, and also the patriotism and loyalty of the Christians and targets priests, nuns and Christian institutions. This discourse brands the minorities as being well off, at the cost of the majority Hindu community who are suffering and therefore the Muslims and the Christians are the enemies of the Hindus. In particular, the Christians are targeted for engaging in conversion by force or inducement, thus manipulating innocent tribals and Dalits, and threatening the demographic strength of the Hindus. A sample of the kind of writing that constructs this discourse on the minorities is given below:

> The minorities are safe only under the BJP. One country, one people is its core ideology. . . But the definition of minorities in India is strangely distorted. Here the minorities are better off than Hindus and were the ruling class for centuries. . . The vote-bank politics has deprived the Hindu his status. This is at the root of the tension in places where conversion is tearing apart the social fabric. In states where the minorities are in majority their tyranny has totally subjugated the Hindu. (Balashankar 2008)

The impact of the minority discourse of the Sangh Parivar was seen vividly in December 2007 in the anti-Christian attacks in Kandhamal district, Orissa, that, according to the All-India Christian Council's (AICC) reports and corroborated by the National Commission for

Minorities' (NCM) report, resulted in 95 churches and 730 houses being destroyed in the clashes and six people seriously wounded, multiple reports of women molested or raped and four people confirmed dead (Bauman 2010: 267). But the ferocity of these riots paled in comparison to the events of the last week of August 2008, when the Dalit Pana Christians experienced the fury of the worst-ever communal rage in Orissa – churches were set on fire, Christian institutions, orphanages and hamlets were destroyed, pastors were attacked, one nun was burnt alive and another was gang-raped. At the height of the violence there were over 20,000 refugees, mostly Christians, in relief camps, while according to the AICC there were over a hundred deaths by November. An opposition party report put the total much higher, though government officials reported in May 2009 that only 42 persons were confirmed dead.

Militant Hinduisation had deeply divided the Adivasis (Kandhas have become increasingly Hinduised) and the Dalits (around 70 per cent of the Panas are Christians) on communal lines in Kandhamal district of Orissa and the Kandha–Pana ethnic divide was available to be converted by the Sangh Parivar into a Hindu–Christian communal confrontation (Kanungo 2008). Chad Bauman argues that the Orissa violence was exacerbated by the involvement of those who intentionally politicised and communalised local tensions, in part by portraying communal identities at both the local and national level as if they were singular, rigid and mutually exclusive (2010: 263–90). The Orissa violence brought to the fore the lack of bargaining power of the scattered Christian minority with the government in a country ruled by vote-bank politics.

At the same time these attacks worked as a catalyst in uniting Christians and giving them a stronger sense of their Christian communitarian identity. When the Sangh Parivar activists attacked churches in Mangalore on 14 September 2008, the church bells were tolled and on hearing the bells big crowds of Christians, especially the youth, gathered at the churches and thwarted the plans of the aggressors. The tolling of the church bells is a powerful symbol for the Christians reminding them that they need to come together as a community in the face of crisis (Prakash 2008). If the attacks against the Dalit Christians in Orissa in August 2008 weakened the Christian community's trust in the state authorities, the subsequent attacks on various Christian places of worship in BJP-ruled Karnataka made the Christians very sceptical of the intent and capability of the state machinery and law enforcement agencies to protect the interests of the minorities.

The report of the Justice B. K. Somasekhara Commission of Inquiry, constituted by the Karnataka government, found that attacks had taken place at various places of worship across Karnataka, particularly in the towns of Mangalore and Davanagere. Some of the attacks were deliberate and well-planned. Clearly, forms of communal antagonism and fundamentalism had been brewing for several years. The commission indicted the district administration functionaries including the corporation, the municipality, the electricity board and the village panchayat authorities for failing to protect the rights of the religious minorities guaranteed under the Constitution, but found no evidence to show that the politicians, the BJP, the Sangh Parivar or the state government were, directly or indirectly, involved in the attacks.

On the other hand, an independent inquiry by Justice (retired) Michael F.J. Saldanha found that each and every one of the attacks was state-sponsored in that it was not only supported by the state but also covered up by the state. Justice Saldanha, Transparency International India (TII) chairman and former judge of Bombay and Karnataka high courts, held the then chief minister B. S. Yediyurappa and the then home minister B. V. Acharya fully responsible for the unfortunate incidents. Justice Saldanha visited 413 places, examined 673 witnesses and collected evidence and testimonies from 2,114 victims after visiting hospitals, courts, police stations, jails and government offices The attacks against Christians in Orissa and Karnataka in 2008 evoked protests not just from within the country but also from several other countries, highlighting the global dimension of the Indian Christian community, and this was noticed again recently in India's Universal Periodic Review at Geneva on 24 May 2012, when UN member countries expressed concerns over India's right to freedom of religion and belief, the anti-conversion laws of different states and the targeting of religious minorities.

Legal and constitutional challenges

When finally laid down in the Constitution, the cultural rights and freedoms of communities were as follows. Article 25 ensures all citizens the right to freely profess, practice and propagate their religion. Article 26 gives every religious denomination the right to establish and maintain institutions for religious and charitable purposes, to manage its own affairs in matters of religion, to own and acquire movable and immovable property and to administer such property in accordance with the law. Article 29 ensures the right of any section of citizens with a distinct language, script or culture of its own to conserve the same. Article 29(2) also prohibits any citizen from being denied admission into any educational institution maintained by or receiving aid from the state on the grounds of religion, race, caste or language.

Article 30 refers to the educational rights of the minorities. It gives to all minorities, whether religious or linguistic, the right to establish and administer educational institutions of their choice. It lays down, further, that with respect to the granting of aid the state shall not discriminate against any educational institution on the ground that it is under the management of a minority, whether based on language or religion.

It is true that minority and majority cultural and religious rights and freedoms were instituted simultaneously in the Constitution and were thus not framed, as it were, against each other. Rather, both are original, equal and valid claims made on the nation-state, which it accedes to, thus protecting – from the start – the autonomy of religion from the state. At the same time, several difficulties emerge and I shall discuss some of them here, especially those with disturbing implications for Christians.

Initially, constitutional debates had discussed the issue of disadvantage in terms of three sections of Indians: religious minorities, Scheduled Castes and Tribes. By the time of the final draft of the Constitution, however, a split had emerged: minorities based on language, culture and religion were pulled together and given the 'cultural' rights and freedoms that have been outlined above; Scheduled Castes and Tribes alone were given 'political' rights: reserved seats in legislatures and 'rights to make economic claims' in the sense of quotas in government employment (to be reassessed after a period of 10 years). They alone were covered later by the provisions of the Prevention of Atrocities Act (1989).

In other words, cultural rights appear as compensation for more substantive political rights that remained unachieved. Indeed, it is argued that the trade-off for the Indian Christian agreement to the proposal to eliminate special representation for minorities was the agreement by the

Hindu 'majority' to the inclusion of the word 'propagate' in Article 25 of the Constitution. The Constitutional Order of 1950 listed Scheduled Castes and Scheduled Tribes using the list employed by the Government of India (Scheduled Castes) Order of 1936. The 1936 order excluded minorities from being counted among the Scheduled Castes because at the time they were covered by the Communal Award. The 1950 order again specifies that no person professing a religion other than Hinduism may be deemed a member of a Scheduled Caste. However, at this time, special representation for the minorities was rejected.

The limitation in the 1950 order has been understood and defended in terms of the logic that religions such as Islam or Christianity claimed the principle of human equality and therefore there could strictly not be any 'Scheduled Castes' in these communities. However, the order was amended in 1956 to include Sikh Dalits and again in 1990 to include Buddhist Dalits, despite the fact that these are also religions that espouse the idea of equality. Thus, it is principally the Dalits of Christian and of Muslim origin that are affected by the exclusion clause of the order at present. In the states, Dalit Muslim or Christian converts are usually classified as Other Backward Classes, but the benefits they receive are limited and they are competing with larger numbers and with those perhaps having access to greater resources. No such discrimination exists, however, with respect to Christians of tribal origin, to whom the category of Scheduled Tribes applies.

Apart from provisions for reservations and certain economic benefits, the legislation on Scheduled Castes and Tribes includes the Scheduled Caste and Scheduled Tribe (Prevention of Atrocities) Act, 1989. This law contains sanctions to protect Dalits, in particular, from violence by caste Hindus. The law, which refuses to recognise Scheduled Caste Christians or Muslims, is blind to the fact that conversion has by no means secured them from discrimination or violence by caste Hindus. Violence against Christian Dalits and Tribals, for instance, has been recorded in many parts of the country. In some areas, as in Andhra Pradesh, Dalit Christians record their identity legally as Hindu. This is not merely to obtain the economic benefit that goes with Scheduled Caste status but, crucially, to ensure themselves the protection of the Prevention of Atrocities Act. In a state such as Andhra Pradesh, caste is a grim reality and violence against Dalits is routine. The legal position on the question of reservation for Dalits from minority communities as well as their exclusion from the provisions of the Atrocity Act consti-tutes a clear example of discrimination based on religion and the exis-tence of such legal disabilities throws the secular identity of the state in doubt.

Problems have also been noted in the cultural rights themselves. For instance, Article 29(2) appears to put limits on the ambit of Article 30. Thus, in 1989, the judges in *Sheetansu Srivastava v. Allahabad Agricul-tural Institute* ruled that a minority institution cannot insist on reserving seats for students of its own community (Ansari 1999). In 1991, though, the Supreme Court argued differently in the St. Stephen's case, allowing minority institutions to act on preference for community candidates, up to the limit of 50 per cent. Ansari (1999: 131), however, points out that the judgment reserves 50 per cent of seats in minority institutions for non-minority candidates in the name of national integration, as schools 'are said to be the melting pot for a nation in the making'. A similar logic is not applied to reserve seats for minorities in non-minority institutions. According to him, this amounts to placing the entire burden of national integration on the minorities. Though it remains unimplemented, in fact, the Ranganath Misra Report (2007), to be discussed later, recom-mended that 15 per cent of seats in non-minority educational institu-tions should be earmarked by law for the minorities (10 per cent for Muslims and 5 per cent for other minorities).

Despite the constitutional protection of the freedom to propagate one's faith, there have been attempts to pass laws restricting the conversion, particularly of Dalits and tribals, to other religions especially Islam and Christianity. Orissa and Arunachal Pradesh, for instance, passed such acts in 1969 and 1978 respectively. Other states recently began to get into the act of bringing in legislation against conversion. There were experiments in Tamil Nadu and in Gujarat. While the constitutional validity of such bills has been questioned, the Supreme Court has declared that states have the right to bring in protective legislation. The Gujarat 'Freedom of Religion Bill' actually stifles the freedom of religious expression selec-tively in that it attempts to limit conversions among the majority Hin-dus. The bill declared that Hindus may convert to Jainism and Buddhism but not to any other faith without explicit permission from the authori-ties. The implication is that Jainism and Buddhism have been treated as

Hindu sects. Islam and Christianity, two 'outside' minority religions are more clearly the targets of this kind of legislation.

Article 48 of the Constitution, part of the Directive Principles of State Policy, enjoin upon the state that it 'shall endeavour to organise agriculture and animal husbandry on modern and scientific lines and shall, in particular, take steps for preserving and improving the breeds, and prohibiting the slaughter, of cows and calves and other milch and draught cattle.' In accordance, several states have cow slaughter prohibition laws, including Gujarat, Karnataka, Jharkhand and Himachal Pradesh. Orissa and Andhra Pradesh permit the killing of cattle other than cows if the animals are not fit for any other purpose. There are certain restrictions in other states, though none in West Bengal and Kerala.

In a recent amended act, the Madhya Pradesh Gau-Vansh Vadh Pratishedh Sansodhan Vidheyak (Madhya Pradesh Prohibition of Slaughter of Cow-Progeny (amendment) Act), the state has put forward a reason for the more stringent sanctions against cow slaughter: that these are in the interest of communal harmony. The amended act provides for harsh punishment: the punishment for cow (and calf) slaughter will now carry a minimum of one year and maximum seven years' imprisonment along with a fine of Rs 5,000. Even storing or transporting beef will now be punishable with a minimum term of six months, which can be extended up to three years. Contentiously, the act grants the police very arbitrary powers. The law states that a 'competent authority' has been empowered to 'enter and inspect any premises' where he has 'reason to believe that an offence under this Act has been, is being, or is likely to be committed', and take necessary action. More crucially, the onus is now on the accused to prove his or her innocence.

As the editorial in *Economic and Political Weekly* of 14 January 2012 pointed out, 'Given the way the police and the legal system function, such a provision is more than likely to be abused as it allows scope for wide interpretation.' The present BJP government in Madhya Pradesh has no clean record of dealing with religious minorities in the state. This act adds considerably to its powers to harass and target them. In effect, as the editorial goes on to say, 'one can see that far from helping communal harmony, the law is likely to inflame passions'. This Act in Madhya Pradesh, as all cow slaughter acts in different states in the country, essentially curtails and criminalises the eating habits – and the religious freedoms contained therein – of Muslims and Christians as well as of Dalits, tribals and a large number of Hindus.

The struggle for reservations

When there are attacks on church institutions and the Christian community and laws adversely affecting the Christians are enacted, the Christian community occupies centre stage in the national minority discourse and Christian identity gets strengthened. At the same time it is also noticed when the minority discourse dwells on the socially backward classes in India, especially the Dalits and the Scheduled Tribes, religious identity weakens or breaks down completely in the face of Scheduled Caste or Scheduled Tribe unity. Such changes are perceived particularly when one looks at discussions and debates surrounding the issue of reservations for Dalit Christians.

The 1950 Order on reservations created a linkage between caste and religion and thus could be said to have divided the entire Dalit community on the basis of religion. This has led the Dalit Christians, supported by the Church, to fight for the same reservation and welfare benefits that are granted to the Scheduled Castes professing Hindu, Sikh and neo-Buddhist religions through different organizations such as the Christian Dalit Liberation Movement, formed in the 1980s and the All India Christian People's Forum comprising of various Christian denominations and NGOs (Stanislaus 2004: 271–91).

This denial of the benefits of reservation to Dalit Christians by the state is countered by innovative strategies, for instance by the Dalit Lutheran Christians of coastal Andhra Pradesh. They employ Hindu names in order to gain access to benefits reserved under the law for Scheduled Castes. Kumar and Robinson argue that the economically extremely deprived Lutherans adopt the Hindu Scheduled Caste identity not only for the benefits of reservation in education and employment it allows them but also, significantly, for the protection offered from oppression and violence by the legal provisions of the Scheduled Castes and Scheduled Tribes (Prevention of Atrocities) Act 1989 (2010: 149–67). This maintaining of a dual identity is not unique to the Lutheran Dalit Christians of coastal Andhra Pradesh but is also found among the rural Christian Vankars in Gujarat (Lobo 2001: 246).

Since the government has denied the Christians the benefits granted to Hindu Scheduled Castes, the Christian Vankars use their Hindu identity in order to get economic benefits and revert to their Christian identity in order to retain their social status.

Christian Scheduled Castes include the Pulayans in Kerala, Pariahs in Tamil Nadu, Tigalas in Karnataka, Malas and Madigas in Andhra Pradesh, Chamars (Ravidasis) in Madhya Pradesh, Uttar Pradesh and Bihar, Vankars from Gujarat and Mahars from Maharashtra (Lobo 2001: 242). The case of the Dalit Christians is special since they face discrimination at three levels. The first level of discrimination, which all Dalits including Dalit Christians face, is from caste Hindus. Several examples of such discrimination can be cited: for instance, caste Hindus in the countryside in Andhra Pradesh do not differentiate between a converted Dalit Christian and a Dalit (Kumar and Robinson 2010: 149–68). All Dalits are meted out the same treatment by those considered high in the caste hierarchy. In Zafferwal village, Gurdaspur district, Punjab, both Dalit Sikhs, known as *Majhoabli Sikh* and Dalit Christians, known as *Issai*, stay side by side in the *thathis* (place of mockery), which is outside the village (Massey 2007: 71).

The second level of discrimination that the Dalit Christians face is from the state. This has already been mentioned earlier. The third level of discrimination that Dalit Christians face is at the hands of fellow Christians who continue to claim caste status even after conversion. This internal discrimination is discussed further below; at the same time it is clear that the second and third levels of discrimination, by the state and at the hands of caste Christians, make the case of Dalit Christians even more complex as compared to other Scheduled Castes.

The National Commission for Scheduled Castes has recommended that reservation should be extended to Dalit Christians and Dalit Muslims. The state governments of Tamil Nadu, West Bengal, Uttar Pradesh, Bihar, Madhya Pradesh, Punjab, Andhra Pradesh and Pondicherry have asked the Indian government to extend Scheduled Caste status to Dalit Christians. However, the Union Government has been regularly postponing giving a reply to the Supreme Court on the issues raised in the writ petitions. When a sizeable proportion of the Christian population, belonging to the Scheduled Castes, are excluded from the process of development this must reflect poorly on the institutional response and the governmental measures apparently aimed at ensuring the equitable socio-economic development of all sections of society.

The efforts and steps to obtain reservation and other Scheduled Caste benefits for the Dalit Christians can be classified under three periods: (1) The period of meeting with political leaders and submitting memoranda (1950s to 1980s), (2) The period of public rallies, strikes, lobbying with political leaders, litigation, private member bills (1990s to 2000) and (3) The period of intense legal battle, lobbying with national and international bodies and leaders, gathering information under the Right to Information Act, demonstrations, collaboration with Dalit Muslims and other human rights groups (2000 onwards) (Arokiaraj 2010: 20). In December 2006 the National council of Dalit Christians, a lay movement of various Dalit Christian movements, conducted a relay hunger strike at the national level to demand Scheduled Caste status for Dalit Christians and Muslims. During the sessions of Parliament in 2007, 2008, 2009 and 2010, this movement, in collaboration with the National Coordination Committee for Dalit Christians, organized rallies and dharnas in New Delhi and were involved in intense lobbying.

The church in India has overtly supported the Dalit and Tribal struggles and in the process has expanded its identity to include these and other marginalized groups:

> The Dalits and Tribals are politically exploited, educationally most backward and socially discriminated against. The Church should be in solidarity with the poor and make a preferential option for them. . . To realize this objective, the Church should join other people of good will and work towards the dismantling of structures like caste and class that cause and perpetuate poverty and oppression. (Catholic Bishops' Conference of India statement on 'The Church in Dialogue', 25th General Body Meeting, Jalandhar, March 1–8, 2002)

The Catholic Bishops' Conference of India (CBCI) at its general body meetings at Jamshedpur in February 2008 and at Guwahati in March 2010 sent signed memoranda to the prime minister urging the Union Government to include Dalit Christians in the Scheduled Caste list. On the other hand, the Dalit Christians continue to accuse the church hierarchy of being ambivalent about their problems and raise issues such as marginalization in admissions and appointments to Christian institutions, discrimination in vocations to priesthood and religious life, and the lack of sharing of power and authority in the church.

The tribes in conflict

Tribal Christians are found mainly in two regional enclaves: northeast India and the Chotanagpur region of central India. In both areas, Christianity entered in the second half of the nineteenth century. The tribals of Chotanagpur area are mainly found in the states of Jharkhand, Chhattisgarh, Madhya Pradesh, Orissa and West Bengal. The tribal Christians here are mainly from the Oraon, Munda, Kharia, Santhal and Ho tribes. Jharkhand with over a million Christians, comprising 4.1 per cent of the total population, had the largest tribal Christian concentration in the Chotanagpur area. Today the tribal Christians of Chotanagpur are spread all over the country, including the Andaman Islands, Assam, West Champaran in North Bihar and North Bengal, besides in many urban centres of north India, especially Delhi.

Tribals who converted to Christianity benefited and developed through the activities of the missionaries in the areas of education, health and welfare, but this also led to conflicts with dominant non-Adivasis. According to Lobo, the work of education, health care and development by the Christians among the Bhils of Gujarat has led to the empowerment of the deprived Adivasis and has also partly resulted in giving voice to Adivasi independence and indigenous revival movements (2010: 211–33). Such movements certainly do not have the backing either of the elite Adivasis or of those who espouse the Hindutva ideology. Also Adivasis empowered by the work of the missionaries might no longer submit to exploitation by non-Adivasi elites such as shopkeepers, money lenders and landlords.

Bhatia links the growth of Christianity in Mizoram with the progress of education since education was delegated to the missions from the start (2010: 169–84). The Mizo church, which is predominantly tribal, has been instrumental in creating and maintaining an educated and aware middle class. This class provided the leadership for Mizoram's political movement. Christianity radically altered Mizo society, creating a highly literate, Westernized and politically aware people. The Mizo middle class is constituted of church leaders, educated members of the government machinery, the political elite, school teachers and medical professionals. Many occupy important positions both in the sacred and secular realms. This explains why Christianity, as a way of life, overshadows and dominates the public and private spheres of Mizo life.

While Dalit Christians face discrimination at three levels, the tribal church in the Chotanagpur area faces double marginalisation (Kujur 2010: 30). First, it has always been in the periphery defending itself from the attacks at the local level by those who accuse it of distorting the traditional culture and dividing the tribal community. In the case of the Oraons of Chotanagpur, there is tension between Christians, non-Christian Sarnas and those seeking to 'Hinduise' the tribals. Conversion to Christianity among the Oraons led to those adhering to the traditional tribal religion, that is, the Sarna Oraons, viewing the Christian Oraons with suspicion because of their betrayal of the parental community. Also under missionary influence the converts had to cut themselves off from all aspects of the old religion and culture.

Fundamentalist Hindu forces such as the Hindu Dharm Sansad or the Rashtriya Swayamsevak Sangh are attempting to 'Hinduize' the tribals by organizing 'home-coming' events for conversion to Hinduism and seeking to de-recognise the tribal identity of Christians and Sarnas who refuse the 'Hindu' label. These Hindutva organisations consider the work of education and health provision among the tribals of Gujarat by the Christians as insidious ways whereby they gain the loyalty of the 'innocent' and 'backward' tribes (Lobo 2010: 230–31). At the same time, the local tribal church faces criticism and censorship from the Orthodox Church hierarchy for its innovations and experimentations in tribal liturgy, tribal theology and tribal ecclesiology.

Tribal Christians are constitutionally entitled to reservation as Scheduled Tribes. Yet due to the gap between intent and implementation, the geographically isolated and marginalised tribals may be pushed to violence. Thus, in the North-East, the sense of alienation from the mainstream led to various nationalist and ethnic conflicts (Fernandes 2012). The Naga National council, the Mizo National Front and other organizations led the struggle for autonomy and sovereignty. Quite often the government treats these disturbances as a law and order problem and action on the ground is inadequate and often counterproductive. Whether in its repressive policing or its non-participative, top-down approach towards Scheduled Tribes, the state response is at best patronising and at worst leading to the creation of dependencies that stymie tribal autonomy. The cultural hegemony of the imposed institutional response compromises the dignity of the tribals and renders them inferior (Heredia 2012).

Internal challenges

Caste divide among Indian Christians: caste first, Christ second

Since the advent of Christian missions in India, Christian groups belonging to various denominations have tussled with the issue of caste. At the same time, it was because of the mass conversions from the latter part of the nineteenth century, through which numerous *avarna* communities joined the Christian fold, that the issue gained centrality. South India was the epicentre of mass conversion movements to Christianity from about 1860 to 1920. This led to a huge growth rate in the Christian population of the Madras Presidency.

The responses from missionaries, colonial officials, scholars, policy makers, public representatives and others on mass conversion movements were mixed in nature, questioning the motives of the converts and how caste would leave its footprint on the future course of Christianity in India and South Asia. There were sharp and strong differences among missionaries in their opinion about Indian caste system and how to deal with it. However, there was scholarly consensus to the effect that the underlying motivations for conversion were a search for improved social status, for a greater sense of personal dignity, self-respect and for freedom from bondage (Oddie 1975; Webster 1992). The groups converted thereby were not victims of the colonial experience; they often ensured that the missionaries served their aspirations or expectations.

Caste continued to prevail among Christians but the 'caste system' in its totality did not exist. In other words, as Dumont (1970) rightly observes, caste exists among Indian Christians in the 'absence of ritual justification'. Discrimination is particularly severe against the erstwhile *avarna* communities. S. M. Michael points out how, in some places, there are separate seating arrangements for the Dalits in churches, while in others liturgical services are performed separately for caste Christians (Michael 2010: 51–74). Sometimes, Dalits are asked to sit on the floor, even where raised seating is available and there are, in some places, two cemeteries and two hearses for dead bodies. In some places, separate queues are formed for receiving Holy Communion.

The church recognises the extent of such discrimination. Archbishop George Zur, Apostolic Pro-Nuncio to India, in his address to the Catholic Bishops' Conference of India (CBCI) in December 1991 said: 'Casteism is rampant among the clergy and the religious. Though Dalit Christians make up 65 per cent of the 10 million Christians in the South, less than 4 per cent of the parishes are entrusted to Dalit priests' (Massey 2007: 74). Of late, Dalit Christianity crystallises this opposition to the caste Christian church hierarchy through its activism and its articulation of a separate and distinct Dalit Christian theology. Dalit Christian theology traces roots back to Latin American Liberation theology but specifically articulates the experiences of Dalits in Indian society. The Dalit Christian movement has the potential to determine the future course of Christianity in India.

The gender divide

Indian Christianity surely gave women some privileges in terms of equal rights of access to sacred places and of organising themselves in the church. Converts to Christianity often viewed it as a religion that promoted gender equality but Christianity could not make any alterations in existing power equations between men and women. More women than men attend Sunday church services across the country. In some parts of South India, such as Andhra Pradesh, Christian women organise themselves to meet their social and theological needs with the help of institutions of the church. Among the Andhra Lutherans, each such unit is called a *sthreela samajam*. The *sthreela samajam* pays special attention to Bible study and urges the adoption of the lifestyle of women named in the Bible such as Ruth, Esther, Rebecca, Miriam, Deborah, Mary and Martha. The women inculcate Christian ideas regarding female roles, and sexuality within the community and advise women on how to conduct themselves both in public and in the private sphere. It is both interesting and problematic that their ideas about female roles, sexuality and public conduct are not completely different from those of other Hindu women in Indian society.

The set of ideas on matters of feminine identity, sexuality and moral conduct believed and practiced by Indian Christian women, particularly in rural India, are in close correspondence with those prevailing in Hindu society. Ideas regarding the 'good' and 'bad' woman are common to Christians and Hindus in many parts of India. The good woman is pure and unselfish. As a wife and mother, she is dutiful, constant and loving. Qualities of tenderness and compassion abound in her. The bad woman, the whore, belongs nowhere and to no one. She rejects family ties or is cast off by her family due to her immoral ways and, hence, is not secure in the legitimate protection of a male authority figure such as father, brother or husband.

Notions of feminine identity, 'good' and 'bad' women and desirable moral conduct constitute the subject matter of *sthreela samajam* teachings in churches. There is a great deal of correspondence between the cultural practices, kinship morality and especially gender values of Christians and Hindus. At the same time, being a Christian adds extra responsibilities on Christian women for they must live up to the expectations of both village moral conduct, which is based both on Hindu religious faith, and also Christian morality. In other words, it may be an extra burden on Christian women that a mix of caste ideas along with Christian sentiments shapes their understanding of proper feminine conduct. Christian women carry the added responsibility of being 'good Christian women'. A good Christian woman must be regular in attending church activities, be attentive to nurturing her children in God's wisdom and, if required, help her husband in agricultural activity besides involving herself in the regular agricultural labour work.

In the contemporary period, the legal position of Christian women has come under greater scrutiny. Legally Christians are treated as a single category; thus, in order to reform any laws they need to come together. But internal social and sectarian differences have been so strong that it was extremely difficult to attain consensus on legal reform. The Catholic Church held up reform of Christian Personal Law for more than a decade, despite great distress to Christian women, because of their position on 'divorce'. Christian missions have historically demonstrated that they were committed to gender equality; they started the first boarding schools for girls when education for girls was viewed as a stigma. Despite such an encouraging historical record, present-day Christians are battling with several gender issues within and outside the church. These include domestic violence, the practice of dowry among Christians, the lack of equal opportunities for women in the church and church-related institutions, the lack of adequate women's representation in pastoral positions, church administration, church-run educational institutions and within the clergy.

Rich and poor Christians: the economic divide

In general, Christians are economically better off in the North-East and in some parts of South and South-West India. Older Christian communities such as the Syrian of Kerala and Goan Catholics are better off compared to Christian groups belonging to various other denominations that came into existence at different periods of time in the more recent past. Indian Christians demonstrate reasonably high urban presence with 23.5 per cent of them in salaried employment. Yet, 66 per cent are rural and of these a significant percentage are in agriculture or work as agricultural labour (Censes 2011). Yet, Christians are among the smallest holders of land. All other religious communities do better than them in terms of agricultural landholdings. Dalit Christians, who have been in the past branded 'rice Christians' implying that their poverty made them susceptible to the handouts and the ideological persuasions of the missionaries, are even today among the poorest of the community. The economic life of these poor Christians has not improved greatly after conversion. They are still, the bulk of them, agricultural labourers and face both the deprivation of poverty and the stigma of caste identity.

New challenges

One of the biggest challenges facing the church from within is the challenge of Dalit and tribal consciousness and the new theological identity that these groups wish to carve out for themselves. The church, which is largely composed of Dalits and tribals, faces the danger of becoming irrelevant to its members and the challenges they confront every day. As Dalit empowerment increases, their resistance within the boundaries of the church begins to reveal the signs of their greater presence.

New breakaway movements, which are another serious challenge to the established churches, also achieve success partly because of this and also because the hierarchy and rigidity of the conventional churches are alienating many members today.

Conclusion

The church today needs to redefine its engagement with its own members, other member churches and with the society outside. Internally, the questions of inequality – of class, caste and gender – need to be addressed. In particular, given the demographic realities of the Indian church, an ecumenical Indian Christianity would be reflective of the concerns of the majority of Christians, who are Dalits and tribals, *and* also allow for the creation of spaces in which these groups invoke their distinctiveness both from each other and from mainstream Christianity.

As concerns external challenges, political reticence and withdrawal will not help the church. With specific reference to the threat of Hindu nationalism, for instance, Indian Christians require not so much to close in on themselves, but to join together with civil society organisations (which are run by a wide range of people of all religious faiths) and other minorities to ensure the protection of India's plural culture and its constitutional commitment to political secularism. In this respect, the church in India can play a central role. With the depth of its establishment and its intellectual and institutional capital, it has the potential for creating a strong network of those working for peace and conflict management. It is through secularism and the struggle against ethnic strife that the Christian church in India will shift from the terrain of its own diffidence to redefine its contemporary social and ethical relevance.

In other words, it is offered here that the joint commitment to social justice (both within and outside its own boundaries) and to secularism will enable the Christian church not only to be more self-aware about its own internal community dynamics but also to face more confidently – and critically – the dangers of majority fundamentalism.

11

POLITICS OF THE 2008 ANTI-CHRISTIAN VIOLENCE IN KANDHAMAL, ODISHA

*Mujibur Rehman**

What I have sought to analyse is the factors that caused the 2008 anti-Christian violence in Kandhamal, Odisha, and also the responses it received from the state, political parties and civil societies. This chapter also seeks to explain how the state's complicity and the role of political parties continue to make Christian populations of not just Odisha but also of other regions vulnerable to future pogroms.[1] Moreover, there are consistent efforts by some state organisations and various Hindutva and non-Hindutva political forces to present this conflict not as anti-Christian violence but as arising out of land conflict. On 13 October 2008, Chief Minister Naveen Patnaik was reported to have said that Kandhamal violence was due to the rift among Scheduled Castes and Scheduled Tribes.[2] Justice S.C. Mohapatra Commission, in its 28-page interim report, also attributed land conflict as one of the factors.[3]

I argue categorically that Kandhamal was a case of an anti-Christian violence. The so-called land dimension given as the dominant explanation is rather secondary, almost in the way such factors are attributed to multi-dimensional conflicts. If land aspect is central to the conflict, we then need to ask: Why did conflicts often erupt between two communities during the Christmas celebrations such as the conflict in 2007? Why does Kandhamal remain under the grip of fear in and around Christmas time even now after so many years? How does one explain instances of church burning if it were a land conflict? And finally, why were only Christian homes and populations targeted? Given that the target group

216

was Christians, and the only targeted place of worship was the region's church, and the time was Christmas period, violence does reflect to its anti-Christian nature.

Kandhamal violence is the first prominent case of anti-Christian violence in modern India, though there were numerous Hindu–Muslim and other types of ethnic violence such as anti-Sikh riots of 1984.[4] Researchers have shed enormous light on these cases. They have propounded several theories attributing the role of state, civil society and other factors such as the Partition of British India; the politics that preceded and ensued thereafter is seen as a dominant factor by many historians. Scholarly investigation on communalism in India has stressed on either culturalist or materialist explanation or the golden mean approach. According to the culturalist view, the communal identity is often characterised as existing prior to or independent of the conflict, whereas the materialistic approach seeks to explain this by attributing to socio-economic or political factors or even the manipulation of masses by state or political elites. The golden mean approach seeks to articulate the argument that addresses the limitation of both these approaches (Shani 2007: 4–13).

This chapter has three major components: the first part discusses Kandhamal's political economy, and analyses in detail about what triggered the conflict; the second part attempts critical reflection on the state's party politics, and how Hindutva parties such as Bharthiya Janata Party (BJP) found its feet in Odisha and grew; and finally the chapter seeks to discuss the larger implications of this conflict for Indian Christians.

Political economy of Kandhamal, and the roots of violence

Kandhamal, one of the 30 districts of Odisha, was created in 1994 by the then chief minister Biju Patnaik.[5] Prior to 1994, Odisha had only 13 districts. The region is called Kandhamal because it is a land of Kandha tribes. The word 'Khanda' is derived from a Telugu word meaning hills. Located in the tribal-dominated western Odisha, it was carved out largely from the Phulbani district, which continues to remain the main town for all administrative and commercial purposes.

According to the Census 2001, 51.96 per cent of Kandhamal's population are scheduled tribes (ST) and 16.89 per cent are scheduled castes

(SC), and others are 31.15 per cent. Out of its total population, 49.80 per cent is male and the remainder is female. The percentage of literates is 43.15 per cent, out of which male literacy is 56.91 per cent and female literacy is 29.49 per cent.[6] Out of one lakh Christians, 60 per cent are converted from SC, known as 'Pana Christians'. The per capita income is Rs 4,730 in the district, where as Odisha's per capita income is Rs 5,264. Kandhamal has only 15 sanctioned police stations with the capacity of 647 personnel looking after 6.48 lakhs of its citizens.

According to the official statistics of the Odisha government, Kandhamal is one of the backward districts in Odisha and the latter is also one of the backward Indian states. In recent years, famine in Kalahandi district drew a great deal of national attention (Jayal 2001). According to the Odisha Human Development Report (HDR) 2004,

> When compared to all India values Odisha per-capita income was three fourths of that of all-India at the beginning of 1980s, became half by the end of 1990s. The contrast becomes stark when the comparisons are made with the states whose growth rates are higher than the national average. For instance the per capita income of Odisha is one third that of Punjab.[7]

The violence against Christians in August–September 2008 in Kandhamal lasted for several weeks, which is not the first one either in Kandhamal or Odisha. In fact, it is not even the first in India. But the global reaction it provoked was unprecedented, particularly from various Western countries and the European Union. Major global leaders such as the former French president Nicolas Sarkozy[8] and the former US secretary of state Condoleezza Rice expressed concern over this violence and raised the issue with Indian leaders such as India's prime minister Manmohan Singh, and BJP leaders, including L.K. Advani, during their interactions. In fact the United States Commission on International Religious Freedom (USCIRF), in its Annual Report 2009, has placed India under its watch list.

The commission notes:

> Nevertheless, several incidents of communal violence have occurred in various parts of the country, resulting in many deaths and mass displacements-particularly members of

Christian and Muslim minorities, including major incidents against the Christian communities within the 2008–09 reporting period. Because the government's response at the state and local levels have been found to be largely inadequate, and the national government has failed to take effective measures to ensure the rights of minorities in several states, the Commission decided to place India on its Watch List in 2009.[9]

What placed Odisha in the global map of violence against Christians is the tragic incident in which Australian missionary Graham Staines was burnt alive together with his two sons on 22 January 1999.[10] While it was mistakenly seen as an isolated incident, the violence against Christians in December 2007 in Kandhamal clearly served as a precursor for the subsequent events. The August–September, 2008 genocidal violence suggests a concerted political design by Hindutva forces led by Rashtriya Swayamsevak Sangh (RSS), Vishwa Hindu Parishad (VHP)[11] and Bajrang Dal (BD). A dangerous political trend is fast emerging in India's political landscape with the potential to rewrite the ground rules on which the relationship among the different religious communities operate, but its emergence and implications for Indian polity calls for careful examination.

Roots of Kandhamal violence and state response

In August–September 2008, the anti-Christian violence took place for the second time, the first being around Christmas in 2007. A commission of inquiry headed by Justice Mohapatra began investigating the violence and has submitted an interim report to the government.[12] Over the years, various political forces of different ideological orientations such as Maoists, members of the VHP or RSS have become active in the region along with traditional political parties. There are also Christian missionary activities involving various forms of missionary and educational initiatives among the tribals. Swami Laxmananda, whose assassination triggered the violence, was a prominent religious figure. Over the years, he had built up a large following in that region by taking part in various religious activities. Swami Laxmananda became controversial gradually owing to his constant criticism of Christian missionaries and Maoist activities. Local Christian leaders share accounts of him leading an angry mob to attack churches in the region. He also founded institutions like *mathas*, a typical Hindu organisation where religious traditions were taught. Some of these institutions were meant for both boys and girls. These activities endeared him to the followers of various Hindutva forces such as RSS, VHP, political parties like the BJP as well as religious-minded Hindus generally. On 23 August 2008, he and a few of his associates were killed by Maoists.[13] Durga Prasad Kar, president of the Odisha unit of the VHP, submitted an intervention petition, leading to the investigation of his death. There were eight attempts on the swami's life between 1969 and 2007.[14] The activities of the swami in the region caused tension between missionaries, local Christians and Hindus, and contributed to the simmering hostility towards innocent local Christians. Though this background is seen as a provocation, the Hindutva agenda aiming to decimate the missionary activities in India is the key motivating factor. VHP, RSS and BD are the real players, but their sister organisations, particularly the BJP as a major political party, contributed directly and often co-ordinated their activities to advance the Hindutva agenda.

At the time when violence erupted in late August 2008, Odisha was governed by a coalition government led by Naveen Patnaik, in which BJP was a coalition partner with Biju Janata Dal (BJD). Since organisations such as RSS or VHP enjoy patronage from the BJP, and their membership overlaps, it is only suggestive of evidence of state complicity in sustaining the violence. Pyari Mohan Mohapatra, a key leader in BJD at the time, who was widely seen as a super chief minister, played a vital role in breaking the coalition with the BJP after a few months, owing to BJP's active role in promoting violence. Finally, BJD contested the 2009 Assembly elections without an alliance with the BJP, and won the majority to form a government on its own.[15]

The state response to the violence was almost inconsequential, and revealed more about its complicity. There are different accounts of this response. Several reports from the government, civil society organisations, both national and international, and also individuals have published about the violence and its impact, containing data on death tolls, property losses and others. According to the data available in the district collector's office, 12 relief camps were established to offer temporary accommodation to the victims. These camps were set up in blocks such as Phulbani, Phiringia, Tikabali, G. Udayagiri, Raikia, K. Nuagaon, Baliguda and Daringibadi. The first set of camps became operational on 28 August 2008 where 6,929 people took refuge. These camps remained operative for almost a year till 26 August 2009. At the height of the violence, there were 25,177 victims residing in these camps. According to the government, 22,02,912 persons were residents of these camps during the entire period, but thousands ran away to different cities in Odisha such as Bhubaneswar and Berhampur. Some moved to other parts of India in places like Delhi, Kolkata or even as far as Kerala. There is no data about the people who chose to run away to other parts of India, but it does dramatically raise the number of victims of this violence. According to the district collector's report, there were a total of 232 churches destroyed, out of which seven were considered big churches and 225 small churches.

Other reports published on this violence include Concerned Citizen's Group Report (2007), National Commission For Minorities Report (2008), Ramakanta Rath Report (2008[16]), Venugopal Report (2009), Women's International League for Peace and Freedom Report (WILPF, 2009) and the state government's report (2008). In these reports, there is a considerable variation in the analysis of not so much what caused the violence, but what prolonged the violence, how relief camps were maintained and on state response to the crisis during and after the violence. There are also considerable differences in their recommendations.

The members of the team that prepared the report titled, 'Concerned Citizen's Group Report' toured different places like Kalinga, Tikabali, Nuogan, Baliguda, Mereka, Paburiam Tiangia, Malikapada, Sarang Guda, Pabingia, Kasipadar, Dimligud, Kasingpada, G. Udayagiri, Mandakia, Boruigia, Nilangia, Bakingia, Raikia and Phulbani. According to the estimate of this report, close to 27,000 people became refugees and 101 churches were burnt. The team was comprised of many activists, journalists and academicians.[17] The report expressed anguish and shock over the manner of negligence by the Odisha state. It recommended several measures to the government. The report also stated,

Hindutva mythogises the demise of Hinduism raising the bogey of 'conversion' and creating a fear that Christianity will swamp

221

Hinduism. Hindu cultural dominance organizes Hindu nationalism. The Sangh Parivar seeks to build a cadre that targets Christians, Muslims, and Dalits. This conflict has been camouflaged
as a tribal versus Dalit one; it is essentially the Hinduised tribals
enacting violence against Dalit Christians. The RSS has 6000
shakhas in Odisha with 1,50,000 cadres. It has 391 Saraswati
Shishu Mandir schools, with 1,11,000 students preparing for
future leadership. Vanvasi Kalyan Ashram runs 1,534 projects
and schools in 21 Adivasi concentrated districts. The Sangh
has initiated 1200 Ekal Vidyalayas in Odisha. The structure to
spread the concept of Hindutva is wide.[18]

The report by National Commission for Minorities (NCM), New
Delhi whose vice chairperson visited Kandhamal between 11 and 13
September 2008, noted the following:

> Some groups did complain that large scale conversion was at
> the root of the disturbances and that the Swamiji's murder was
> only the trigger that set off the seething unrest that was already
> brewing in Kandhamal. While exact figures of the number con-
> verted are hard to come by, there is no doubt that the Chris-
> tian population has registered a larger increase than that of the
> Hindu population. But although the Freedom of Religion Act
> has been in existence for about 40 years, not a single case has
> been registered under this Act for forced conversion in Kandha-
> mal. If indeed conversions by force or fraud were responsible for
> the feelings against Christians, it is absolutely amazing that the
> provisions of an Act designed precisely to address such conver-
> sions have never been invoked. It gives rise to the suspicion that
> conversion had really very little to do with the problem.[19]

It is obvious from the report's formulation that violence is not an
intra-ethnic conflict among the rival tribes that the government sought
to present consistently through its various organisations. Meanwhile,
the Women's International League for Peace and Freedom (WILPF),
together with WISCOMP[20] (New Delhi) sent a team comprised of
Annelesie Ebbe, Ila Pathak, Jharana Pathak and Mujibur Rehman. The

report also recognises the anti-Christian violence character, and this particular report titled 'Whithered Women's Rights' highlights the women's conditions after the violence.[21]

Party politics and anti-minority agenda

After India's independence in 1947, Odisha's politics was characterised by multi-party politics, but the Congress party was the dominant player from the beginning mainly because it led the freedom movement. Its presence in Odisha's tribal region was rather limited. A political party, Ganatantra Parishad (GP), whose leadership was dominated by former princes, offered a major challenge to the Congress party together with socialist and communist parties.

None of the major parties of Odisha since 1947 pursued communal agenda as part of their ideology. Though Jana Sangh existed, it barely had any political presence. Jana Sangh did take part in elections, but never managed to secure even close to 1 per cent vote in the Assembly elections. For instance, in Assembly election held in 1967, Jana Sangh could muster only 0.54 per cent of the total votes polled. In 1971 the party's position marginally improved: 0.70 per cent and in 1974, it had a significantly lower vote share, which was 0.41 per cent of the votes polled. Jana Sangh subsequently morphed into Bharathiya Janata Party (BJP) in its new incarnation in 1980.[22] The BJP acquired electoral strength much later in Odisha, compared to its rise at the national scene or in other states like Madhya Pradesh or Uttar Pradesh. The electoral history of state elections indicate BJP's rise from the 2000 elections as a rather new phenomenon. In 1980, BJP garnered only 1.36 per cent of the votes; in 1990, BJP fielded 63 candidates, garnered 3.56 per cent of the votes and won two seats. It lost deposit in 54 seats. In the 2000 Assembly elections, out of 63 of its candidates 38 won, with a vote share of 18.20 per cent. In 2004, it won 32 seats with a vote share of 17.11 per cent. But the BJP's presence as part of Naveen Patnaik's coalition government between 2004 and 2009 created political opportunities for Hindutva organisations to expand and consolidate their social bases.

Although the dominant political parties such as the Congress party, Ganatantra Parishad, socialist and major communist parties (CPI(M) and CPI) did not have any anti-minority political agenda, it does

Assembly Elections: Orissa

Year

Name of the Party	1951 Seats Won(%)	1957 Seats Won(%)	1961 Seats Won(%)	1967 Seats Won(%)	1971 Seats Won(%)	1974 Seats Won(%)	1977 Seats Won(%)	1980 Seats Won(%)	1985 Seats Won(%)	1990 Seats Won(%)	1995 Seats Won(%)	2000 Seats Won(%)	2004 Seats Won(%)	2009 Seats Won(%)
BJP	-	-	-	0 (0.54)	0 (0.70)	0 (0.41)	-	0 (1.36)	1 (2.60)	2 (3.56)	9 (7.88)	38 (18.20)	32 (17.11)	6 (15.05)
INC	67 (37.87)	56 (38.26)	82 (43.28)	31 (30.66)	51 (28.18)	69 (37.44)	26 (31.02)	118 (47.78)	117 (51.08)	10 (29.78)	80 (39.08)	26 (33.78)	38 (34.82)	27 (29.10)
BJD	-	-	-	-	-	-	-	-	-	-	-	68 (29.40)	61 (27.36)	103 (38.86)
CPI	7 (5.62)	9 (8.40)	4 (7.98)	7 (5.26)	4 (4.79)	7 (4.87)	1 (3.57)	4 (5.09)	1 (3.31)	5 (2.98)	1 (1.71)	1 (1.22)	1 (0.77)	1 (0.51)

Source: Election Commission of India

not imply that these parties were committed to minority welfare or minority upliftment. In the early years until the 1971 elections, Odisha had a significant presence of the Left parties of different ideological persuasions such as socialist parties, Communist Party of India (Marxist) [CPI(M)] and Communist Party of India (CPI). Even now these parties continue to exist but barely have electoral strength of any significance. But a remarkable number of civil society organisations led by the Left-leaning activists have made progressive political agenda visible in Odisha's mainstream politics and media. Some of these organisations have played a significant role in fighting the Hindutva forces in recent years. Some of the key players of Odisha politics such as Harekrushna Mehtab, Surendra Nath Dwivedi, R. N. Singh Deo, Nandini Satpathy, Biju Patnaik and J. B. Patnaik are not associated with an anti-minority agenda in a manner politicians like Narendra Modi, Bal Thackeray or L. K. Advani are known in India's electoral politics.

Naveen Patnaik, the leader of Biju Janata Dal (BJD), was running a coalition government with BJP as Odisha's chief minister at the time Kandhamal violence occurred in 2008. Late Mr. Biju Patnaik, after whom the BJD is founded, was fiercely opposed to any alliance with Hindutva parties. In the 1989 Parliamentary elections, when all the major non-Congress parties stitched together an electoral alliance with the BJP, Biju Patnaik firmly opposed the move and yet won a majority of Lok Sabha seats from Odisha for his party. While Naveen Patnaik may claim that BJD represents Biju Patnaik's legacy, the fact is that the most important legacy of secularism was deeply compromised by the party when it entered into an alliance with the BJP; it was not able to control recurring violence against the Christians. During the 2009 elections, the coalition between the BJP and the BJD fell apart. The BJD officially claimed that it was the Kandhamal crisis that caused the rift between the two long-standing allies. This, however, cannot explain the inadequate state response to Kandhamal violence, which many believe is because of the BJP's role as a coalition partner in the state government at the time. However, current separation augurs well for the secular politics of Odisha but in no way suggests that the threat to Odisha's secular polity or minorities is over.

Evolution of Odisha and religious minorities

Odisha is an example for inter-religious peace in modern India, and generally not notorious for ethnic violence like other states such as Uttar Pradesh, Bihar, Gujarat or Maharashtra. Like many other regions of India, Odisha is multi-religious, but Hindus are a dominant majority. Muslims, Christians and people of other religions constitute a small fraction of Odisha's otherwise peace-loving minority communities.

Christians are only 2.4 per cent of Odisha's population according to the Census of India, 2001. However, there were sporadic incidents of ethnic violence, mainly involving Hindus and Muslims, in Odisha since 1947. These incidents can be described as skirmishes or riots at best, but such incidents neither took genocidal shape nor ever involved Christian communities. Dozens of churches have been standing in major cities of Odisha like its old capital, Cuttack, and the current capital, Bhubaneswar. In various parts of the state, there are missionary-run schools and colleges. There are evidences of missionary activities in all parts of Odisha, though more actively in tribal areas since the colonial times. Furthermore, the state remained largely free from any general impact of violence of Partition of 1947 that rocked the neighbouring states West Bengal or Bihar severely.

Yet, there are Hindu fundamentalist organisations active in the state. Many of these organisations have grown rather rapidly in the past two decades or so together with the growth of the BJP. Historically, there was barely any violence against even the Muslims, the most prominent religious minority of India against which violence is generally seen in many parts of India. Odisha's Muslim population is only 2.1 per cent, and mainly concentrated in regions like Bhadrak, Kendrapada and Cuttack. These regions have seen occasional communal disturbances, but never acquired alarming proportions like Gujarat 2002 or Mumbai 1992/93. Even during Babri Masjid demolition in 1992 only minor incidents were reported from Cuttack. This violence against Christians is a rather new phenomenon, and has spread to different regions in Odisha, and outside to states like Karnataka, Tamil Nadu and Kerala in recent years.

To grasp the complexity associated with the unique nature of ethnic violence, we need to know how Odisha came to exist, and how it remained largely free from the communal politics that swept large parts of North and East India. The current geographical shape of Odisha is an outcome of centuries of evolution marked by invasion, colonial rule and political movements. During these years, its name as well as its geographical shape underwent several changes. Historical research suggests that after the Aryans occupied the coastal region of Odisha, they pushed the native inhabitants to the inside hilly region. It was named Kalinga then, which existed with three divisions. Odisha was much larger and this was particularly true during the rule of the Cheti king Kharavela in the first century BC. King Kharavela's empire extended from Mathura in the north up to Godavari (in present-day Andhra) in the South, and from the Saurashtra coast to the east coast, besides Burma and Southeast Asia. This was perhaps politically the most glorious moment for Odisha. During these years of evolution, it was ruled mainly by regional kings and its economy was not been as bad as it became later (Mohanty, 1990; Mehtab, 1960).

Odisha came under the Afghan rule in 1568 marking the end of Odisha's relative period of prosperity. During the remainder of the century, it was the regular war site between Afghans and Mughals until 1611 when Mughals eventually began to rule the state. The Mughal rule lasted until 1751. After the Mughal rule, Marathas established their rule over the state, which also gradually weakened and several local kings began to rule its various regions until 1803 when the British took over, marking a new era in its history.[23]

The geographical entity of modern Odisha is a result of the politics of the colonial era in the early part of twentieth century. Madhusudhan Das, a noted barrister and a charismatic leader, led a mass political movement with the help of his political party, Utkal Sammilani, independent of the Congress party. He embraced Christianity. A statement once made by a relatively unknown Bengali writer, 'Oriya ekta bhasa naye' (Oriya is not a language) became a rallying cry for a separate Oriya state movement, leading to its creation on 1 April 1936. The idea of Odisha, along with Sindh as a separate state, was floated on a white paper prepared by the British in 1933, as a sequel to the report of the Simon Commission. It is thus the first state to be created on the basis of a separate language, and inspired state reorganisations across linguistic lines in post-independent India. The State Reorganization Commission Report (1956) did not alter its boundaries. However, a prolonged popular agitation for the inclusion of Oriya-speaking areas, Sareikala and Kharsuan, took place, which were allowed to remain with Bihar. Like other regions of India, the state welcomed people of all faiths and allowed them to settle down over the centuries, and continues to do so. What helped in creating a welcoming ambience is the particular variety of Hindu religion represented by the Jagannath cult. It is worthwhile to remember that a legendary devotee of Lord Jagannath is a Muslim, known as Bhakta Salabega.

Implications for Indian Christians

In the history of India's ethnic violence, this Hindu–Christian conflict opens a completely new chapter. In the West, Muslims and Christians are perceived to be at loggerheads, but their relationships have been largely conflict free in India in recent decades. This is generally true in the post-independent India. Among the reasons that have led to this conflict-free relationship is the manner in which prominent Muslim thinkers look at Christianity and Christians, namely leaders like Sir Sayed Ahmed Khan[24] and poet Iqbal. Sir Syed Ahmed Khan realised that a deep intellectual understanding of Christianity is a pre-condition to advance the cause of mutual respect and friendship between two world religions. He undertook meticulous research, and produced a commentary on the Holy Bible in three volumes titled *Tabiyan Al-Kalam*, a first of its kind. The first volume focused on the Bible, the second on the Genesis up to Chapter Eleven and the third commented on Mathew 1–5.[25] This cannot be the only reason for ethnic peace between Muslims and Christians in India, and there are other factors that would distinguish the patterns of relationships between Muslims and Christians as vastly different from the relationship between Muslims and Hindus. Given that British rule was never seen as Christian rule, the relationship of a ruler and subject, and stories of humiliations and atrocities associated with Hindu–Muslim question is generally never raised between Muslims and Christians in India. Furthermore, Muslims never perceived any threat from the Christians in India as the latter is a much smaller minority as opposed to the Hindu majority. Among others, these are some of the factors that explain why Muslim–Christian relationships have been conflict free thus far.[26]

Unlike the Muslim–Christian relationship, the Hindu–Christian relationship is rather long, convoluted and ridden with tensions. There are cases of anti-Christian violence during the colonial as well as postcolonial period. During the colonial days, there were several Hindu–Christian communal troubles, particularly during the 1820s and 1830s. These are mostly sporadic incidents occurring at various times in the Madras Presidency.

One particular case worth recalling is the violence against Christians in Tirunelveli district (present-day Tamil Nadu) in 1845. It was a direct outcome of the reaction to the conversions. As it is widely known that Christian missionary activities did not enjoy direct patronage of the British Empire owing to the Sepoy Mutiny 1857, which was triggered owing to the East India Company's interference in native religions. Interestingly, according to Frykenberg, there was hostility towards Christians and Christian missionaries as part of a policy of the Raj. He writes:

In many ways, at unofficially, Company's raj was a Hindu raj . . . This being so, it is hardly surprising that official attitudes towards Christians and Christian missionaries was less than cordial. Exceptions tended to be opportunistic and pragmatic. As urgent needs arose, Christians on the ground would be readily exploited by British officials. (Frykenberg 2003: 55)

In the absence of state patronage, the missionary activities largely remained autonomous, and Christians remained a very small minority at the time of independence, and politically almost insignificant in modern India in the larger politics of religious minorities, whereas Muslim elites and clergies not just drew attention but also received dominant fraction of political patronage before the 2014 election.

However, there are reports of incidents of anti-Christian violence after 1947. One of the first incidents of anti-Christian anger became evident in 1952 after 4,000 Adivasis converted to Christianity in the Surganju district in Madhya Pradesh and Madhya Bharat (a tribal region that was incorporated into the former). This led to a debate on minority rights and freedom of religion, particularly the latter. Niyogi Committee was set up to inquire into this matter under the chairmanship of a retired judge of Madhya Pradesh High Court, Bhawani Shankar Niyogi, and was called the Christian Missionaries Activities Inquiry Committee. Ironically, Christian organisations protested against the investigation of missionaries and their activities. The committee visited the Christian hospitals, schools, churches, hostels and leprosy homes, and interviewed 11,360 persons in 700 villages, and received 375 written replies, out of which only 55 were from Christians. In 1956, two volumes of the report were submitted.[27]

Just as Gujarat was part of an experiment against the Muslims in 2002, Kandhamal 2008 needs to be seen as part of the experiment against Christians. The ideology of the Hindutva organisations as anti-Muslim is well known. In their attempt to make India a Hindu state, they have been anti-Christian as well, but the political manifestation of being anti-Muslim has been generally prominent since the early years of the RSS. In recent years, there are instances of Christians in Gujarat being the target of violence. What is striking is that there has been an increase in the incidents of violence after the BJP came to power in Gujarat in 1998. Some of the incidents involve tearing and burning of the holy Bible in Rajkot, church burning in Dangs, exhuming of the body of a Christian in Kapadvanj, disruption of religious services in Pipalwad, among others. In addition, there are regular campaigns by the Hindutva organisations through propaganda in vernacular newspapers and distributions of handbills.[28]

In the larger context, it could be argued that Indian Christians are now a new enemy for Hindutva organisations all over India. Christians, like Indian Muslims, have been for past several decades bearing a heavy loss to life and property. Hindutva votaries have seemingly decided to deal with this by using a three-pronged strategy: the first is to develop organisations like schools and hospitals in the areas where they find active missionary organisations; and second, by tampering with the Freedom of Religion Act in different states, making the missionary activities almost impossible. There are evidences of this measure visible in states like Gujarat, Madhya Pradesh and Rajasthan where the BJP is in power. The third- strategy is organising genocidal violence of the Kandhamal type in different parts of India. It is obvious that Christians in India are going to be target of organised discrimination in the coming years, and they are going to live with anxiety and fear in a manner Muslims do in different parts of India.

Conclusion

The Kandhamal violence is indeed a reflection of a pernicious political trend emerging in India. It is not an isolated incident. Violence of this gravity cannot occur without the collusion of the state. The political economy of the region characterised by massive illiteracy, and mass unemployment is hospitable to the recruitment of militant wings of various fundamentalist organisations such as VHP and RSS. The tardiness of the inquiries by both commissions indicate the state's unwillingness to address this issue with urgency.

As our analysis shows, this is not purely a land-conflict story, instead a genocidal politics organised by fundamentalist organisations like VHP and RSS and others, backed by the BJP. A consensus for this violence among Hindutva organisations is evident in their decision to pass anti-conversion law in states like Madhya Pradesh and Rajasthan. These laws stand against the constitutionally guaranteed religious freedom. In some ways, these laws offer required ideological justification for violence, whose abrogation alone would help enrich the meaning of minority rights in India. The manner in which Kandhamal violence triggered violence in other parts of India like Karnataka, Tamil Nadu and Kerala indicates enduring threats to the religious freedom and future possibilities of genocide against the minorities.[29] A strong case for the ban of both BD and the VHP does exist, but this measure is not enough to defeat the Hindutva politics ideologically, for which a concerted campaign is required in which media and civil society have to play a pro-active role in a systematic and long-term fashion. Christians today are as vulnerable as Muslims, and their life, liberty and property will remain a target of violence. If minorities remain in fear, Indian democracy will fail and forces weakening the moral foundations of Indian democracy need to be strengthened.

Notes

1 The impact of this violence began to spread to other parts of India such as Karnataka and Kerala.
2 'Kandhamal violence is due to SC–ST rift', *Indian Express*, 13 October 2008. SC: Scheduled Castes; ST: Scheduled Tribes.

3 'Land disputes, negligence cited as factors in Kandhamal', in www.christian-today.com, 2 July 2009. Justice Mohapatra Commission was set up to enquire into violence that took place in 2007, which was a precursor to the 2008 violence.

4 There are some cases of anti-Christian violence in the 1950s and 1960s, but they were never compared to the Hindu–Muslim violence either in frequency or size.

5 Biju Patnaik, former chief minister of Odisha, was a towering political leader of national importance, and had a long, chequered political career. Biju Janata Dal (BJD), now the ruling party, was named after him after his death in 1998. Naveen Patnaik, one of his two sons, heads the party and currently is the chief minister of Odisha.

6 Report on Kandhamal, Government of Orissa, Bhubaneswar, 2008.

7 Orissa Development Report, Government of Orissa, Bhubaneswar, 2004, p. 43.

8 'European envoys meet Kandhamal victims', *The Times of India*, 16 November 2009.

9 United States Commission on International Religious Freedom (USCIRF), Annual Report, Washington, 2009, p. 1.

10 'Odisha: CBI arrests two in Australian missionary murder case', *The New Indian Express*, 17 May 2013.

11 For a detailed analysis of these organisations and the threat they pose to India include Jaffrelot (2005), Katju (2003), Katzenstein (1979), Anderson and Dalme (1987), Hansen (2001) and Ghosh (2000).

12 Justice Mohapatra meanwhile has passed away. The Commission is now headed by Justice Naidu. In a recent interview with the author, Justice Naidu has said that reports will be out in a few months.

13 'Maoists killed swami: Police', *The Telegraph*, 18 May 2011. Sabyasachi Panda, secretary of the underground Maoist organisations, had given an interview to the media accepting the blame that Maoists were directly involved in the murder of the swami.

14 Ibid.

15 Pyari Mohan Mohapatra has recently fallen apart with the chief minister, and now runs his own party. He revealed to the author in an interview he gave as part of a visiting delegate of WILPF that prepared a report on women victims of violence.

16 Another report is prepared by a prominent writer and bureaucrat Ramakanta Rath who completed writing it on 25 October 2008. This report is based on his tour to different parts of Kandhamal. Unlike other reports, Ramakanta Rath disagrees that it is mainly an anti-Christian violence. He notes: 'A major cause of the recent as well as earlier disturbances has been the occupation of land of the Scheduled Tribes by others. Securing jobs on the basis of false caste certificates.' The Government of Odisha also prepared a report

of its own. This report also did not look at it as an anti-Christian violence. The report observes: 'In order to have a proper perspective-it is important to appreciate that the ongoing conflict in Kandhamal district has its genesis in the age old ethnic divide and discord between Kandha (one of the Schedule Tribes) and Pana (one of the Schedule Caste) communities.' According to this report, the administration set up relief camps in block headquarters of all the affected blocks, such as at Tikabali, G. Udaygiri, Raikia, K, Nuagam, Balliguda, Daringibadi, Phulbani, Phiringia, Kotagarh and Tumudibandh. According to the state government estimate, the highest number of persons in relief camps was 25,177 on 4 September 2008, but gradually number declined to 6,574 on 6 January 2009. On this day, there were six camps running in four different blocks such as Tikabali, G. Udaygiri, Raikia and K. Nuagaon.

17 Seema Mustafa, Sagari Chhabra, Amit Bhaduri, Vincent Manoharan, Manoranjan Mohanty, Kamal Chenoy and few others were part of the team. This team was made up of academics, journalists and activists.

18 Report on Kandhamal by Concerned Citizen's Group, New Delhi, September 2008.

19 Report by the Vice Chairperson of the National Commission for Minorities to Orissa, 13 September .2008, New Delhi.

20 Women in security, conflict management and peace (WISCOMP).

21 Women are generally the worst victims of this type of violence. For a conceptual understanding of this analysis, see Butler (1990). For specific case stories, see Saba Gul Khattak on Afghan women, Urvashi Butalia on women victims during the Partition, Mary O'Kane on women in Burma in Behera, ed., Gender 2006).

22 See Jaffrelot (2005).

23 There is a detailed discussion about Odisha's evolution in Mahtab (1960). Also see Mohanty (1989, 1990).

24 A vast number of literature is produced on that period of Muslim politics and the role of Sir Sayed Ahmed Khan. A good sample includes Hasan (2006) and Leyfeld (1996).

25 Ridgson (2001:1–31). For a detailed discussion on Muslim–Christian relations, see Mahony (2001:212–48).

26 There are recent reports of conflict between Muslims and Christians, though much smaller in scale, from the state of Kerala, which has significant Muslim and Christian population.

27 Report of the Christian Missionary Activities Enquiry Committee, Madhya Pradesh, 18 April 1956, 3 Vols. (Indore, Madhya Pradesh, Government Publication, 1956).

28 Lancy Lobo, *Globalization, Hindu Nationalism, and Christians in India*, Rawat Publications, New Delhi, 2002.

29 See Rehman (2008).

12

UNITED PROGRESSIVE ALLIANCE (I) AND INDIA'S MUSLIMS

Redefining equality of opportunity?

Heewon Kim

One of the most remarkable features of Indian states' responses to 9/11 was the uniformity of approach towards Muslim minority communities. The dramatic developments, and the 'War on Terror', were accompanied by an outlook that, by and large, pathologised Muslim minority communities around the discourses of terror, identity politics and religiously self-imposed isolation (Saggar 2009). In the West, this outcome was attributed in large measure to the politics of multi-culturalism, a libertarian political creed that had undermined collective citizenship by fostering identity politics. Thus, for example, in the aftermath of the 7 July 2005 (7/7) bombings in central London, British public opinion appeared to agree on one thing: that multi-culturalism was dead and that it was militant Islam that had killed it off (Singh and Tatla 2006:1). Almost universally across the West, the rise of Islamophobia has been accompanied by a political backlash to build 'social cohesion' and re-establish traditional national values. Whilst the securitisation of Muslim minority communities reflected the hard edge of this policy, state-led efforts to examine causes of Muslim under-achievement and disadvantage, and how these could be better addressed by anti-discrimination policies mirrored the 'softer', integrationist intent. Nearly all states in Europe have adopted policies that include a mixture of these approaches, with the initial emphasis on securitisation being superseded by a renewed policy interest in disadvantage and discrimination suffered by Muslim minorities (Klausen 2005).

In developing countries somewhat similar processes have been evident, too. In India, the growth of communalism since the early 1980s reached its climax in the Gujarat riots of 2002, which saw the death of 5,000 Muslims and the further displacement of 100,000 into relief camps in state-sponsored pogroms (Singh 2004). The events in Gujarat were the culmination of almost two decades' of aggressive mobilisation by the Hindu right that led to the emergence of the Bharatiya Janata Party (BJP) as a national force. Although the BJP-led National Democratic Alliance (NDA) was defeated in the 2004 Lok Sabha elections, its impact on public policy towards religious minorities was lasting in significantly changing terms of trade of India's national identity and the place of religious minorities within it (Adney and Sáez 2005).

The Congress-led United Progressive Alliance (UPA), which came to power in 2004, was committed to reversing this process. The UPA's common minimum programme (CMP) gave major prominence to secularism. Of its 'six basic principles of governance', two included a commitment to preserve, protect and promote social harmony and to enforce the law without fear or favour to deal with all obscurantist and fundamentalist elements who seek to disturb social amity and peace, [and] to provide full equality of opportunity, particularly in education and employment for scheduled castes, scheduled tribes, other backward classes (OBCs) and religious minorities (GOI 2004:2–3).

These overarching objectives were set within specific proposals that included: measures to reverse the communalisation of education under the NDA, especially in higher education; 'to implement the Places of Worship (Special Provisions) Act, 1992 and seek a negotiated settlement on Ayodhya'; to enact a comprehensive law to deal with communal violence; 'to establish a Commission for Minority Educational Institutions that will provide direct affiliation for minority professional institutions to central universities'; to achieve the social and economic empowerment of minorities through education; to establish a national commission to address the welfare of socially and economically backward religious and linguistic minorities (including the possibility of reservation); to adequately fund the national Minorities Development Corporation; 'to provide constitutional status to the Minorities Commission and the recognition of Urdu under Articles 345 and 347 of the Constitution'; 'to revive the National Integration Council so that it meets at least twice a year'; and, 'to take the strictest possible action, without fear or favour, against all those individuals and organisations, who spread social discord, disturb social amity, and propagate religious bigotry and communal hatred' (ibid.: 5–11).

Many of the above proposals were also present in Congress's own manifesto. The Congress, it declared,

> believes in *affirmative action for all religious and linguistic minorities*. The Congress has provided for reservations for Muslims in Kerala and Karnataka in government employment and education on the grounds that they are a socially and educationally backward class. *The Congress is committed to adopting this policy for. . . Muslims and other religious minorities on a national scale.* (Indian National Congress 2004, emphasis added)

These proposals, moreover, were set in a context in which secularism was identified as the 'key issue' because the BJP was 'systematically undermining the very essence of Indian civilisation and destroying the very idea of India'. 'The Congress', the party's manifesto warned, 'recognises that this is not a moment for a narrow pursuit of power': rather, it was '*a moment to consolidate all forces subscribing to the fundamental values of our Constitution*' (ibid.: emphasis added). In short, directly or indirectly, state secularism and anti-communalism featured prominently in the UPA's CMP and the Congress's manifesto and was tied to three commitments: to 'de-communalise' some of the policy initiatives of the previous NDA; to develop policies to empower (religious) minorities; and to ensure effective and impartial governance that upheld state secularism.

The existing literature on the first UPA (2004–09), or UPA (I), administration's record in power is distinguished by four different approaches. First, the Congress-led support for anti-communal and pro-religious minorities' policies, it is argued, was motivated primarily by the desire to re-establish the party's traditional link with these communities. After almost a decade in the wilderness, Congress needed to offer tangible electoral incentives to rebuild the relationship with minorities, especially Muslims (Wilkinson 2012). Second, that the Congress's approach towards minorities was part of its much broader strategy of building post-clientistic politics. With party organisation in disarray, post-clientistic politics offered a new approach, especially in using targeted development programmes at specific social constituencies (Manor 2012). Third, the Congress's policies represented more of continuity than a radical departure. Although the argument and the discourses changed, it is suggested, the Congress-led UPA was simply executing the tried and tested policy prescriptions of the past. What was different, for instance with reference to affirmative action, was the terms in which the debate was articulated (Bajpai 2011). Finally, one comprehensive evaluation of UPA's performance in power concludes, somewhat convincingly, that the 'UPA experience suggests that *ideology* matters' (Sáez and Singh 2012: 151). Whereas UPA's delivery on the proposed manifesto programme significantly fell short, it was, nonetheless, quite adept in creating deep blue water between itself and the NDA. It was an ideological outlook that embraced a plural, multi-cultural vision of the nation and a distinct political style, one that has privileged quiet diplomacy, and a traditional emphasis on consensus. Both the ideology and the style enabled the Congress to accomplish a shift to reservation-based identity politics – a policy that had always been an anathema to the party. Congress's conversion was so complete that it exuded the zeal of neophyte in embracing the case for Muslim reservations and creating a new architecture for equal opportunities for religious minorities (ibid.: 152).

Although the four perspectives outlined above provide a general overviews of UPA's policies, they offer few meaningful insights into which policies were adopted and why. They tell us little, for instance, about how the UPA was able to use institutional discretion to implement some of the policies on religious minorities that were clearly contentious or how institutional barriers also frustrated policy implementation.[1] An institutional-based policy grounded approach, which also seeks to track how policy was formulated, implemented or remained unimplemented would offer a more rounded assessment of UPA's record than is available hitherto. This is particularly the case with reference to the policies on religious minorities as they often strike at the very heart of the conception of the nation, with policy failure being ascribed to broader, intangible factors.

In this chapter, which is part of research on institutional policy analysis of UPA's policies on religious minorities with special reference to the

Muslim community,[2] we reflect on the extent to which the UPA succeeded in creating new public discourse on equality of opportunity for religious minorities in India. We do so by focusing in particular on four substantive reports that underpinned the UPA's policy formation process: the Sachar Committee Report (SCR 2006), the Ranganath Misra Commission Report (RMR 2007), Equal Opportunities Commission Report (EOC 2008) and the Kundu Committee Report (KCR 2008). The chapter is organised in three sections. Section one offers an outline of how equality of opportunity was framed within the Constitution of India, and the long-term implications of excluding religious minorities from affirmative action. Section two outlines core elements of the new framework within which UPA's policies were framed. Finally, section three offers some suggestions on how institutional-based policy analysis offers a more relevant point of departure for examining the UPA's record than existing frames of policy analysis.

Equality of opportunity and the Constitution

The starting point for an understanding the framing of equality of opportunity is the making of the Constitution of India. In essence the Constitution embraces dual conception of equality: one based on the generic principle of non-discrimination, and another rooted in 'protective equality' for seriously disadvantaged groups. These two approaches represent 'competing equalities', but ones that are historically rooted in the Indian social formation and are products of historical evolution (Galanter 1984).

As a secular, modern text, the Indian Constitution recognises individual rights associated with liberal democracy. As a corollary, it established a strong principle of non-discrimination. Articles 15 and 16 prohibit the state from discriminating on the grounds of religion, race, caste, descent, place of birth or any of them generally in state's actions. More specifically, they prohibit discrimination on such grounds 'in matters relating to employment or appointment to any office under the State' (RMR 2007: 4). The principle of non-discrimination is further enshrined in procedural equality embedded in Articles 14–16 that commit the state to combat discrimination. Non-discrimination was thus one of the 'core principles guiding the development of a democratic nation state in India' (Verma 2012: 69).

Alongside the principle of non-discrimination, which is an essential requirement of liberal democracy, the Constitution also recognises the need for positive discrimination for disadvantaged groups. Articles 15 permits the state to make 'any special provisions for women, children [and] any socially, educationally backward class of citizens' and Scheduled Castes (SC) and Scheduled Tribes (ST) (RMR 2007: 4–5). Article 16 further enables the state to make provisions for reservations in appointments of posts in favour of 'any backward class of citizens which, in the opinion of the state, is not adequately represented in the services under the State' (ibid: 5). Whereas the former provision has become the bedrock of affirmative action in employment and education (and reservation of seats in the legislatures) for SC and ST, since 1950 the latter article, especially at the level of states, has justified the extension of reservations (employment, education) to other backward classes.

It is important to acknowledge that provision for affirmative action were constructed largely in response to the political claims of formerly untouchable castes and against similar claims voiced by religious minorities. Partition and the creation of Pakistan severely circumscribed the claims of minority rights, which were limited to cultural and linguistic sphere. However, in contrast the project of democratising Hindu society resulted in the re-designation of SC and ST, who before the Government of India Act (1935) were defined as 'other minorities', as part of the majority (Hindu) community. Affirmative action provisions for these groups, as outlined above, were justified on the grounds that they were necessary to address historic exclusion and victimisation in the Hindu society. Religious minorities were excluded from these provisions as the criteria for reservations were defined primarily with reference to caste, tribe and backwardness. Poor Muslims, Christians, Sikhs and Buddhists were deemed to be outside the remit of these provisions because of the egalitarian precepts of these faiths.[3] The Constitution in taking an ideological construction of caste that identified it with Hinduism – as opposed to a sociological one – created a sharp new boundary between Hindus and non-Hindus while excluding equally disadvantaged groups (poor Muslims, Christians, Buddhists and Sikhs) because such claims were seen to intertwine group rights with religion. In sum, the Constitution rejected the political claims of religious minorities, recognised the cultural and linguistic rights of all minorities, and in introducing affirmative action provisions for SC and ST, set up the project of democratising Hindu society. The last measure did not just create a structural imbalance in the equality of opportunity for protected minorities; it would have a pro-found impact on the evolution of Indian democracy (see Singh 2014).

In the period after Independence the tensions inherent in this struc-tural imbalance would manifest themselves, on the one hand, in the demands from SC and ST and OBC to increase the scope of reserva-tions, and demands from the poor of religious minorities, on the other, that their exclusions from these provisions on grounds of religion was a form of religious discrimination. Yet, the criteria for SC and OBC were clearly defined by the overarching emphasis on caste within the Hindu tradition; and when this was challenged, the courts continued to err in favour of the hegemonic understanding of these categories. One nota-ble variation from this norm was the practice of reservation for OBC at national and state levels. At the national level the criteria for OBC were only effectively established by the Mandal Commission, which conceded that religious communities like the Muslims had 'backward classes' that should be given reservation. But in the pre-Mandal period, states' interpretation of OBC criteria was largely influenced by history, tradition and regional peculiarities, so that some states like Karnataka and Kerala included Muslims under the OBC category. But even these breakthroughs were unable to make significant bridgeheads: the rise of the Hindu right in the 1980s and 1990s along with mobilisation of Dalit communities following the implementation of the Mandal Commission Report (1990) further marginalised the case for considering the case of poor and socially excluded religious minorities. In fact as Dalitisation of Indian politics in the 1990s and 2000s occurred at pace, the need to effectively address the shortcomings in equality of opportunity for religious minorities, especially India's Muslims, were brought home by 9/11 and the riots in Gujarat.

UPA (I) and a new framework of equality of opportunity for religious minorities with special reference to Muslims

It has been persuasively argued that the tenure of the first UPA admin-istration marked something of a radical departure in the approach to equality of opportunity for religious minorities as framed within the Constitution (Khaitan 2008). In the policies, political discourses, official commissions and report, and the use of institutional discretion, there was, it is suggested, a perceptible shift from the focus on national integration, which had characterised the earlier construction of religious minorities, to justice and equality. Discourses of social inclusion, diversity and anti-discrimination underpinned this change. This change was most evident in the desire to shift the debate with reference to India's Muslims from the politics of identity to the politics of development and social exclusion. Religious minorities were to be enabled to share fully the glow of citizenship in India's developing economy, and the core elements of this framework included: (i) recognising religion as a category of social exclusion; (ii) establishing a level-playing field for religious minorities on par with SC, ST and OBC; (iii) ensuring that service delivery reflects the principle of proportionality; (iv) institutionalising the monitoring of equality of opportunity and promotion of social diversity; and (v) addressing the concerns of religious minorities about security and communal violence.

Religion as a category of social exclusion

As noted previously, the dominant approach after 1950 towards religion's claim for public space was defined by the Nehruvian state that emphasised secularism and development. Often the state assiduously rejected minority claims because of the assumed religious intent as, for example, in the case of the Sikh campaign for a Punjabi Suba (creation of a Punjabi-majority province). Indeed, minority claims in particular were regularly stigmatised as 'communal', 'separatist' and encouraging 'fissiparous' tendencies (Singh 2000: Chapter 3). Ironically, such use of language readily intersected with discourses of Hindutva on minorities and contributed substantially to the rise of the BJP.

However, the SCR on the socio-economic conditions of Indian Muslims published in November 2006 'marked an important shift in the popular/political discourse on India's religious minorities' (Jodhka: 297). The SCR addressed directly the development deficit among Muslims by opening 'up new ways of talking about religious minorities' (ibid.), a subject of intense public debate. These 'new ways' included *inter alia* taking socio-economic-religious categories seriously, recognising the level of deprivation among some of these communities, especially Muslims, and developing new approaches to address this under-development.

Surprisingly, notwithstanding the wealth of data available to the Planning Commission and other executive agencies, for political and ideological reasons these data, especially on development and disadvantage, had not been aggregated for religious minorities. As the SCR observed:

> While the perception of deprivation is widespread among Muslims, there has been no systematic effort since Independence to analyse the condition of religious minorities in the country. Despite the need to analyse the socio-economic and educational conditions of different Socio Religious Categories (SRCs), until recently appropriate data for such an analysis was not generated by Government agencies. (SCR 2006: 2)

One of the major achievements of the SCR was to utilise these data to examine the condition of socio-religious communities. In doing so, it was a significant act of *recognition* within the secular, scientific establishment that disadvantaged communities exist among religious communities. This shift from recognition to accepting socio-religious communities as social categories worthy of serious policy programmes marked a begrudging acknowledgement that the life chances of some communities were also determined by their religious identities (UK). 'Indeed', as Jodhka has noted, 'the proposals put forward by the Sachar Committee for amelioration of the Muslim population are premised on the assumption that religious identity be treated as a relevant category in the State policy and perspective on development' (Jodhka 2009: 298).

By utilising religious identification as relevant socio-religious community, the SCR was able to demonstrate the scale of disadvantage suffered by Indian's Muslims. This included, among other things, very poor representation in state governance and employment, both at the national and state levels, a dismal provision for education, infrastructure, security in areas of Muslim settlement; an extremely improvised support from financial services for Muslim enterprises, and widespread perception of wholesale religious discrimination, resulting in ghettoisation, an inward, identity-centred community (SCR 2006). Whilst most socio-religious communities, including SC and ST, were showing noticeable evidence of improvement on key performance indicators, such as education, evidence for similar developments within India's Muslim communities was difficult to find. As the SCR concluded:

> Our analysis shows that while there is considerable variation in the conditions of Muslims across states (and among the Muslims, those who identified themselves as OBCs and others), the *Community exhibits deficits and deprivation in practically all dimensions of development. In fact, by and large, Muslims rank somewhat above SCs/STs but below Hindu-OBCs, Other Minorities and Hindu – General (mostly upper castes) in almost all indicators considered. Among the states that have large Muslim populations, the situation is particularly grave in the states of West Bengal, Bihar, Uttar Pradesh and Assam* . . . In addition to the 'development deficit', the perception among Muslims that they are discriminated against and excluded is widespread, which exacerbates the problem. (SCR 2006: 237, emphasis added)

The scale of the 'problem' was such that it could no longer be ignored. In addressing the 'development deficit' among Muslims, the SCR also proposed measures beyond the conventional conceptual tool-box of Indian approach to disadvantage. In addition to community-specific programmes aimed at education, infrastructure and self-help measure support by private and public sector undertakings, the SCR recommended four initiatives that had the potential to redefine the equality of opportunity. First, it proposed the creation of a National Data Bank for establishing transparent, generally accessible and relevant data on SRC so their engagement in public and private programmes could be better evaluated. Second, this data would then be evaluated by an Assessment and Monitoring Authority, which would highlight areas of concern for further development. Third, to better enhance the framework of equality of opportunity, the SCR recommended a more decisive shift from non-discrimination to anti-discrimination by recommending a policy borrowed from the English experience to legislate more effectively against direct and indirect discrimination (religious and non-religious). This legislation, the SCR suggested, would be overseen by an EOC. Finally, to combat discrimination in all its form, the committee proposed the construction of diversity index (DI) that would measure diversity in critical areas such as employment in the public and private sectors and housing. The degree of organisational diversity would become the new marker of willingness to embrace diverse, plural and equal opportunities-driven modern India (ibid.: Chapter 12).

Religious minorities and SC, ST and OBC – a new level-playing field

As well as the new approaches to better ensure equality of opportunity and promotion of diversity, a key feature of UPA's framework was to erase the structural barriers between religious minorities and SC, ST and OBC in the recognition of 'protective equality'. By creating a new level-playing field in which religious minorities were included in the protective, developmental provisions of affirmative action in employment and service delivery, the UPA sought to eradicate the anomalies that had persisted as ineradicable barriers. Potentially, this thrust challenged the very essence of the constitutional settlement; in the event, though the UPA was frustrated in this objective, it was able to bring to the fore the underlying inequities that confronted religious minorities.

Alongside the Sachar Committee, on 29 October 2004, the UPA government established the Ranganath Misra Commission (National Commission for Religious and Linguistic Minorities). Its remit was to:

> Suggest [a] criteria for identification of socially and economically backward sections among religious and linguistic minorities; to recommend measure for the welfare for the socially and economically backward sections among religious and linguistic minorities, including reservation in education and employment; and, to suggest the necessary constitutional, legal and administrative modalities required for the implement of its recommendations. (RMR 2007:1)

The commission's report ultimately became embroiled in a bitter controversy, so much so that was not tabled in Parliament until after the

2009 general elections. This, as we shall see later, is generally interpreted as a lack of faith on part of the UPA. Conversely, it can be reasonably argued that the commission's recommendations touched a raw nerve in the nation's psyche, mobilising the latent opposition to the proposal, including, surprisingly, among SC, ST and OBC, the constitutionally acceptable subalterns. It was this opposition, as much the lack of political will among the UPA, which ultimately frustrated the translation of these proposals into policy.[4]

At the core of Misra Commission's proposal was to establish a level-playing field between poor religious minorities and SC, ST and OBC in terms of the provisions for 'protective equality'. To this end, the commission opted for a criteria of socially and economically backward in keeping with that defined for the majority (Hindu) community with 'no discrimination whatsoever between the majority community and minorities; and the criteria now applied for this purpose to the majority community', it insisted, 'must be unreservedly applied also to all the minorities' (ibid.: 149). The logical extension of this principle, the commission argued, was that sections and groups among minorities that are regarded as 'inferior' (lower castes) 'should be treated as backward' in the same ways as their 'counterparts in the majority community are regarded as backward' (ibid.). Thus SC and ST equivalent among the religious minorities should be brought into the SC and ST 'net' of affirmative provisions. And being consistent with this recommendation based on de-linking caste from religion, and a recognition of caste as a general feature of Indian society were, in the commission's view, the need to delete paragraph three of the Constitution (Scheduled Caste) Order (1950), 'which originally restricted the SC net to the Hindus and later opened it to Sikhs and Buddhist' but still excluded Muslims, Christians, Parsis and Jains (ibid.: 154). In making caste religiously neutral, moreover, the commission was insistent that a change in an individual's religion, for example conversion to Islam or Christianity, should not affect his or her SC status. In sum, the constitutional logic of restricting reservations to former Hindu untouchables (SC and ST) was now to be extended to religious minorities, including to the followers of those religions that officially proclaimed an egalitarian creed.

By making caste religiously neutral, the RMR opened up the possibilities of reservations in central and states' employment for religious minorities. Given the extent of under-representation of religious minorities in state employment, especially Muslims, the RMR suggested that 15 per cent 'of posts in all cadres and grades under the Central and State governments should be earmarked' for Muslims (10 per cent) and other minorities (5 per cent). Such an action, it argued, was consistent with Article 16(4) of the Constitution, which provides the enabling provision for reservations for SC and ST.[5] In the event this proved difficult to implement, the RMR recommended that 8.4 per cent of the 27 per cent OBC quota be reserved for religious minorities with 6 per cent earmarked for Muslims and 2.4 for non-Muslims (ibid.: 153).

In addition to the need for reservation for religious minorities to square the circle of unequal opportunities, the RMR proposed a raft of legal and institutional measures which, among other things, included: firm protection for minority rights to education; the need for statutory status for the judicial enforcement of the prime minister's 15-point programme for minorities; a parliamentary committee on constitutional policy for minorities; a national committee for monitoring the educational and economic development of minorities; the establishment of state-level minorities commissions and welfare departments in all those states and union territories where these do not exist of now; and the decentralisation of all minority-related schemes to the district-level mechanism with corresponding structures for minority representation and engagement (ibid.: 154–55). The real policy thrust behind these measures was to place the provision for religious minorities on par with other groups, and to do so in ways that reflected existing policy conventions and new approaches innate in contemporary understandings of addressing equality opportunity.

Proportionality in service delivery

Another basic dimension of this approach was that alongside affirmative action for poor sections of religious minorities, the principle of proportionality in service delivery should apply. In the development of equal opportunities policies to address the disadvantage suffered by black and ethnic minorities in the United States and the United Kingdom, there was increasing recognition that services provided by the state and parastatal organisation to these groups should be both beyond direct and indirect discrimination and that these service budgets should be proportionally allocated to the target group, for example, black and ethnic minorities, to reflect at least their proportion in the population (see Ball and Solomos: 1990). This principle had been conceded for SC and ST in the Tenth Five-Year Plan (2002–07), but extending it to religious minorities required circumventing the constitutional barriers against religious-based actions.

Although the case for a sub-plan for minorities in the Eleventh Five-Year Plan (2007–12) was rejected (Hasan: 54), the proposals that emerged from the SCR, RMR, and other related initiatives were to recognise the need for proportionality within the limits of executive and legislative action. The flagship measure which was at the centre of this drive was the prime minister's 15-point programme. A new version of an early initiative launched by Indira Gandhi, the 15-point programme for the welfare of minorities, was launched in January 2006 with the specific aim of improving the education opportunities for minorities; ensuring an equitable share for religious minorities in economic activity and employment; improving the living condition of minorities; and preventing and control of communal riots (MoMA 2006). This initiative drew on resources allocated to other programmes, and where possible, aimed to ensure that 15 per cent of the total outlay was earmarked for minorities. In 2007–08 the newly created Ministry of Minority Affairs (ibid.) identified 90 minority concentration districts (MCDs) for which a multi-sector development programme (MSDP) was launched to address the 'development deficit in education, skills development, employment, sanitation, housing, drinking water and electricity supply' (Press Information Bureau, 2009).

The case for proportionality was also made for some of the high-profile UPA government programmes – Bharat Nirman (creation of basic rural infrastructure), National Rural Employment Guarantee Act (NREGA), Mid-Day Meal Scheme, Sarva Shiksha Abhiyan (Education for All Movement), Total Sanitation Campaign, National Rural Health Mission, Integrated Child Development Services, Polio Eradication and Jawaharlal Nehru Urban Renewal Mission – aimed at poverty reduction (RMR 2007: 91–2). Monitoring data available for some of these programmes indicated that take-up by religious minorities, notably Muslims, is significantly below the mean (ibid.: Chapter 7); and in seeking to correct this imbalance through better distribution and monitoring, the case was also made for extending this approach to the activities of public sector units, banks and private contractors dependent on official contracts. In following this approach these recommendations were both building on the existing policies of leveraging change by using the state sector, but also drawing on comparative experience of the United States and the United Kingdom where contract compliance has been used as an effective tool for better promoting equal opportunities among third parties.

(vi) Institutionalising equality of opportunity and promotion of social diversity (equal opportunities commission and diversity index)

A further innovation in creating a level-playing field for religious minorities was the proposal to create an EOC and a DI. Both proposals emerged from the recommendations of the SCR, but their origins were to be found in like structures and policies in other liberal democracies. It was recognised that India's case was unique insofar as the Constitution conceded the principle of 'competing' equalities, but major development had taken place in other liberal democracies (United States, United Kingdom, Canada, South Africa, Malaysia) in addressing competing social disadvantages around race, ethnicity, gender and tribe that were worthy of serious reflection. Some of these countries (e.g. the United Kingdom), moreover, like India, were faced with competing structures for promoting equality and the task of how to integrate these (for race, gender, religion) within a singular overarching framework of equalities legislation (EOC 2008).

The starting point for these proposals was the SCR's contention that in contemporary India as more complex challenges were emerging around disadvantage and discrimination, often around the existence of multiple axes of disadvantage, new thinking was needed on 'how to handle the interaction effects of more than one axes of disadvantage' (EOC 2008:12). The expert group that examined this subject proposed an EOC with a focus on eradicating discrimination against 'deprived groups' identified by an objective deprivation index and defined by 'sex, caste, language, religion, disability, descent, place of birth, residence, race or any other' grounds (Khaitan 2008:9). The EOC was to be the executive body that would initially focus on two domains: education and employment. However, its overall remit was one of policy intervention and coordination:

> the Commission will have advisory and consultative functions with government departments, private enterprises and autonomous institutions in respect of equal opportunity practices for which the EOC will evolve Equal Opportunity Practices Codes in different sectors and regions . . . The Commission's overall role would thus be to work towards ensuring the elimination of discrimination and denial of equal opportunities in all walks of life. (EOC 2008: 40–1)

Whilst the EOC would focus on advocacy, monitoring, and where necessary, group grievance redressal, a more direct effort to promote social diversity in the public and private sector was proposed by the KCR, which recommended the creation of an expert group on diversity index to oversee the encouragement of diversity in education, employment and housing societies. 'The case for increasing social diversity in the public sphere', the report noted, can be built on the notion of a fair demographic representation for all groups of population. Groups that are subjected to discrimination in society tend to get under-represented (as compared to their proportion in the population) in several public spheres. This leads to inequity and alienation resulting in resentment and frustration among the excluded population (KCR 33).

The report's key recommendation was to establish a DI with which to measure the 'diversity gap' of in public spaces of particular social groups – religion, caste, gender – in proportion to the population who are eligible to enter the institution. Significant under-representation of any category, the report suggested, should be addressed through incentivisation in the allocation of state funding to institution (e.g. universities in the private and public sector), corporate social responsibility, backed with threat of affirmative action (public and private sector), and 'incentives to builders for housing complexes to have more "diverse" resident population to promote "composite living spaces" for "socio-religious" communities' (ibid.: VIII).

Religious minorities, security and communal violence

The UPA, as we have noted above, sought to create clear blue water between itself and the NDA by defining its position on secularism and the place of religious minorities within Indian nationhood. Tackling communalism and providing security to minorities was a cornerstone in this commitment that was forged on the back of pogroms in Gujarat, but also the rising wave of communal violence in the 1980s and 1990s. At the heart of the new deal for religious minorities was to guarantee security from communal violence.

Most assessments of the UPA on this front argue that very limited progress in fulfilling this commitment. In Gujarat the Congress-led UPA trod wearily in bring the perpetrators of violence in Gujarat to book. In fact the UPA appeared to skirt around Narendra Modi than directly confront him, and this was in no small measure due to Congress' electoral weakness in the state where the party had to tread carefully in not appearing to be alienate its Hindu votes. In Odisha, similar political considerations also appear to have been in play in the coalition's management of the anti-Christian violence (2007–08). This began at the end of 2007, but new wave of attacks against Christians was triggered in 2008, resulting in the displacement of 50,000 Christians. The nature of this violence and the inadequate response of the local state administration called into question the ability of the Centre to ensure basic law and order in the state. And similar ambiguity and vacillation was also demonstrated with reference to two long-running inquiries: into the demolition of the Babri Masjid mosque and the anti-Sikh riots in Delhi in 1984. Whereas the Liberhan Commission's report into the Babri Masjid was only made available in June 2009, after being selectively leaked to the chagrin of the BJP, the Congress' handling of the anti-Sikh riots culminated in serious embarrassment for the party in the May 2009 Lok Sabha elections (see Sáez and Singh 2012: Chapter 5).

Yet, it would be seriously misleading to suggest that the UPA approach towards anti-communalism was 'only' guided by electoral or partisan party considerations. For one, data on incidents of communal riots during the regime recorded an appreciable decline compared with the previous administration and majority Congress governments.

For another, in developing an effective approach to security the UPA had not only to overcome the need to build necessary political support but also inherent legal and administrative barriers to creating a clear model framework. Thus the failure of the Communal Violence (Prevention, control and Rehabilitation of Victims) Bill (2005) was one illustrative example. The bill was framed as a piece of model legislation that would make it difficult for perpetrators to instigate communal violence and, in the event of such incidents, ensure the prompt rehabilitation of victims. Its provisions, among other things, included giving more powers to the police to deal with rioters and effective measures to bring the guilty to book, including the provision for special courts. Authorities were to be empowered to declare certain areas as communally disturbed and constitute them as single judicial-zones in which the police could take preventative measures such as the controlling the movement of vehicles and people in such areas. The bill also placed heavy sanctions on police officers for neglect of duty while doubling the rate of punishment under the Indian Penal Code (*Times of India*, 24 August 2010).

The reasons for the failure of this bill to reach the statute book require more detailed evaluation. Social activists and lawyers criticised it on the ground that what was lacking was not legislation but a political commitment to effectively control outbreaks of communal violence. For them the bill was seriously flawed because it made no provisions for official authorities for the non-exercise of power to prevent or control communal violence. Indeed, the assumptions of the bill were so seriously 'flawed that it [could] not be remedied by amending a few components' (*The Tribune*, 17 June 2007). These shortcomings with the drafting of the bill, however, need to be placed within the broader framework of policy formation in this area that embraces judicial, administrative and parliamentary constraints.

Re-thinking the UPA (I) experience: an institutional policy analysis approach

It is undoubtedly the case that the UPA's policies towards religious minorities need to be situated within the broader framework of the administration's general approach to equality of opportunity that also

included gender, OBC, affirmative action and poverty reduction programmes (see Bajpai 2011; Verma 2012). However, within this overarching framework the concerns of minorities were addressed both in general
and specific terms. Generally, in seeking to better integrate religious
minorities within the India's growing economy, the justification offered
alluded to social justice, the need for inclusive growth and to address
persistent disadvantage. Specifically, the efforts to assuage the concerns of minorities, especially Muslims, needed a level-playing field, to
eradicate discrimination in the ideological construction of caste, which
excluded religious minorities (Muslims and Christians) from accessing
the benefits of reservations. The preference for reservations for religious
minorities, for example in the case of the RMR, may well derived from
experience of such reservations with SC and ST, and the recognition
that they entail low 'enforcement costs and [are] easily identifiable and
achievable, even if [they are] rigid targets' (Khaitan 2008: 12). It was
almost certainly the outcome of an institutional approach, a form of
path-dependency, to the subject which has become firmly established
within the Indian polity as a norm. Indeed, this pattern of institutional
response to issues of social disadvantage was aligned with new policy
innovations designed to tackle discrimination and disadvantage; and
these new approaches, as we have seen above, were both designed to
complement the conventional institutional modes of path-dependency
and provide more creative solutions to intractable issues of social justice. In short, in the new framework of equality of opportunity evolved
by UPA's policy formation process envisioned a distinct approach to the
religious minorities predicated on tried and tested methods such as reservations but also new innovations borrowed from comparative experience that would encourage and 'buy' social justice without producing
obvious 'winners' and 'losers'.

There is a general consensus that taken together the policy initiatives
proposed by the four commissions and committee reports considered
above marked the 'official' recognition of the need for new thinking
in better promoting equality of opportunity for religious minorities,
one which required a noticeable shift in conventional approach to the
subject. Yet, to what extent these proposals were, if at all, acted upon
during the UPA's administration is entirely different matter. By and
large the assessments of UPA's record in office, as we have noted above,

is one which merely contrasts outcomes with manifesto and CMP commitments (Sáez and Singh 2012). But this checklist approach provides only limited insights into how institutional discretion was used to advance such policies, why particular policy packages were selected, and the judicial, administrative and political constraints on implementing the new framework. Thus a more rounded understanding of UPA's performance in this area, therefore, is required, one that would place at centre stage the role of institutions as both facilitators of change, often by creating scope for executive action, but also as limiting agents in defining the boundaries of such change. A more nuanced appreciation of how institutions – administrative, judicial, political – both leveraged policy change, and frustrated it, would provide a more satisfactory account of understanding of public policy in this difficult area than is so far available.

Policy analysis in Indian politics is overwhelmingly biased towards initiation or failure (see Sáez and Singh 2012: 149–53). Policy initiatives are often identified with potential political pay-offs, for example, the ability to capture existing vote-banks, or create new ones. Consequently, political manifestos, either before or after elections, invariably came under this spotlight. At the other end of the policy analysis, considerable effort has been devoted to examining policy failure: that is, why policies fail to deliver, especially in the field of development (Corbridge et al. 2005). Implementation here not only focuses on design and execution, but the Centre–state divide and the political alignment in the Centre and the states at a time when the general movement is towards regionalisation. While these structural givens are useful in providing the context for policy failures and successes, they do not provide detailed insights into three questions: why particular policy preferences are selected for implementation (and non-implementation); why there are variations in outcome for similar policies, not only at the level of the states but within the Centre's policy field itself; and how the process of policy change can be better understood in ways that recognises successes as well as failures.

Absence from much policy analysis, both in India and elsewhere, is the reluctance to draw on institutional theory that accepts the role of institutions as an independent variable (Boin and Kuipers 2008).

Institutionalism comes in many forms – normative, historical, empirical (and even rational choice!) – but common to all its sub-schools is that it

> purports to explain behavior – be it of individuals, small groups, organisations and nation-states or international relations – in terms of institutions. Intuitionalists believe that orderly behavior is extraordinary, because so many factors (biological and social) predict selfish behavior that would result in chaos. (ibid.: 46)

Whilst we do not have the space here to further develop the institutionalist approach, it is undoubtedly the case that India's key structures – administrative, legislative, and judicial – play a critical role in policy success or failure. These institutions intervene not only as executors of the political will, but also as evaluators, monitors, instruments of executive or legal discretion, as well as being the upholders of embedded institutional cultural values rooted in the constitutional settlement at Partition. They, above all, provide 'institutional surroundings in which politicians and policymakers make their decisions' (ibid.: 44), and provide a relationship between themselves and their members that can be '*constraining* in nature, as the institution defines the parameters of (in)action and labels alternative forms of behavior as deviant' (ibid.: 47). However, an institution can also have an 'enabling effect' by 'providing guidance in deciding between various courses of action and determining the way employees use their discretion' (ibid.: 47).

By operationalising an institutional-based policy analysis to the highly contested area of UPA's policies towards religious minorities we can develop a more fine-grained mode of analyses of how policy implementation and (non-implementation) was undertaken. It will, moreover, enable us to bring out much more sharply the centrality of institutions in determining the successes and failures of policy implementation in this area. To what extent, for instance, institutional discretion was used to better promote equal opportunities for religious minorities in employment and service delivery when legal judgments and coalition politics (political constraints) limited the scope for policy implementation. And to what extent did institutional interests mitigate or facilitate the new innovations in equal opportunities policies that sought to complement the conventional approaches to the subject.

Conclusion

This chapter has attempted to argue that a new assessment is required of UPA's policies towards religious minorities intended to improve the equality of opportunity. In some ways the UPA's response in this field was part of a general states' reaction to 9/11 to address the concerns of Muslim minorities. At the same time, however, there was a very specific Indian aspect to this response rooted in the construction of secular conception of nationhood and developmentalist vision of 'protective equality', which excluded religious minorities from sharing the affirmative action provisions available to lower caste Hindus. In seeking to re-address this balance, the UPA sought both to shift the discourse on religious minorities from identity politics, associate with broader issues of nationhood and national integration, to development and justice, and encourage complementary methods of delivering social justice to all social groups, including religious minorities. Clearly at the level of policy initiation, as demonstrated by the evaluation of the reports of commissions and committees outlined above, it was recognised that there is a need to remove the anomalies against the rights of minorities to access provisions available to OBC, SC and ST. How these recommendations were then implemented, or not implemented, in areas of employment, service delivery, and for developing a robust anti-discrimination and anti-communal violence approach, needs to be examined in more depth. Critical to any such analysis is the role of key institutions – the administration, judiciary and the legislature. Appropriately undertaken, an institutional-based policy analysis approach has the potential to highlight the limits and possibilities in these difficult areas as well as provide firm pathways for radical change in the future.

Notes

1 Institutional-based policy analysis approach is discussed at length in the conclusion. For more details of the literature, see Boin and Kuipers (2008) and Chubb and Moe (1990).

2 This chapter is based on Heewon Kim's research, the UPA and equal opportunities with special reference to the Muslim community. This research, as the chapter outlines, seeks to evaluate the UPA(I)'s record by using an institutional-based policy analysis approach. This orientation draws heavily from the comparative experience, notably of the United States and the United Kingdom, in designing, implementation and evaluating equal opportunities and the role of institutions in shaping these processes.

3 Following political mobilisation, Sikh SC were brought under the provision in 1956, and Buddhist in 1990.

4 This aspect of the research is currently being investigated.

5 Nothing in this article shall prevent the state from making any provision for the reservation of appointments or posts in favour of any backward class of citizens which, in the opinion of the State, is not adequately represented in the services under the state.

REFERENCES

Abreu, Savio. (2009) 'The Making of a Christian Minority', *Seminar* (October) 602: 64–69.

Adhikari, G. (1943) *Pakistan and National Unity*, Bombay: Labour Monthly. File CPI-31/1932, PC Joshi Archives, JNU. The full text of the resolution is also available at http://www.unz.org/Pub/LabourMonthly-1943mar-00093.

Adney, Katharine and Lawrence Sáez, eds (2005) *Coalition Politics and Hindu Nationalism*. London: Routledge.

Ahmad, Ishtiaq. (2012) *The Punjab: Bloodied, Partitioned and Cleansed*. New Delhi: Oxford University Press.

Ahmad, J. (2011) *Speeches and Writings of Mr. Jinnah*, Vol. 1, p. 267; cited in Venkat Dhulipala; 'Debating Pakistan in Late Colonial North India', *Indian Economic and Social History Review*, 48/3.

Aiyar, Mani Shankar. (2004) *Confessions of a Secular Fundamentalist*. New Delhi: Penguin.

Alavi, Hamza. (1998) 'Ironies of History: Contradictions of the Khilafat Movement', in Mushirul Hasan (ed.), *Islam, Communities and the Nation: Muslim Identities in South Asia and Beyond*. New Delhi: Manohar.

Ali, A. (1992) 'The Quest for Cultural Identity and Material Advancement: Parallels and Contrasts in Muslim Minority Experience in Secular India and Buddhist Sri Lanka', *Journal Institute of Muslim Minority Affairs*, 13 (1, January): 33–57.

Ambedkar, B.R. (2006/1943) *Mr Gandhi and the Emancipation of the Untouchables*. New Delhi: Critical Quest. First published in 1943.

Ambedkar, B.R. (2008/1945) *Gandhi and Gandhism*, New Delhi: Critical Quest. First published in 1945.

Ambedkar, B.R. (1946) *Pakistan or the Partition of India*. Bombay: Thacker and Company.

Anderson, Perry 2012. *Indian Ideology*. Delhi: Three Essays Collective.

Ansari, M.T. and Deeptha Achar, eds (2010) *Discourse, Democracy and Difference: Perspectives on Community, Politics and Culture*. New Delhi: Sahitya Akademi.

Arendt, Hannah. (1951) *The Origins of Totalitarianism.* New York: Harcourt, Brace and Co.

Arokiaraj, Cosmon G. (2010) 'Dalit Christian Struggles for Equal Rights and the Way Forward', *Jeevadhara* XLI(241): 14–25.

Arokiaraj, Cosmon G. (2010) 'The NCRLM Report – Additional Term of Reference, A Ray of Hope for the Socially Excluded Dalit Christians and Dalit Muslims', *Catholic India* 22(2): 32–39.

Baixas, Lionel. (2008) *Thematic Chronology of Mass Violence in Pakistan, 1947–2007.* Online Encyclopedia of Mass Violence [online], published on 24 June 2008, http://www.massviolence.org/Thematic-Chronology-of-Mass-Violencein-Pakistan-1947–2007.

Bajpai, Rochna. (2002) 'Conceptual Vocabularies of Secularism and Minority Rights in India', *Journal of Political Ideologies*, 7(2): 179–97.

Bajpai, Rochna. (2009/10) 'Constitution-making and Political Safeguards for Minorities: An Ideological Explanation', *Journal of Contemporary Thought* 30 (Winter): 57–87.

Bajpai, Rochana. (2011) *Debating Differences: Group Rights and Liberal Democracy in India.* Delhi: Oxford University Press.

Balashankar, R. (2008) 'Are Minorities Safe in BJP-Ruled States?', *Economic Times* (22 Sept).

Ball, Wendy and John Solomos, eds (1990) *Race and Local Politics.* Basingstoke: Macmillan.

Bauman, Chad. (2010) 'Identity, Conversion and Violence: Dalits, Adivasis and the 2007–08 Riots in Orissa', in Rowena Robinson and Joseph M. Kujur (eds), *Margins of Faith: Dalit and Tribal Christianity in India*, pp. 263–90. New Delhi: Sage Publications.

Bhana, Surendra, and Goolam Vahed. (2005) *The Making of a Political Reformer: Gandhi in South Africa 1893–1914.* New Delhi: Manohar.

Bhatia, Lakshmi. (2010) 'Contradiction and Change in the Mizo Church', in Rowena Robinson and Joseph M. Kujur (eds), *Margins of Faith: Dalit and Tribal Christianity in India*, pp. 169–84. New Delhi: Sage Publications.

Boin, Arjen and Sanneke Kuipers. (2008) 'Institutional Theory and the Public Policy Field: A Promising Perspective for Perennial Problems', in Jon Pierre, B. Guy Peters and Gerry Stoker (eds), *Debating Institutionalism*, pp. 42–65. Manchester: Manchester University Press.

Bose, N.K. (1967) *Selections from Gandhi.* Ahmedabad: Navajivan Publications.

Bourdieu, P. (1986) 'The Forms of Capital', in J. Richardson (ed.), *Handbook of Theory and Resources in the Sociology of Education*, pp. 241–58. Westport, CT: Greenwood Press.

Bourdieu, P. and L.J.D. Wacquant. (1992) *An Invitation to Reflexive Sociology.* Cambridge: Polity Press.

Brass, Paul R. (2003) *The Production of Hindu-Muslim Violence in Contemporary India.* New Delhi: Oxford University Press.

Brown, Judith M. (1989) *Gandhi: Prisoner of Hope*. New Haven: Yale University Press.

Caplan, Lionel. (1987) *Class and Culture in Urban India: Fundamentalism in a Christian Community*. Oxford: Clarendon Press.

Casolari, Marzia. (2000) 'Hindutva's Foreign Tie-up in the 1930s: Archival Evidence', *Economic and Political Weekly*, 35/4: 218–28. Available at http://www.sacw.net/DC/CommunalismCollection/ArticlesArchive/casolari.pdf.

Census of India. (2001) *Population Profiles*, RGI, from http://delhiplanning.nic.in/Economic%20Survey/ES2007–08/T18.pdf.

Census of India. (2011) *Distribution of Population by Religions*, Drop-in-Article, from http://www.censusindia.gov.in/CensusWebResults.aspx?cx=0129180389 26302546381%3Ajjz7p38u6ma&cof=FORID%3A9&q=Distribution%20 of%20Population%20by%20Religions&sa=Search#156.

Chandra, Bipan. (1984) *Communalism in Modern India*. Delhi: Vikas.

Chandra, Sudhir. (1992) *The Oppressive Present: Literature and Social Consciousness in Colonial India*. New Delhi: Oxford University Press.

Chatterjee, Partha. (1998) 'Secularism and Toleration', in Rajeev Bhargava (ed.), *Secularism and Its Critics*. New Delhi: Oxford University Press.

Chaube, Shibani Kinkar. (1973) *1999 Constituent Assembly of India: Springboard of Revolution*. New Delhi: Manohar Publishers.

Chaube, Shibani Kinkar. (2012) 'Communalism and Secularism in India', in Shibani Kinkar Chaube (ed.), *Politics of Nation Building in India*. New Delhi: Gyan Publishing House.

Chiriyankandath, James. (2002) ' "Creating a Secular State in a Religious Country": The Debate in the Indian Constituent Assembly', *Commonwealth and Comparative Politics*, 38(2): 1–24.

Chubb, J.E. and T.M. Moe. (1990) *Politics, Markets and America's Schools*. Washington, DC: The Brookings Institution.

Comaroff, Jean. (1985) *Body of Power, Spirit of Resistance: The Culture and History of a South African People*. Chicago: University of Chicago Press.

Corbridge, Stuart, Glyn Williams, Manoj Srivastava and René Véron. (2005) *Seeing the State: Governance and Governmentaility in India*. Cambridge: Cambridge University Press.

Crossman, Brenda and Ratna Kapur. (2001) *Secularism's Last Sigh? Hindutva and the (Mis)Rule of Law*. New Delhi: Oxford University Press.

Dalmia, Vasudha. (1997) *The Nationalization of Hindu Traditions: Bharatendu Harishchandra and Nineteenth-century Banaras*. New Delhi: Oxford University Press.

Das, Durga. (1969) *From Curzon to Nehru and Afterwards*. London: HarperCollins.

Datta, M.D. (1953) *The Philosophy of Mahatma Gandhi*. Madison: The University of Wisconsin Press.

Datta, Saikat. (2006). 'Muslims and Sikhs Need Not Apply', *Outlook* November 13.

Davies, Horace B. (1978) *Towards a Marxist Theory of Nationalism*. New York: Monthly Review Press.

Dayal, John. (2008) 'New Islands of Underdevelopment', *Communalism Combat* 14 (132, June): 7–13.

Dumont, Louis. (1970) *Religion, Politics and History in India: Collected papers in Indian Sociology*. Paris: Mouton Publishers.

Dutt, R. Palme. (1940) *India Today*. Bombay: People's Publishing House.

Engineer, Asghar Ali and Narang, Amarjit S., (eds.). (2006) *Minorities and Police in India*. Delhi: Manohar.

Equal Opportunities Commission (EOC). (2008) *What, Why and How?* GOI: Ministry of Minority Affairs.

Fernandes, Walter. (1988) *The Role of Christians in National Integration*. New Delhi: Indian Social Institute.

Fernandes, Walter. (2012) 'Challenges to Theology from the Social Reality of Northeast India', Unpublished paper presented at the Seminar on Tribal Theology in Northeast India, Guwahati, organized by NESRC, Guwahati and Tribal Study Centre, ETC, Jorhat, 17–19 April.

Forrester, Duncan. (1979) *Caste and Christianity: Attitudes and Policies on Caste of Anglo-Saxon Protestant Missions in India*. London: Curzon Press.

Frazer, J.G. (1957) *The Golden, Abridged Edition*, Vol. I. London: Macmillan and Company Limited.

Galanter, Marc. (1984) *Competing Equalities: Law and the Backward Classes in India*. Berkeley, CA: University of California Press.

Gandhi as told in his own words. Paris: UNESCO.

Gandhi, M.K. (1921) *Young India*: 17 June.

Gandhi, M.K. (1925) *Young India*, 5 March.

Gandhi, M.K. (1929) *Young India*, 21 March.

Gandhi, M.K. (1937) *Harijan*, 1 January.

Gandhi, M.K. (1994) *Gandhi and Communal Problems*, compiled and edited by Pradip Pachpinde. Bombay: Centre for Study of Society and Secularism.

Gandhi, M.K. (1997) in Anthony Parel (ed.), *Gandhi: 'Hind Swaraj' and Other Writings*. Cambridge: Cambridge University Press.

Gandhi, M.K., (1999) *Collected Works of Mahatma Gandhi*, Vol. 7. New Delhi: Publications Division, Government of India.

Gandhi, M.K., (1999) *The Collected Works of Mahatma Gandhi*, Vol. 14. New Delhi: Publications Division, Government of India.

Gatade, Subhash. (2008) 'Terrorism's New Signature: Enter Hindutva Terrorists', *Mainstream*, Vol XLVI, No 6.

Geertz, Clifford. (1993) *Interpretation of Cultures: Selected Essays*. Hammersmith: Fontana Press.

Government of India. (2004) *National Common Minimum Programme for the Government of India*. http://pmindia.nic.in/cmp.pdf.

Grover, Vrinda. (2004) 'Prejudice and Democracy: Law, Police and Anti-Sikh Massacre, 1984', Paper presented at the Workshop on 1984 Anti-Sikh Pogroms, Coventry University, 30 October. Unpublished.

Grover, Vrinda. (2006) 'Role of Police in Anti-Sikh Massacre, Delhi' in Engineer and Narang (eds.).

Guha, Ramachandra. (2007) *India after Gandhi: the History of the World's Largest Democracy*. London: Picador.

Hambrick, D.C. (2007) 'Upper Echelons Theory: An Update', *Academy of Management Review*, 32: 334–43.

Hansen, Thomas B. (1999) *The Saffron Wave: Democracy and Hindu Nationalism in Modern India*. Princeton, NJ: Princeton University Press.

Hardiman, David. (2003) *Gandhi in His Time and Ours: The Global Legacy of His Ideas*. Columbia: Columbia University Press.

Harriss-White, Barbara. (2003) *India Working*. Cambridge: Cambridge University Press.

Hasan, Zoya. (2009) *Politics of Inclusion: Castes, Minorities, and Affirmative Action*. Oxford: Oxford University Press.

Heredia, R.C. (2012) 'Tribals at the Margins: Inferiorised Identity, Violated Dignity', Unpublished paper presented at the Seminar on Tribal Theology in Northeast India, Guwahati, organized by NESRC, Guwahati and Tribal Study Centre, ETC, Jorhat, 17–19 April.

Hazarika, Sanjoy. (2012, first published 1994) *Strangers of the Mist, Tales of War and Peace from India's North East*. New Delhi: Penguin.

Hazarika, Sanjoy and Charles Chasie. (2009) *The State Strikes Back: India and Naga Insurgency*. Washington, DC: East-West Centre.

Hazarika, Sanjoy and Preeti Gill. (2011) Bearing Witness: Report on the Impact of Conflict on Women in Nagaland and Assam. New Delhi: Centre for North East Studies and Policy Research, and Heinrich Boll Foundation.

Indian National Congress. (2004) *Election Manifesto 2004*. http://www.indian-elections.com/partymanifestoes/party-manifestoes04/congress.html.

Iyer, Raghavan, ed. (1986) *The Moral and Political Writings of Mahatma Gandhi*. New Delhi: Oxford University Press.

Iyer, Raghavan. (1991) *The Essential Writings of Mahatma Gandhi*. New Delhi: Oxford University Press.

Jodhka, Surinder S. (2009) 'Institutionalising Equality: Contexts and Meanings of Equal Opportunity Commission', *Indian Journal of Human Development*, 3(2): 297–304.

Juergensmeyer, Mark. (1991) *Radhasoami Reality: The Logic of a Modern Faith*, Princeton, NJ: Princeton University Press.

Kahneman, D. (1973) *Attention and Effort*. Englewood Cliffs, NJ: Prentice-Hall.

Kahneman, D. (2011) *Thinking, Fast and Slow*. London: Penguin Books.

Kanungo, Pralay. (2008) 'Hindutva's Fury against Christians in Orissa', *EPW* (September 13) XLIII(37): 16–19.

Karandikar, M.A. (1968) *Islam in India's Transition to Modernity*. New Delhi: Orient Longman.

Kaur, J. (2004) *Twenty Years of Impunity: The November 1984 Pogroms of Sikhs in India*. A Report by ENSAAF with Foreword by Barbara Crossette. London: Nectar Publishing/Bookmarks.

Kent, Eliza F. (2004) *Women: Gender and Protestant Christianity in Colonial South India*. New York: Oxford University Press.

Khaitan, Tarunabh. (2008) 'Transcending Reservations: A Paradigm Shift in the Debate on Equality', *Economic and Political Weekly*, 20 September, pp. 8–12.

Khan, Arshi. (2006) 'Police Prejudice against the Muslims' in Engineer and Narang (eds.).

Klausen, Jytte. (2005) *The Islamic Challenge: Politics and Religion in Western Europe*. Oxford: Oxford University Press.

Kooiman, Dick. (1990) *Conversion and Social Inequality: The London Missionary Society in South Travancore in the 19th Century*. Amsterdam: Free University Press.

Kripalani, Krishna, ed. (1969) *All Men Are Brothers: Life and Thought of Mahatma*.

Kumar HM, Sanjiv. (2013) 'Constructing the Nation's Enemy: Hindutva, Popular Culture and the Muslim "other" in Bollywood cinema', *Third World Quarterly, Vol 34, Issue 3*, pp. 458–69.

Kundu Committee Report (KCR). (2008) *Report of the Expert Group on Diversity Index*. Ministry of Minority Affairs, Government of India.

Lahiri, Prateep K. (2009) *Decoding Intolerance – Riots and the Emergence of Terrorism in India*. New Delhi: Roli Books.

Lobo, Lancy. (2001) 'Visions, Illusions and Dilemmas of Dalit Christians in India', in Ghanshyam Shah (ed.), *Dalit Identity and Politics*. New Delhi: Sage Publications.

Lobo, Lancy. (2010) 'Christianization, Hinduisation and Indigenous Revivalism', in Rowena Robinson and Joseph M. Kujur (eds), *Margins of Faith: Dalit and Tribal Christianity in India*, pp. 211–34. New Delhi: Sage Publications.

Luthera, V.P. (1964) *The Concept of Secular State and India*. Calcutta: Oxford University Press.

Macpherson, W. (1999) *The Stephen Lawrence Inquiry: Report of an Inquiry by Sir William Macpherson of Cluny*. London: Stationery Office.

Mairet, Gerard. (2010) *The Fable of the World: A Philosophical Inquiry into Freedom in Our Times*. Kolkata: Seagull Books.

Malhotra, John. (2012) 'Tough Questions on Religious Freedom at UN Human Rights Periodic Review', *ChristianToday India* (June 4), from http://in.christiantoday.com/articles/tough-questions-on-religious-freedom-at-un-human-rights-periodic-review/7353.htm.

Manickam, S. (1988) *Studies in Missionary History: Reflections on a Culture-Contact*. Madras: The Christian Literature Society.

Manor, James. (2012) 'Did the Central Government's Poverty Initiatives help to Re-elect it?', in Lawrence Sáez and Gurharpal Singh (eds), *New Dimensions of Politics in India: The United Progressive Alliance in Power*, pp. 13–25. London: Routledge.

Mantel, Hilary. (2012) *Bring Up the Bodies*. London: Henry Holt and Co.

Marx, Karl. (1981/1859) *A Contribution to the Critique of Political Economy* (with an introduction by Maurice Dobb). London: Lawrence and Wishart. First published in 1859.

Marx, Karl and Friedrich Engels. *The Communist Manifesto*. First published in 1948.

Marx, Karl and Friedrich Engels. (1973) *Selected Works*, Vol. 1. Moscow: Progress Publishers.

Massey, James. (2007) 'An Analysis of the Dalit Situation with Special Reference to Dalit Christians and Dalit Theology', *Religion and Society* (September-December) 52(3&4): 56–86.

Mazower, Mark. (1999) *Dark Continent: Europe's Twentieth Century*. London: The Penguin Press.

McDonough, Sheila. (1994) *Gandhi's Response to Islam*. New Delhi: D.K. Print World.

Menon, V.P. (1956/1961) *The Story of the Integration of the Indian States*. Calcutta: Orient Longman Ltd.

Ministry of Minority Affairs. 2006. http://minorityaffairs.gov.in/pm15point.

Mitta, M. and H.S. Phoolka. (2007) *When a Tree Shook Delhi: The 1984 Carnage and its Aftermath*. New Delhi: Roli Books.

Mitta, Manoj. (2011) 'Where is judicial objectivity?' *The Times of India*, June 5.

Mosse, David. (2012) 'Caste and Christianity', *Seminar* (May) 633: 58–62.

Mosse, George. (1989) 'Fascism and the French Revolution', *Journal of Contemporary History*, 24/1.

Mundadan, A.M. (1984) *Indian Christians: Search for Identity and Struggle for Autonomy*. Bangalore: Dharmaram Publications.

Nanda, B.R. (1990) *Gandhi and Religion*. New Delhi: Oxford University Press.

Nauman Naqvi. (2012) 'A Secret South Asian meta-utopia', *Seminar # 632*, New Delhi.

Neumann, Franz. (1963) *The Structure and Practice of National Socialism, 1933–1944*. New York. A pdf file may be read here: http://www.unz.org/Pub/NeumannFranz-1942–00027.

Oddie, Jeffrey. (1991) *Hindu and Christian in South-east India*. London: Curzon Press.

Parsons, Talcott. (1922/1956) 'Introduction', in Max Weber (ed.), *The Sociology of Religion*. Boston: Beacon Press.

Pearl, Martyn and Pritam Singh. (1999) *Equal Opportunities in the Curriculum*. Oxford: Oxford Brookes University.

Peel, Quentin. (2013) 'Germany on Edge over Trial of neo-Nazis', *Financial Times*, 6 May.

Peer, Gazala. (2013) 'When the Indian nation's "conscience" was satisfied', Kafila website February 15 (http://kafila.org/2013/02/15/when-the-indian-nations-conscience-was-satisfied-gazala-peer/)

Pickett, J.W. (1933) *Christian Mass Movements in India: A Study with Recommendations*. New York: The Abingdon Press.

Pirson, Michael and Shann Turnbull. (2011) 'Corporate Governance, Risk Management, and the Financial Crisis: An Information Processing View', *Corporate Governance: An International Review*, 19 (5): 459–70.

Portes, A. and J. Sensenbrenner. (1993) 'Embeddedness and Immigration: Notes on the Social Determination of Economic Action', *American Journal of Sociology*, 98 (6): 1320–50.

Press Information Bureau. (2009) http://pib.nic.in/newsite/erelease.aspx?relid= 56407.

Puniyani, Ram. (2005) *Religion, Power and Violence: Expression of Politics in Contemporary Times.* New Delhi: Sage Publications.

Qureshi, Naeem M. (1999) *Pan-Islam in British Indian Politics: A Study of the Khilafat Movement, 1918–1924.* Leiden: Brill.

Rafiq Dossani and Henry S. Rowen. (2005) *Prospects for Peace in South Asia.* Stanford, CA: Stanford University Press.

Ranganath Misra Commission Report (RMR). (2007) *Report of the National Commission for Religious and Linguistic Minorities.* GOI: Ministry of Minority Affairs.

Rauoof, A.A. (1944) Meet Mr. Jinnah. Lahore: Sh Muhammad Ashraf.

Renan, Ernst. (1882) What Is a Nation? The essay is downloadable here: http:// ig.cs.tu-berlin.de/oldstatic/w2001/eu1/dokumente/Basistexte/Renan1882EN-Nation.pdf.

Robinson, R. (1998) *Conversion, Continuity and Change: A lived Christianity in Southern Goa.* New Delhi: Sage Publications.

Robinson, R. (2003) *Christians of India.* New Delhi: Sage Publications.

Robinson, R. (2010) 'Indian Christians: Trajectories of Development', in Gurpreet Mahajan and Surinder S Jodhka (eds), *Religion, Communities and Development: Changing Contours of Politics and Policy in India*, pp. 151–72. New Delhi: Routledge.

Robinson, R. and Joseph M. Kujur, eds (2010) *Margins of Faith: Dalit and Tribal Christianity in India.* New Delhi: Sage Publications.

Ronghaka, D. (1985) 'Love Mizoram', p. 41, 42; and cited by Sajal Nag, in 'Construction of National Question in North-East India, 1946–1950', presented at the Centre for Social Studies, Surat, January 1993.

Rosenberg, Arthur. (2012) 'Fascism as a Mass-Movement', *Historical Materialism* 20; 1. A pdf copy is available here: http://www.sacw.net/article2756.html.

Sachar Committee Report (SCR). (2006) *Social, Economic and Educational Status of the Muslim Community of India.* Prime Minister's High Level Committee, Government of India.

Saggar, Shamit. (2009) *Pariah Politics: Understanding Western Radical Islamism and What Should Be Done.* Oxford: Oxford University Press.

Sandel, Michael J. (1998) 'Religious Liberty: Freedom of Choice or Freedom of Conscience', in Rajeev Bhargava (ed.), *Secularism and its Critics.* New Delhi: Oxford University Press.

Savarkar, V.D. (1999) *Hindutva: Who Is a Hindu?*, 7th ed. Mumbai: Pandit Bhakle.

Sayeed, Khalid Bin. (1963) 'Religion and Nation Building in Pakistan', *Middle East Journal*, Vol. 17, No. 3.

Sen, Amartya. (2006) *Identity and Violence: The Illusion of Destiny*. London: Penguin.

Sen, Ronojoy. (2010) *Articles of Faith: Religion, Secularism and Indian Supreme Court*. New Delhi: Oxford University Press.

Setalvad, M.C. (1990) 'Secularism,' Patel Memorial Lectures, 1965. *Patel Memorial Lectures (Combined) 1955–85*. New Delhi: Publications Division, Ministry of Information and Broadcasting, Government of India, pp. 473–503.

Sethi, Manisha. (2013) 'Sinful Liberals and the War against Jihadi Terror: Manisha Sethi Responds to Praveen Swami', Kafila website http://kafila.org/2013/05/09/sinful-liberals-and-the-war-against-jihadi-terror-manisha-sethi-responds-to-praveen-swami/, accessed on May 8, 2013.

Sharma, Jyotirmaya. (2003) *Hindutva: Exploring the Idea of Hindu Nationalism*. New Delhi: Viking.

Sherwani, L.A., ed. (1969) *Pakistan Resolution to Pakistan*. Karachi: National Publishing House Limited.

Shiva Rao, B. (1967a) *The Framing of India's Constitution: Select Documents*, Vol. II. New Delhi: Indian Institute of Public Administration.

Shiva Rao, B. (1967b) *The Framing of India's Constitution: Select Documents*, Vol. III. New Delhi: Indian Institute of Public Administration.

Shiva Rao, B. (1967c) The *Framing of India's Constitution: Select Documents*, Vol. IV. New Delhi Indian Institute of Public Administration.

Shiva Rao, B. (1968) *The Framing of India's Constitution: A Study*. New Delhi: Indian Institute of Public Administration.

Simeon, Dilip. (1986) 'Communalism in Modern India: A Theoretical Examination' *Mainstream*, December.

Simeon, Dilip. (1994) 'Tremors of Intent: Perceptions of the Nation and Community in Contemporary India', in Ania Loomba and Suvir Kaul (eds), *On India: Oxford Literary Review*, Vol. 16 (1–2).

Simeon, Dilip. (2013) 'The Law of Killing: A Brief History of Indian Fascism', in Jairus Banaji (ed.), *Fascism: Essays on Europe and India*. Three Essays Collective.

Singh, Arvinder. (1999) *Industrial Transition in an Agricultural Surplus Region: A Study of Punjab*. PhD thesis, Jawaharlal Nehru University and Centre for Development Studies, Trivandrum (Kerala).

Singh, Gurharpal. (2000) *Ethnic Conflict in India: A Case-Study of Punjab*. Basing-Stoke: Macmillan Press.

Singh, Gurharpal. (2004) 'State and Religious Diversity: Reflections on Post-1947 India', *Totalitarian Movements and Political Religions*, 5(2): 205–25.

Singh, Gurharpal. (2014) *India's Troubled Democracy: Communalism, Corruption and Social Exclusion*. (London Hurst and Co. 2016).

Singh, Gurharpal and Darshan S. Tatla. (2006) *Sikhs in Britain: The Making of a Community*. London: Zed Books.

Singh, Patwant. (1985) 'The Distorting Mirror', in Patwant Singh and Harji Malik (eds), *Punjab: The Fatal Miscalculation*. New Delhi: Crescent.

Singh, Pritam. (1984) 'AIR and Doordashan Coverage of Punjab after the Army Action', *Economic and Political Weekly*, 8 September.

Singh, Pritam. (1985) 'Government Media and Punjab', *Economic and Political Weekly*, 12 January.

Singh, Pritam. (1985) 'Role of Media', in Amrik Singh (ed.), *Punjab in Indian Politics*. New Delhi: Ajanta Publishers.

Singh, Pritam. (2005) 'Hindu Bias in India's 'Secular' Constitution: Probing Flaws in the Instruments of Governance', *Third World Quarterly*, 26(6): 909–26.

Singh, Pritam. (2008) *Federalism, Nationalism and Development: India and the Punjab Economy*. London/New York: Routledge.

Singh, Pritam. (2009) 'In Remembrance: Patwant Singh and Ram Narayan Kumar', *Journal of Punjab Studies*, 16(2): 295–301. http://www.global.ucsb.edu/punjab/journal/v16_2/articles/8-Obituaries16.2.pdf.

Singh, Pritam. (2010) *Economy, Culture and Human Rights: Turbulence in Punjab, India and Beyond*. New Delhi: Three Essays Collective.

Smith, Donald Eugene. (1998) 'India as a Secular State', in Rajeev Bhargava (ed.), *Secularism and Its Critics*. New Delhi: Oxford University Press.

Somasekhara, B.K. (2011) Final Report of Justice B.K. Somsekhara Commission of Inquiry, 28 January, Bangalore.

Stalin, J.V. (1913) *Marxism and the National Question*, Section 1, available at http://www.marxists.org/reference/archive/stalin/works/1913/03.htm.

Stanislaus, L. (2004) 'Empowering the Oppressed in Society' in S. Ponnumuthan and others (eds), *Christian Contribution to Nation Building: A Third Millennium Enquiry*. Cochin: Documentary Committee of CBCI-KCBC.

Tejani, Shabnam. (2008) *Indian Secularism: A Social and Intellectual History, 1890–1950*. Bloomington: Indiana University Press.

Tendulkar, D.G and Khan Abdul Gaffar Khan. (1967) *Faith Is a Battle*. Bombay: Gandhi Peace Foundation.

The Hindu (2013a). 'How the Centre and the Police Have Shielded Sajjan Kumar since 1984'. 8 May, http://www.thehindu.com/news/national/how-the-centre-and-police-have-shielded-sajjan-kumar-since-1984/article4693431.ece?homepage=true.

The Hindu (2013b) 'There Is a Case for Commuting Bhullar Sentence', M.B. Shah. 21 April, http://www.thehindu.com/news/national/there-is-case-for-commuting-bhullar-sentence-mb-shah/article4637577.ece.

The Tribune. (2013) '1984 riots a blot on nation', February 24.

The Tribune. (2013a) 'Prez guard job only for Rajputs, Jats and Sikhs', October 3.

Trevelyan, G.M. (1959) *A Shortened History of England*. Harmondsworth, Middlesex: Penguin.

Tversky, Amos and Daniel Kahneman. (1974) 'A Judgement under Uncertainty: Heuristics and Biases', *Science*, 185. Also reproduced in Kahneman 2011 as an Appendix.

Verma, Vidhu. (2012) *Non-Discrimination and Equality in India: Contesting Boundaries of Social Justice*. London: Routledge.

Vijapur, Abdulrahim and Mohibul Haque. (2006) 'Endangered Minorities in India: Understanding the Role of Police', in Engineer and Narang (eds.) 2006.

Webster, C. B. John. (1991) *The Dalit Christians: A History*. New Delhi: ISPCK.

Wellman, David T. (1993) *Portraits of White Racism*. New York, NY: Cambridge University Press.

Wells, H.G. (1922) *A Short History of the World*. Harmondsworth, Middlesex: Penguin.

Wilkinson, Steve. (2012) 'The UPA and Muslims', in Lawrence Sáez and Gurharpal Singh (eds), *New Dimensions of Politics in India: The United Progressive Alliance in Power*, pp. 68–78. London: Routledge.

Wilkinson, Steven I. (2004) *Votes and Violence: Electoral Competition and Communal Riots in India*. Cambridge: Cambridge University Press.

Wilson, Kottapalli. (1982) *Twice Alienated: Culture of Dalit Christians*. Hyderabad: Booklinks.

Wright, T.P., Jr. (1981) 'The New Muslim Businessmen of India: A Prospectus for Research', Conference Paper on the 7th European Conference on Modern South Asian Studies, School of Oriental and African Studies, University of London, July 1981.

Primary sources

All India Reporter (AIR) 1975 SC 1788.

August 15 — 'To the People of Pakistan: Communist Party's Appeal'; File CPI-117; P.C. Joshi Archive.

Bleeding Punjab Warns by Dhanwantri and P.C. Joshi; P.C. Joshi Archives, (JNU), File CPI/108, pp. 5–6.

Concise Oxford English Dictionary. 1999. New Delhi: Oxford University Press.

Constituent Assembly Debates. 1950. New Delhi: Manager of Publications, The Government of India, Vol. V.

Lok Sabha Debates. 1976. New Delhi: Lok Sabha Secretariat, 25 October 1976, c. 58.

'On his 79th Birthday – Our Homage and Our Pledge', File CPI-117; P.C. Joshi Archive, Jawaharlal Nehru University Library.

Parliamentary Debates Part II, Vol.VII, 1959. New Delhi: Manager of Publications, Government of India.

Savarkar's Kanpur address in Hindu Rashtra Darshan, pp. 122–25; a collection of presidential speeches: http://liberalpartyofindia.org/communal/Hindu-Rashtra-Darshan.pdf; p. 123.

The Statesman, New Delhi, 21 August 1961.

Who Rules Pakistan? (Communist Party Publication, Bombay, 1948), File CPI/147; P.C. Joshi Archive.

INDEX

269

INDEX

England 15–16
EOC 238, 244, 248–49, 260
equality of opportunity 9, 234–35, 238, 240–41, 243–44, 248, 251–52, 255
eradicating discrimination 35–6, 46–7
ethics 130, 139
Ethnic Conflict and Civic Life (Varshney, Ashutosh) 3
ethnic groups 32–5, 42, 57, 59, 101; white 34, 42, 44
ethnic minorities 246–47
Evidence of institutional communalism in India 34
Evolution of Odisha and religious minorities 226
extermination 53–4
Extremist Hindu organisations 142, 144

federation, 16, 64–5, 67
forgiveness 2, 145
Freedom of Religion Act 222, 230
free India 64–5, 67–8, 143, 145
fundamental rights sub-committee 18–19

Gandhi 11, 20, 30, 48, 82, 129–43, 145
Gandhi and communal problems 141
Gandhi and religious fanaticism 8
Gandhi's concept of religion 134
Gandhi's philosophy of non-violence 131
Gandhi's position on communalism and religious fanaticism 8
Gandhi's religion 134
Godhra 153, 155
Golden Temple 41, 49
government, civilian 180
government agencies 106, 242
government drafts 160
Government of India Act, 1935 70
Governor 176–7
Gujarat 6, 89, 99, 101, 108, 119–23, 146–7, 153, 156, 230; violence in 3, 108, 121, 204–10, 226, 230–235, 250
Gujarat carnage 147, 151

Gujarat: The Making of a Tragedy (Varadarajan, Siddharth) 3
Gujarati Muslims 92, 100
Gujarat riots 89, 92, 107, 235
Gujarat violence 109, 116, 127
Gyanendra Pandey 186, 191

Harsh Mander 9, 142
Hazarika 169–71, 179, 183
Hindu bias 36–7, 40, 49
Hindu–Christian communal confrontation 200
Hindu–Christian conflict 228–29
Hindu–Christian relationship 232
Hindu cloth merchants 94; to damage property of Muslim competitors 94
Hindu communalism 81, 186; institutional 47; institutionalised 45; modern 186, 195
Hindu communalists in India 50
Hindu communal parties and organisations 47, 184–5
Hindu communal politics 185
Hindu community 137, 199, 239
Hindu culture 82, 86, 114
Hindu fundamentalism in India 8
Hindu identity 113, 207
Hindu India 67, 213
Hindu Indian American 101
Hinduisation 104, 110
Hinduised tribals enacting violence 222
Hinduism 76, 84, 104, 106, 114, 117, 119–20, 130–1, 203, 210, 221, 222, 239
Hindu labels 187, 215
Hindu Mahasabha 17, 60–1, 63, 78, 184
Hindu majoritarian dominance in India 33
Hindu majority 17, 35, 62, 88, 228
Hindu Marriage Act 21
Hindu–Muslim 91, 183, 187
Hindu–Muslim amity and brotherhood 10
Hindu–Muslim communal discourse 73
Hindu–Muslim feud 81

Smith, Donald Eugene 22
SOP *see* standard operating procedure
South Asian American Leaders of
Tomorrow (SAALT) 115
South Asian Progressive Action
Collective (SAPAC) 115
standard operating procedure
(SOP) 176
state authorities 144, 147
state elections 92
State governments 6, 176
state institutions 41
state population 196
state religion 18
state secularism 236
survivors of mass communal
violence 144
Swaminarayan Hinduism 119–27
Swami, Sahajanand 119

Tribal Christians 209
tribes in conflict 209–11

ULFA *see* United Liberation Front
of Asom
UN Commission on Human
Rights 115
Union of Soviet Socialist Republics
(USSR), 17
United Liberation Front of Asom
(ULFA), 175
united national front (UNF), 64
United Progressive Alliance (I) (UPA
(I)) 9; equality of opportunity
248–9; equality of opportunity and
constitution 238–42; institutional

policy analysis approach 251, 255–56;
religious minorities 240–50;
security and communal violence
250–3; social exclusion 241–44
Universal Periodic Review (UPR) 198
UPA government programmes 247–8
UPR *see* Universal Periodic Review
US Immigration and Naturalization
Service 110

Vajpayee, Atal Bihari 181
Vanavasi Kalyan Ashram (VKA) 85
Veer Jaimal va Krishna Kanta (Gupta,
Ganga Prasad) 189
Veer Patni (Gupta, Ganga Prasad) 189
Veer Varangana va Aadarsha Lalana
(Gupta, Ganga Prasad) 192
VHP *see* Vishwa Hindu Parishad
vicarious nationalism, 187
Vishwa Hindu Parishad (VHP), 8, 85,
88, 101
VKA *see* Vanavasi Kalyan Ashram
*Votes and Violence: Electoral Competition
and Ethnic Riots In India* (Wilkinson,
Steve) 3

Western history 16
Women's International League for
Peace and Freedom (WILPF) 221

Youth Solidarity Summer (YSS)
114
YSS *see* Youth Solidarity Summer

*Ziauddin Burhanuddin Bukhari v.
Brijmohan Ramdass Mehra* 14